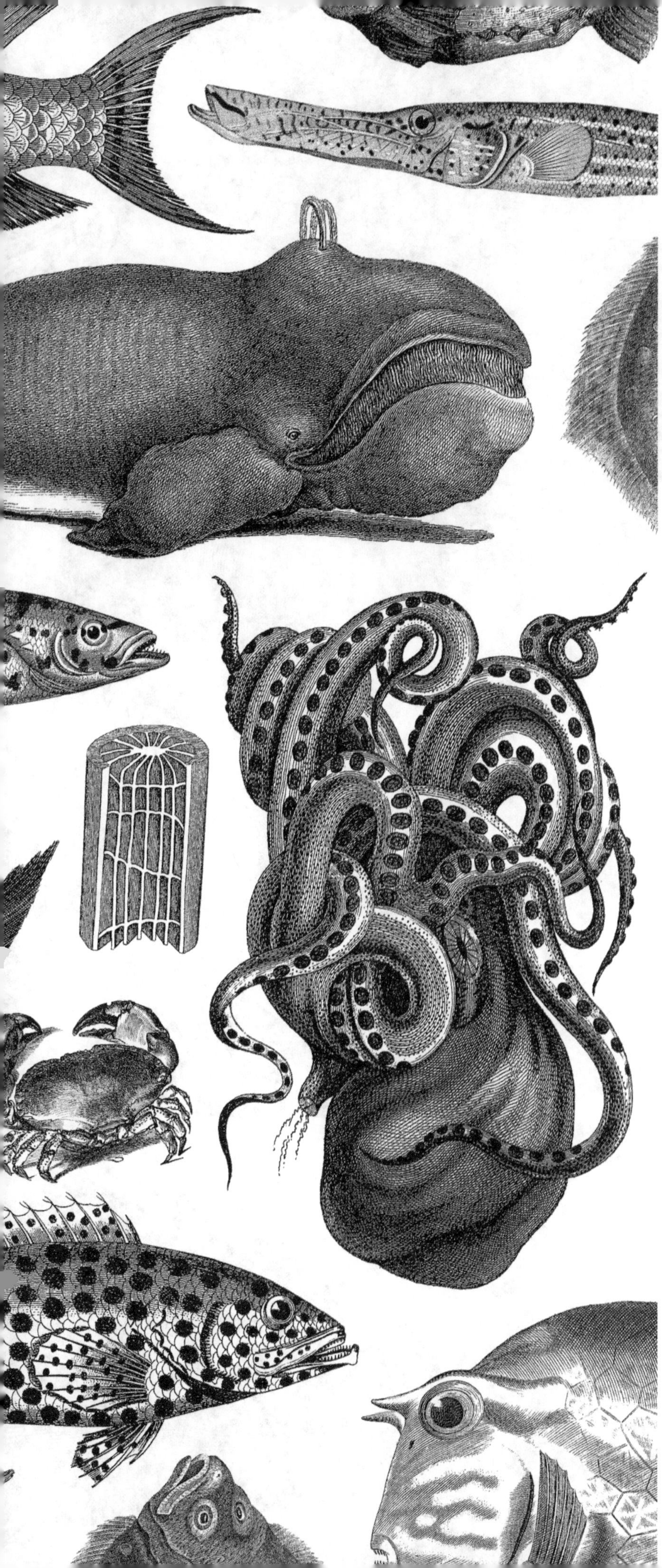

VOLUME NUMBER ONE

SEA-LIFE &
MONSTERS
OF THE DEEP

AN IMAGE ARCHIVE FOR
ARTISTS *And* DESIGNERS

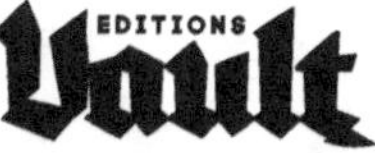

EDITIONS Vault

INTRODUCTION

The oceans are home to an unimaginable variety of creatures, from the tiniest plankton to the mightiest whales. This diversity is a source of endless fascination and inspiration for artists. The ocean is also a place of great beauty, with its gentle waves and sunlight playing on the surface. But beneath the surface lies a world of mystery and terror, where fearsome predators prowl and strange creatures lurk in the darkness. This dark side of the ocean is also a rich source of inspiration for artists, who can use it to create works that are both beautiful and disturbing. Sea-life and Monsters of the Deep is an excellent reference book for artists looking to take inspiration from the ocean. It contains detailed illustrations of a wide range of sea creatures, both real and imaginary. Whether you're looking for ideas for a new painting or sculpture, or just want to learn more about the amazing creatures that inhabit the oceans, Sea-life and Monsters of the Deep is an essential book for any artist's library.

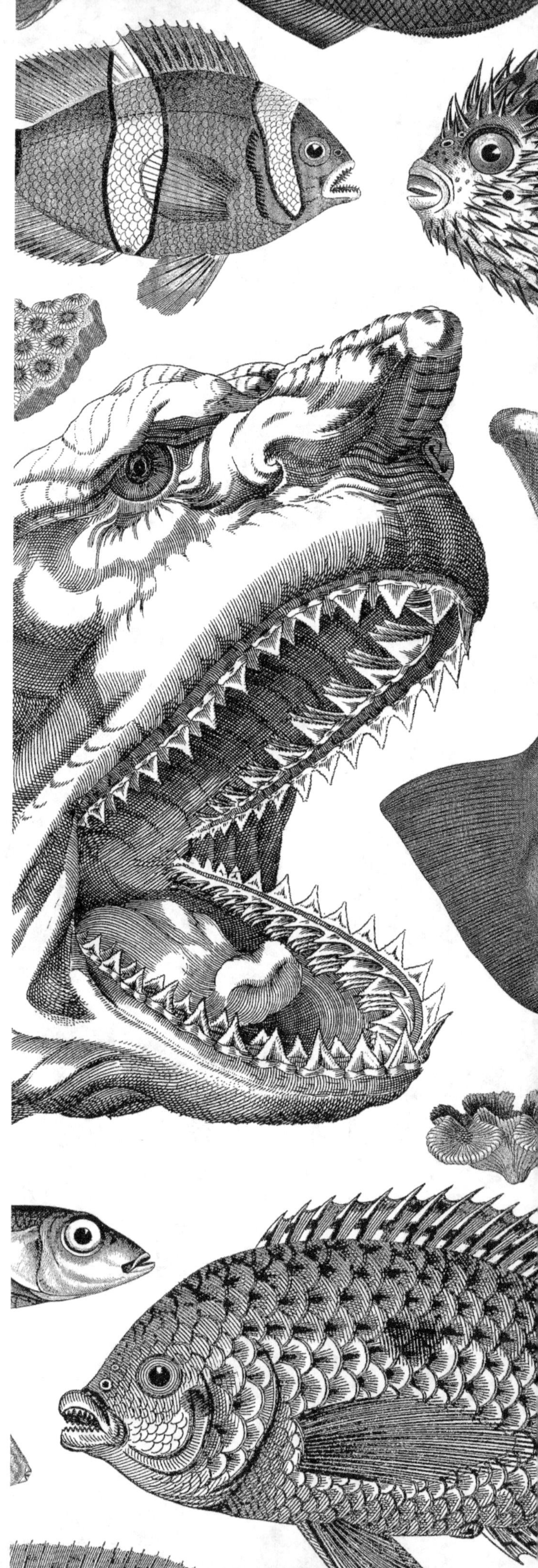

TABLE OF CONTENTS

Sharks & Rays	01-08
Whales, Dolphins and Porpoises	09-14
Fish	15-57
Eels	58-60
Seahorses	61-62
Worm Shell	63
Crustaceans	64-70
Cephalopods	71-84
Turtles	85-86
Seals & Walruses	87-88
Starfish	89-90
Corals	91-96
Shells	97-98

DOWNLOAD YOUR FILES

Downloading your files is simple. To access your digital files, please go to the last page of this book and follow the instructions.

For technical assistance, please email:
info@vaulteditions.com

Copyright

Copyright © Vault Editions Ltd 2022.

Bibliographical Note

This book is a new work created by Vault Editions Ltd.

ISBN: 978-1-925968-94-1

SEA-LIFE & MONSTERS OF THE DEEP

VAULT EDITIONS

01

02

03

04

05

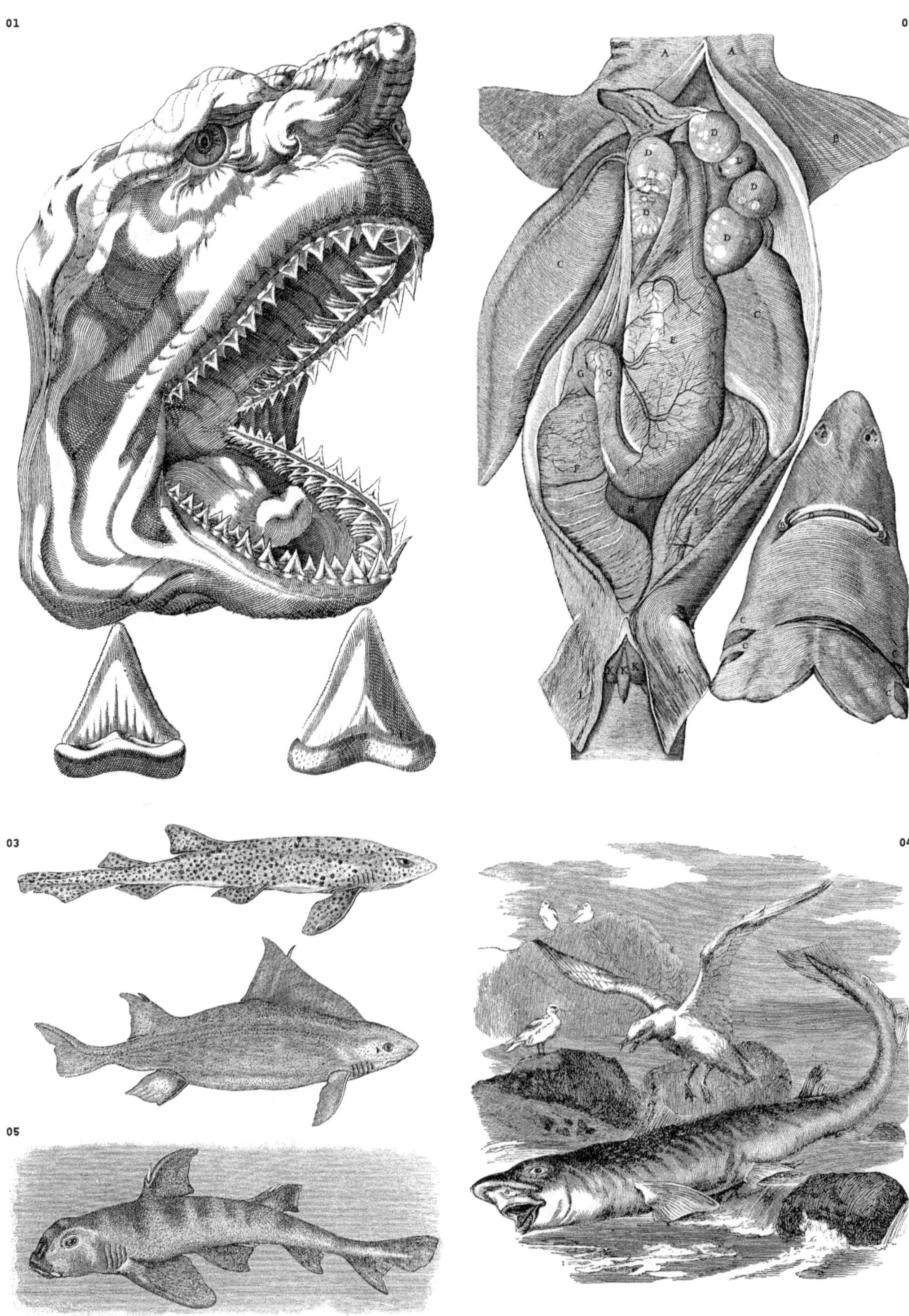

06

07

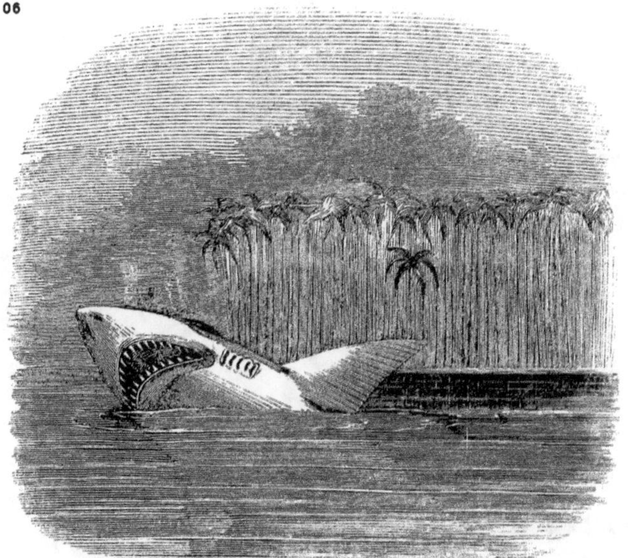

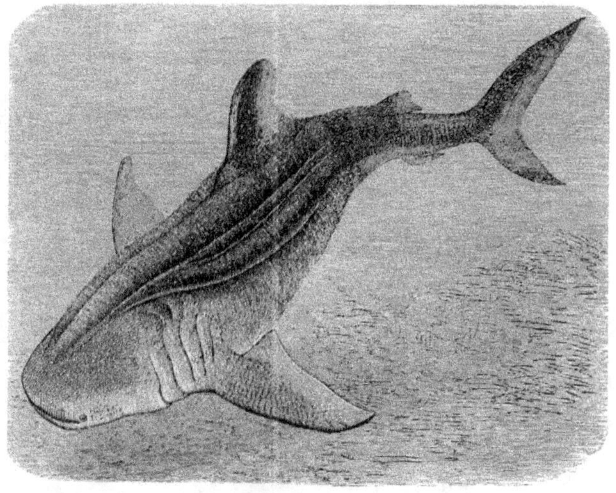

08

09

10

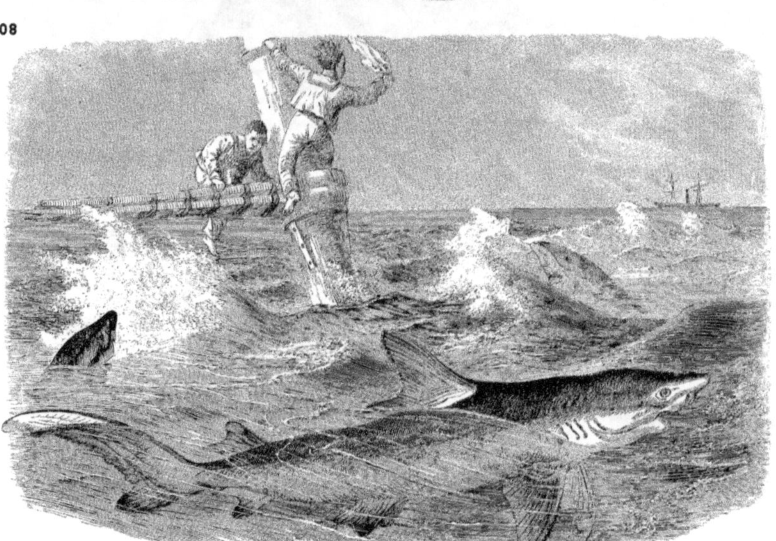

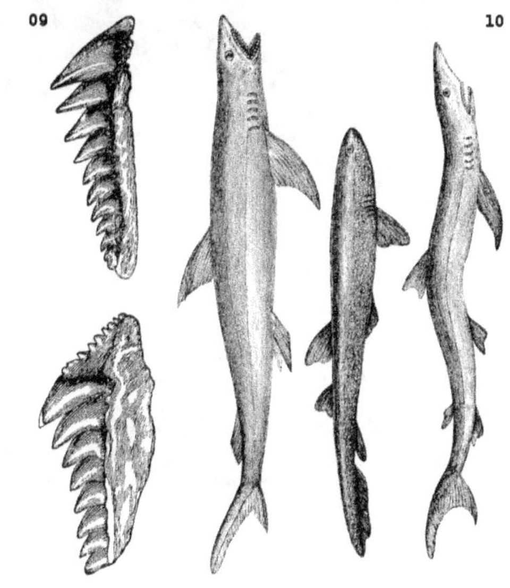

11

12

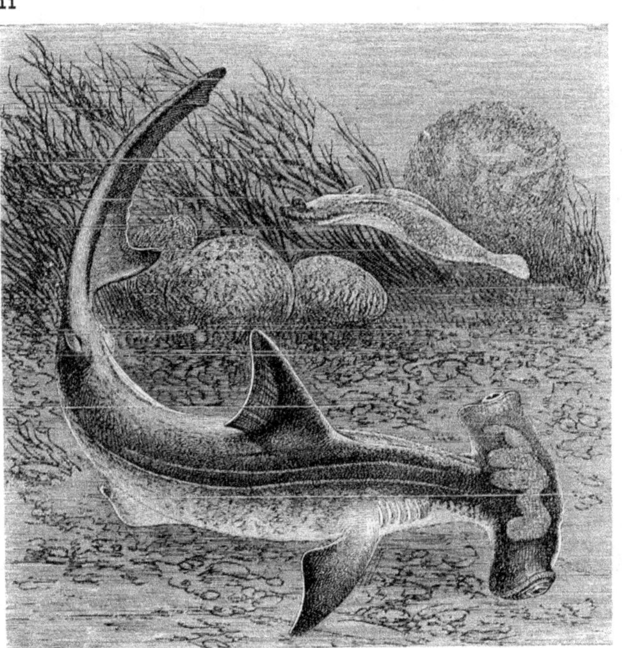

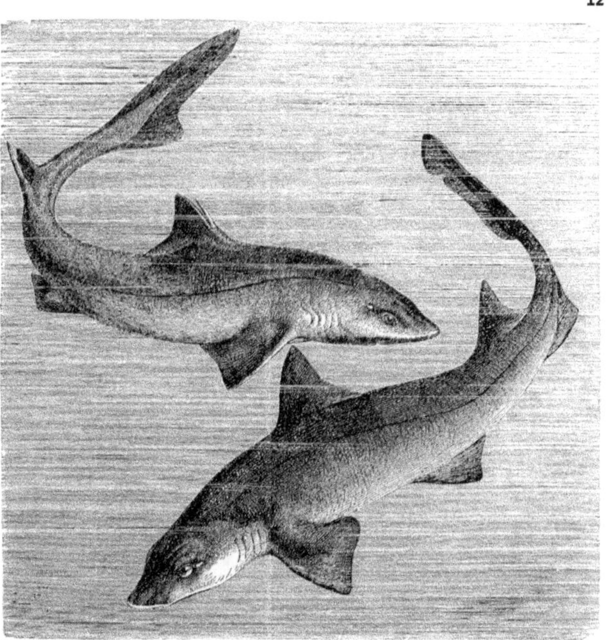

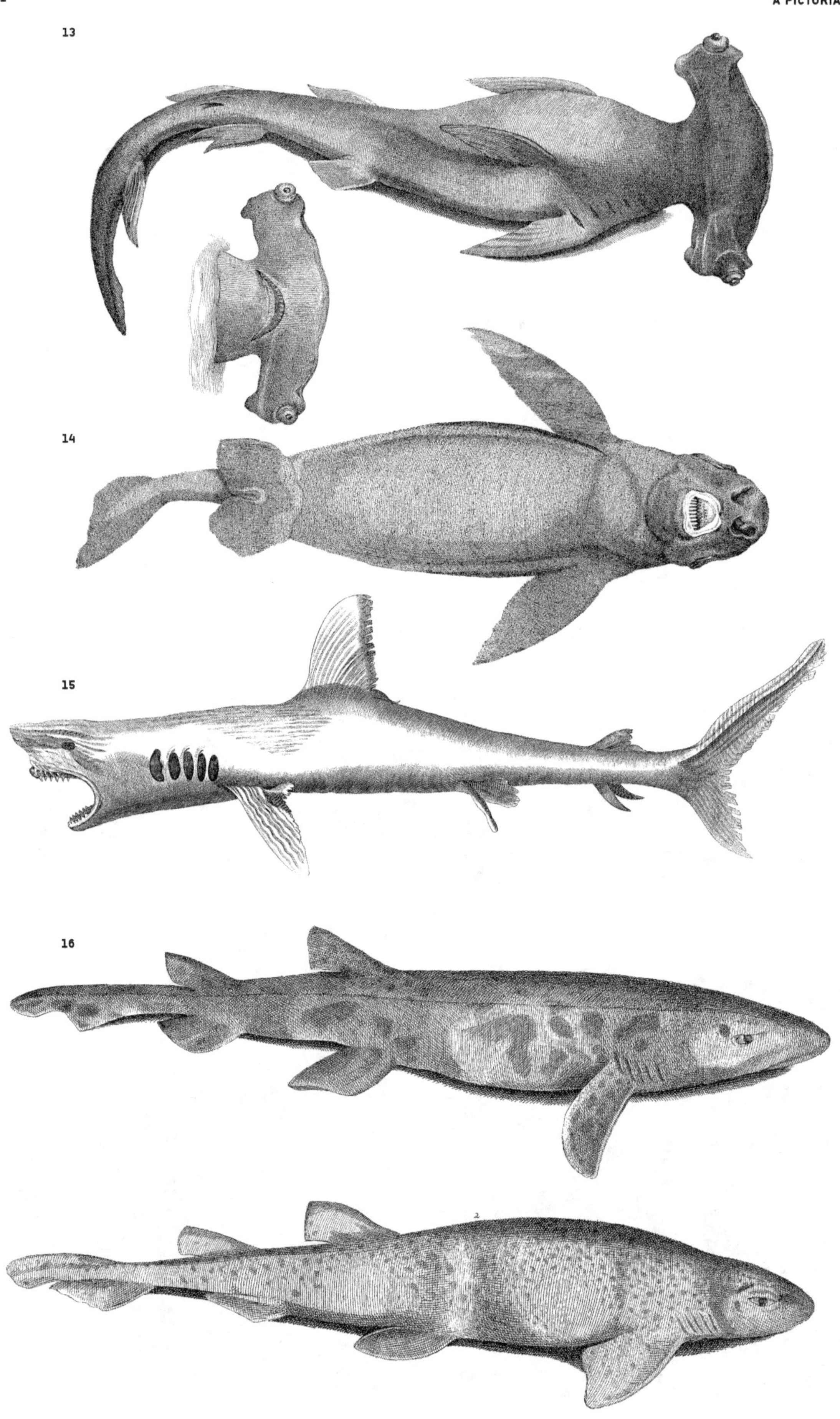

13

14

15

16

17

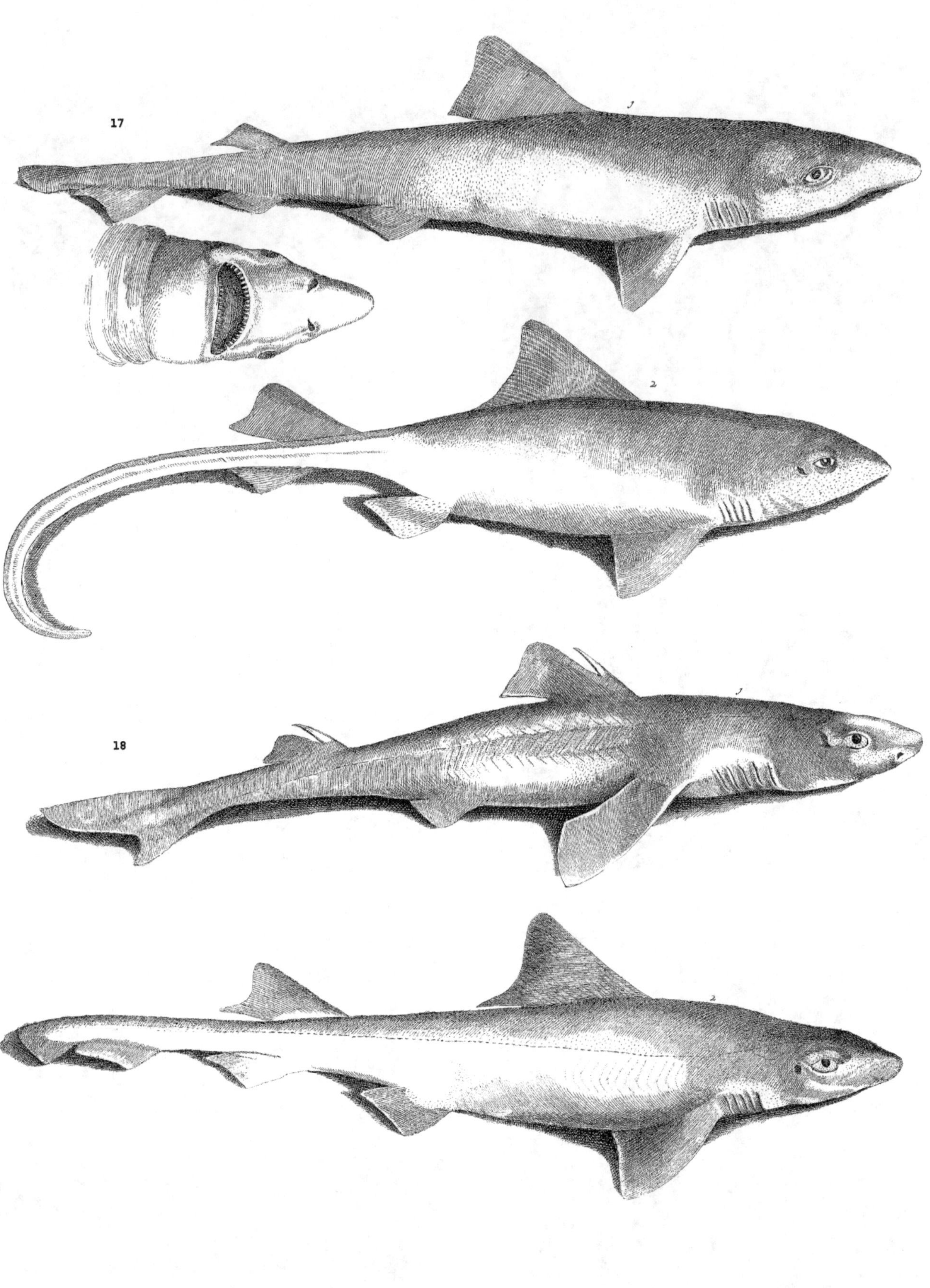

18

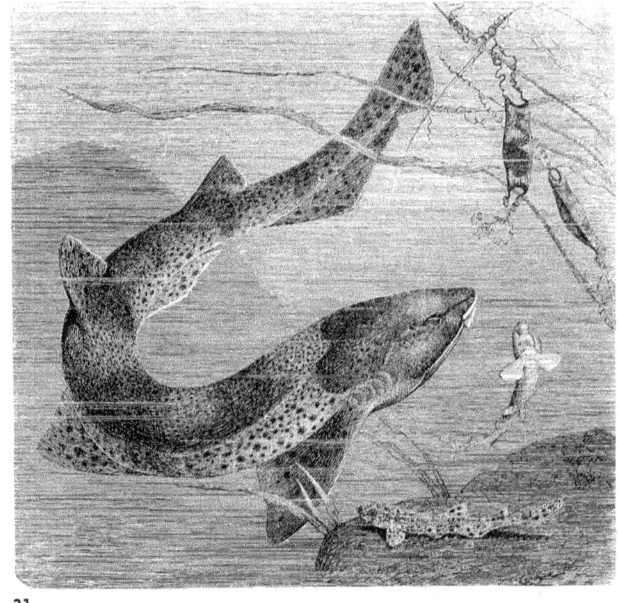

<19

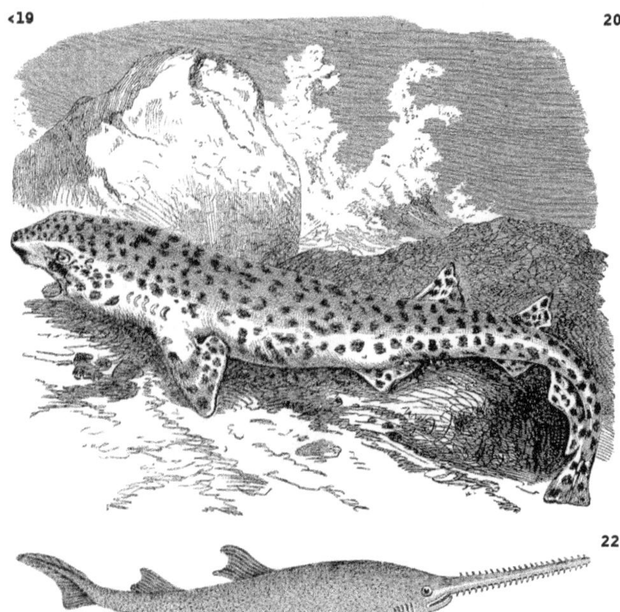

20

22

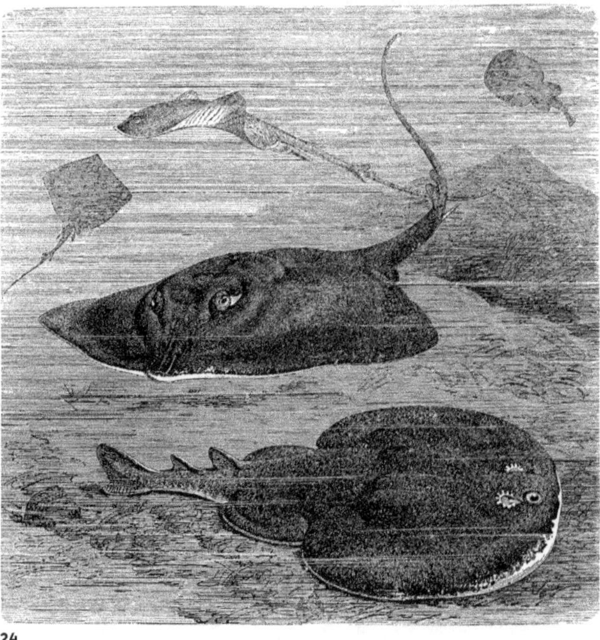

21

23

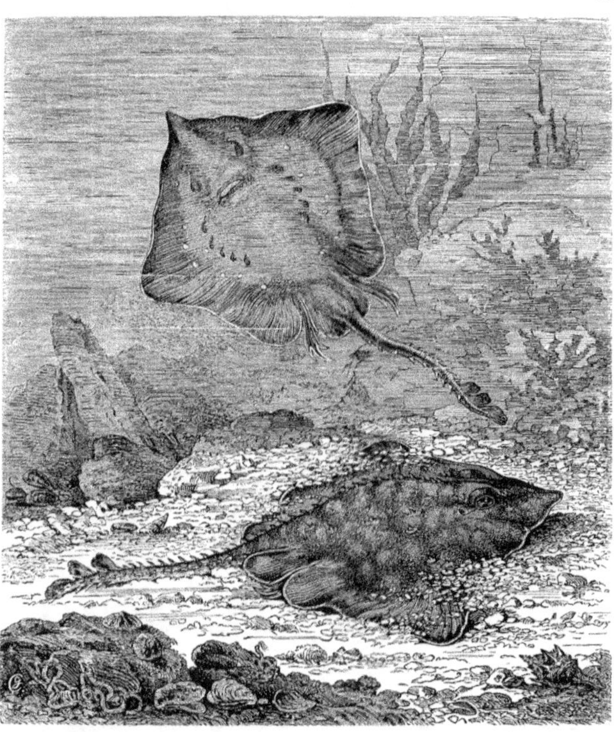

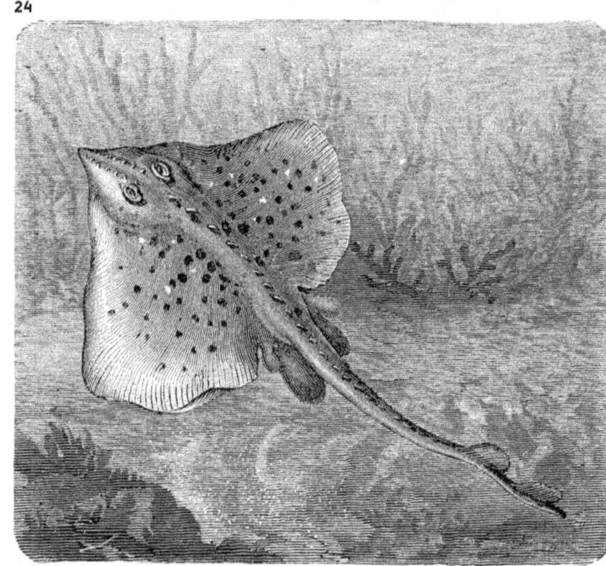

24

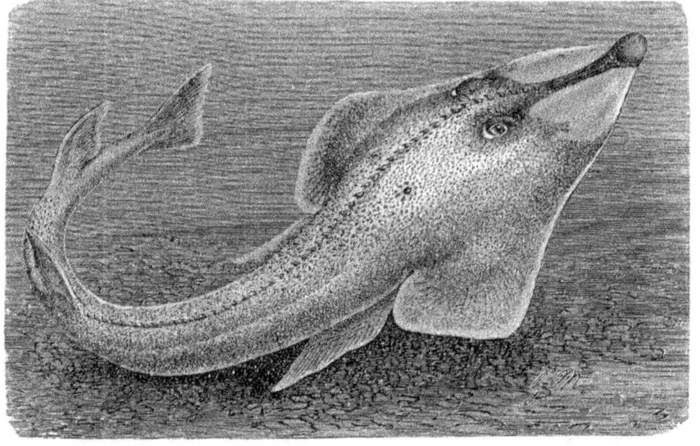

25

26

27

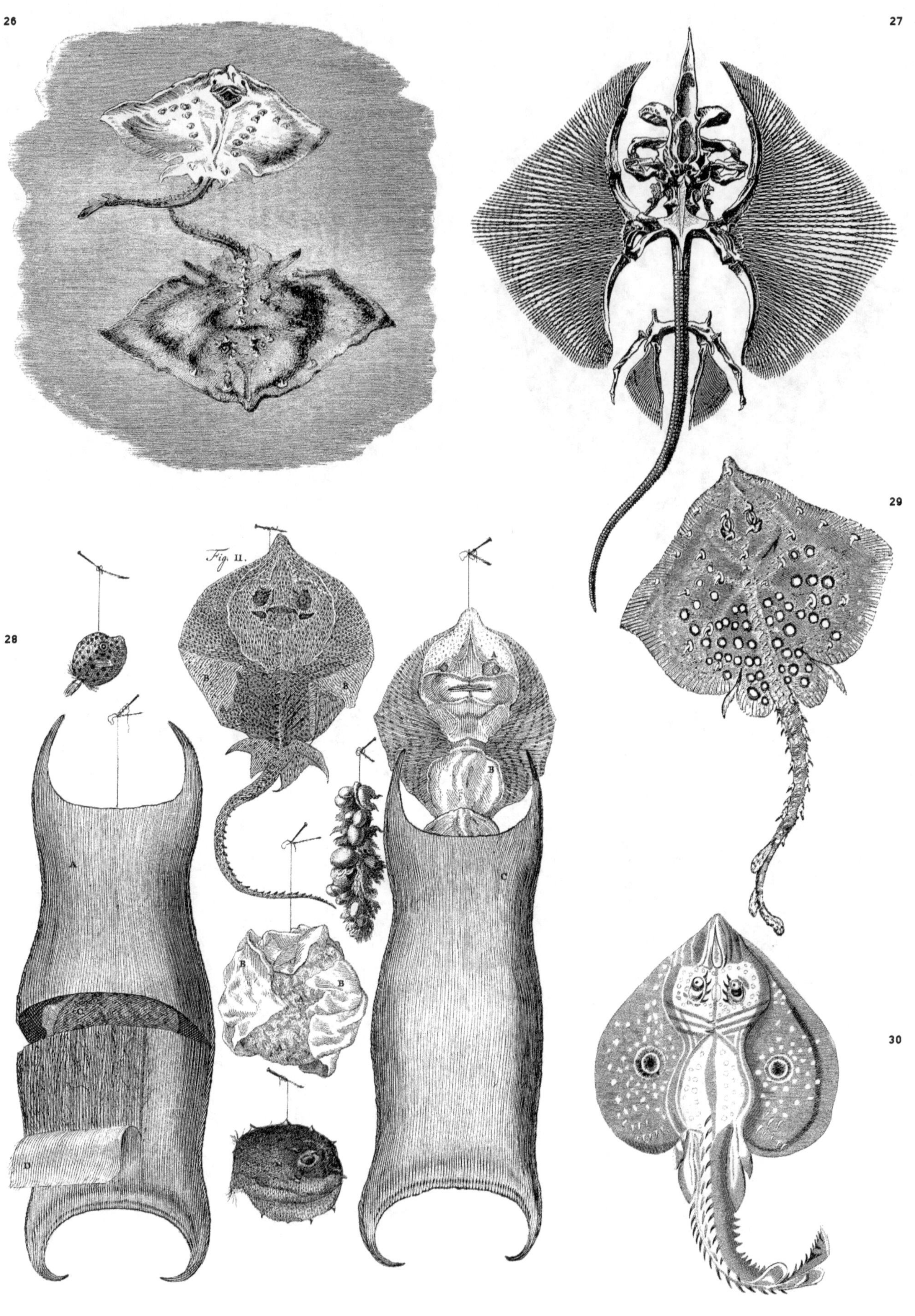

28

29

30

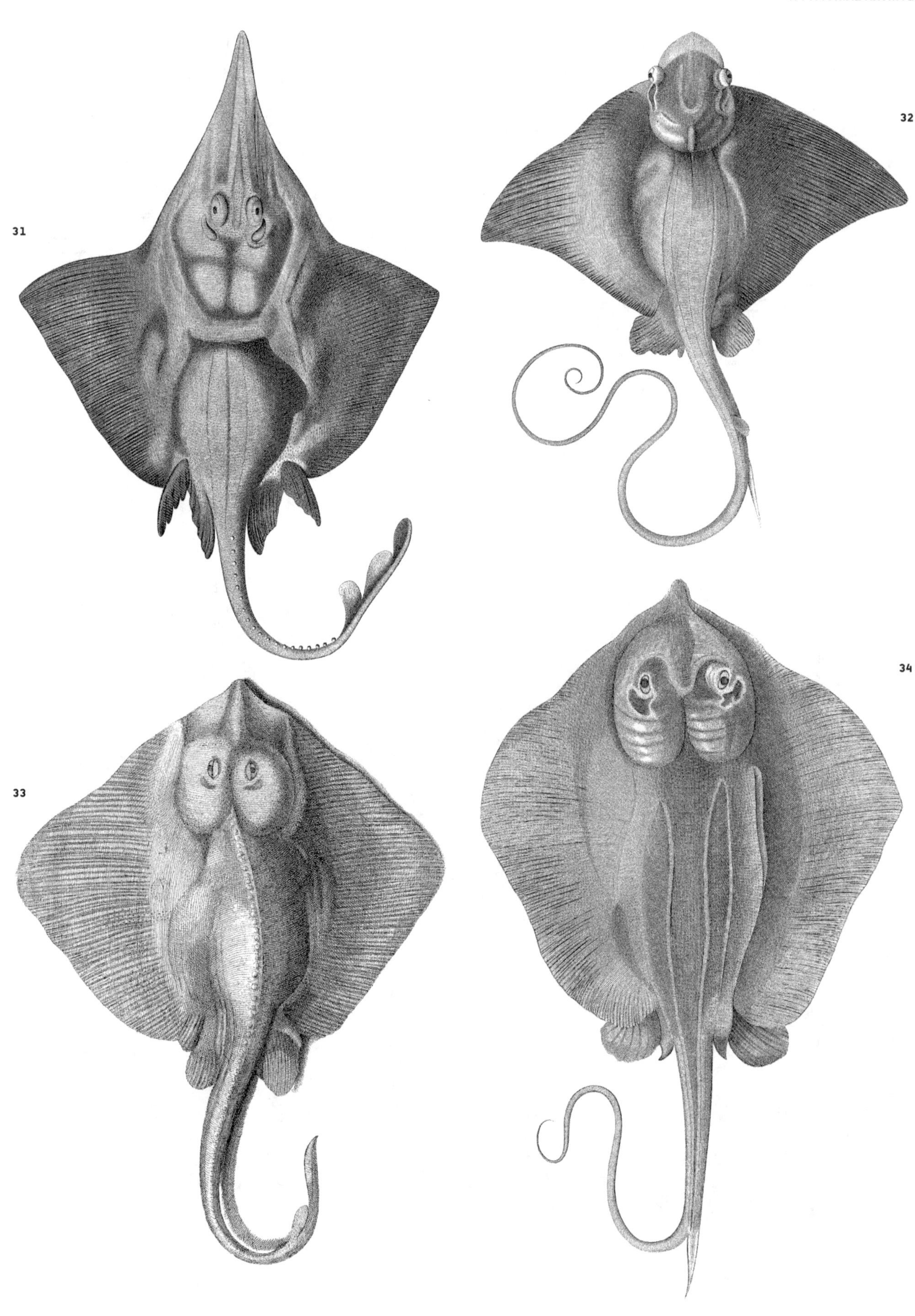
31
32
33
34

35

36

37

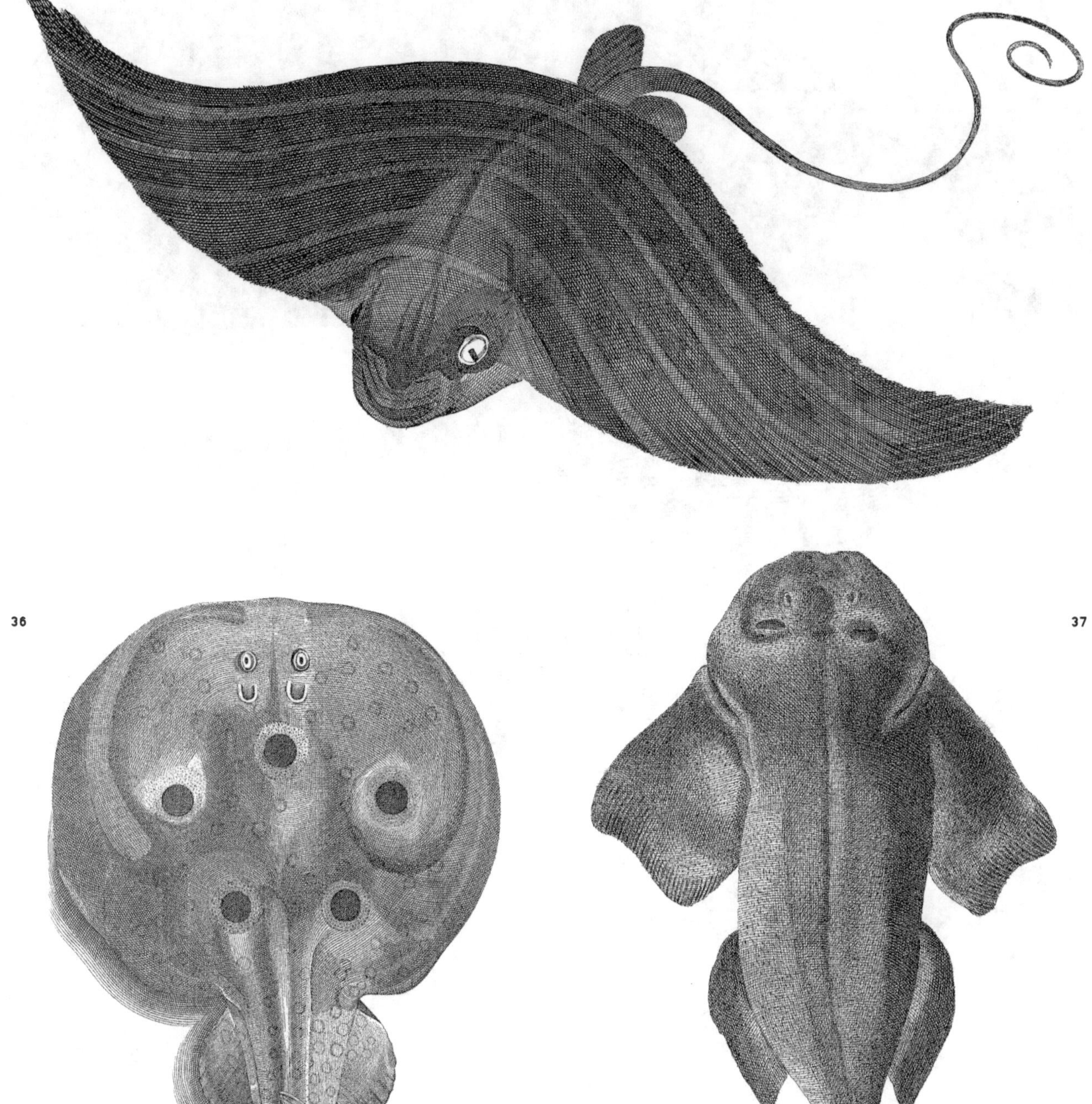

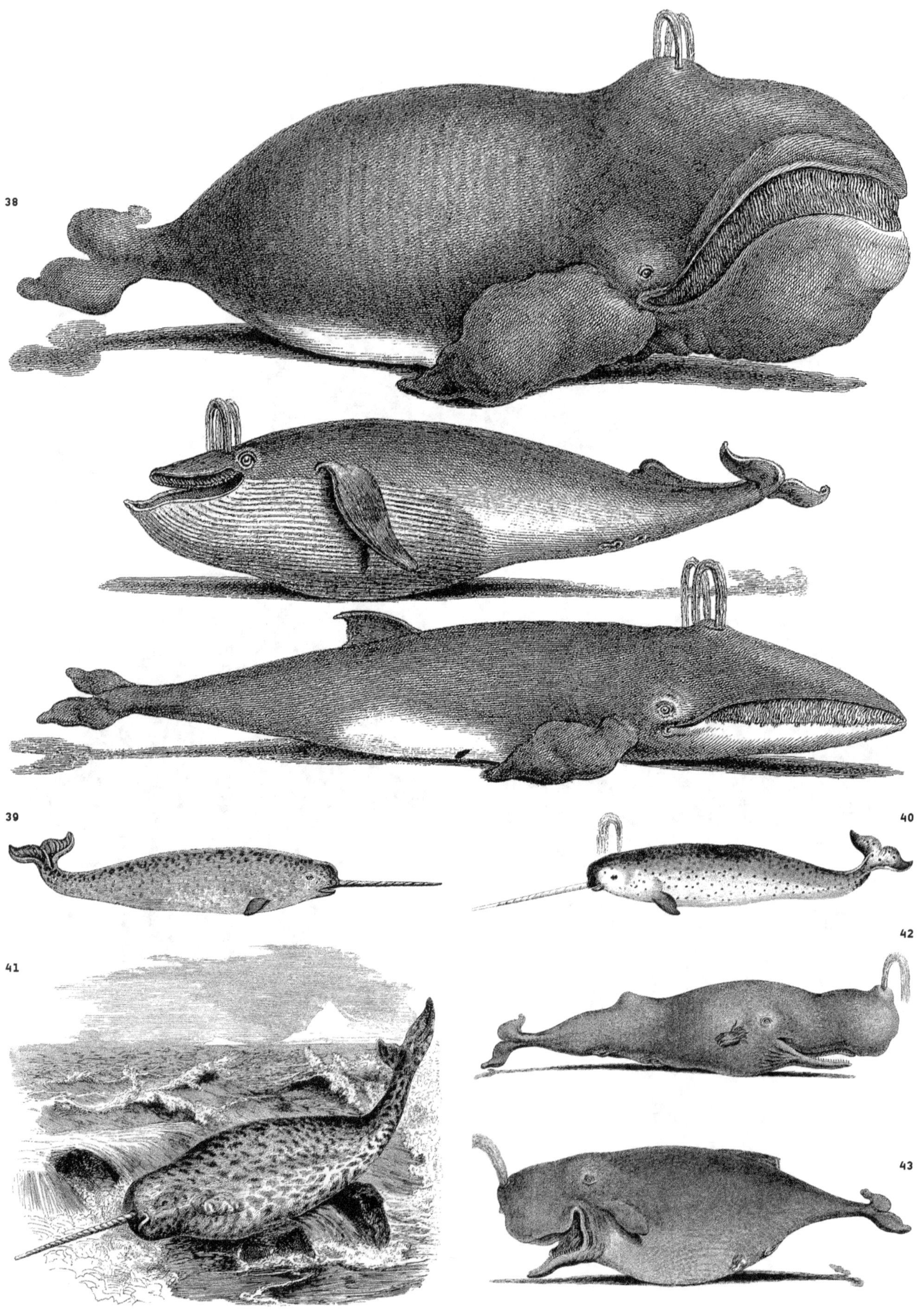

38

39

40

41

42

43

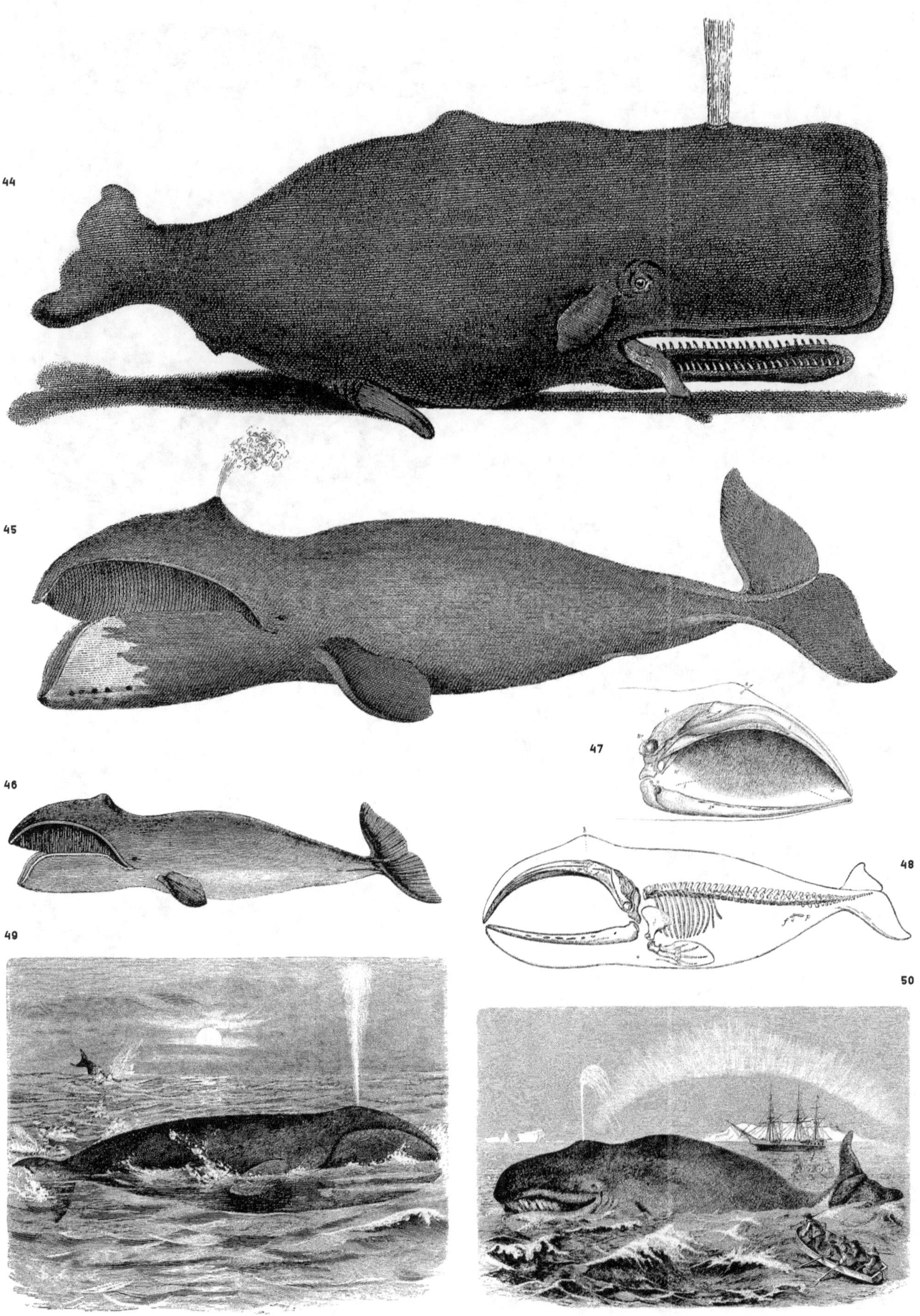

44
45
46
47
48
49
50
SEA-LIFE & MONSTERS OF THE DEEP

51
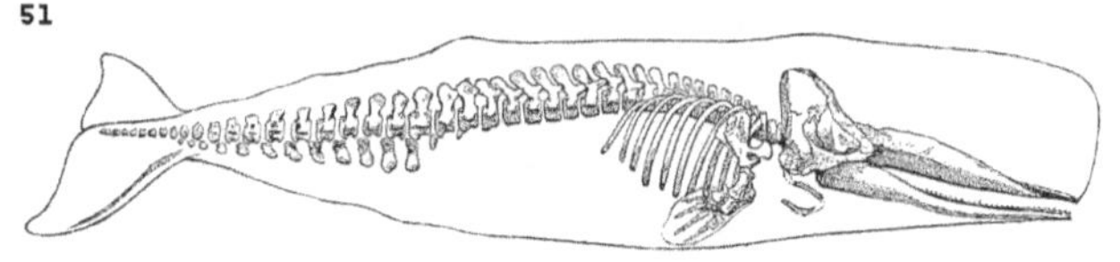

52
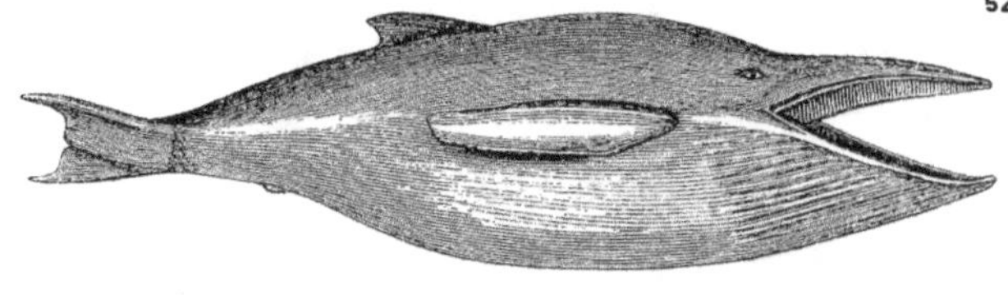

53
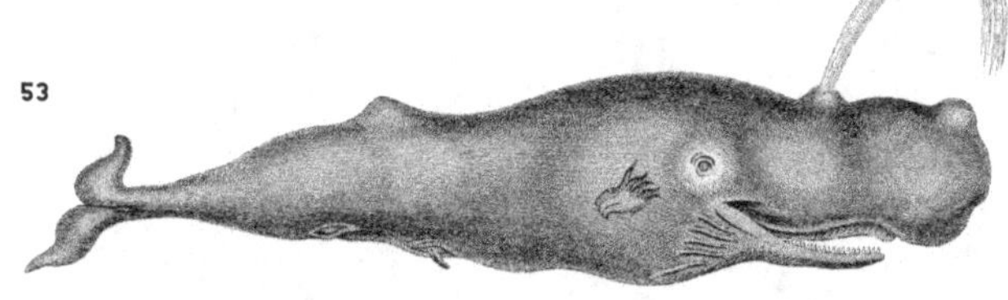

54
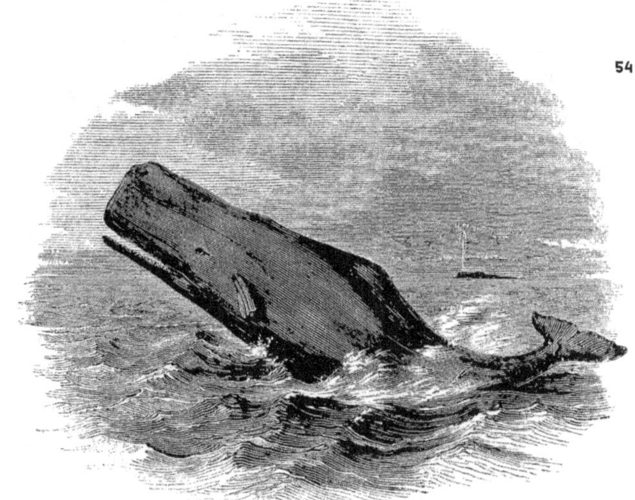

55
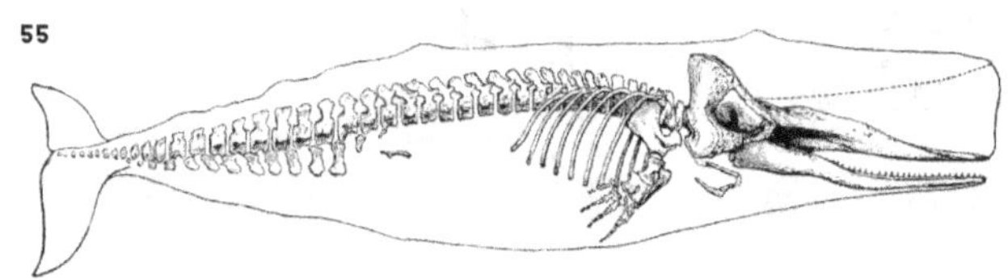

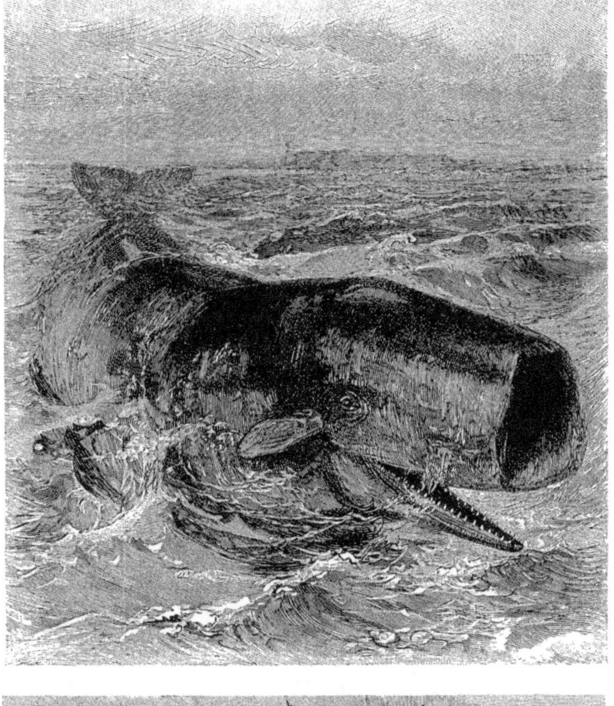

<56

57
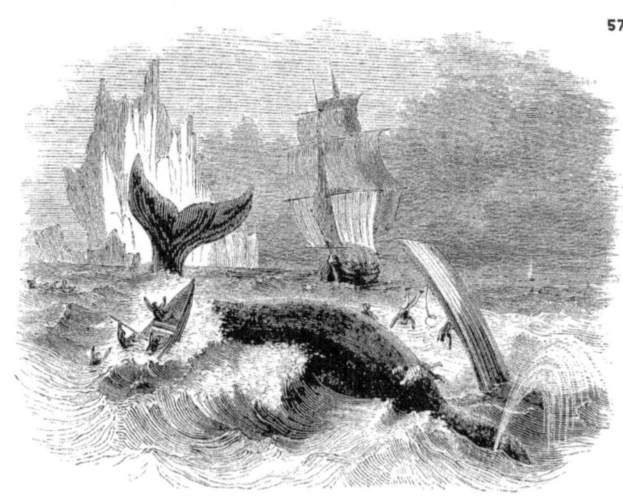

<58

59
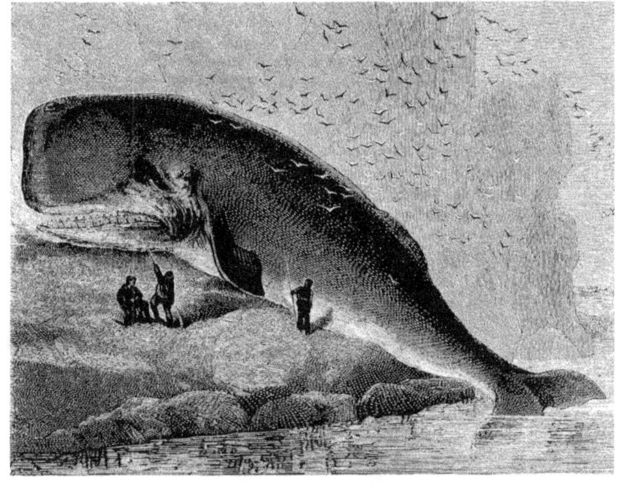

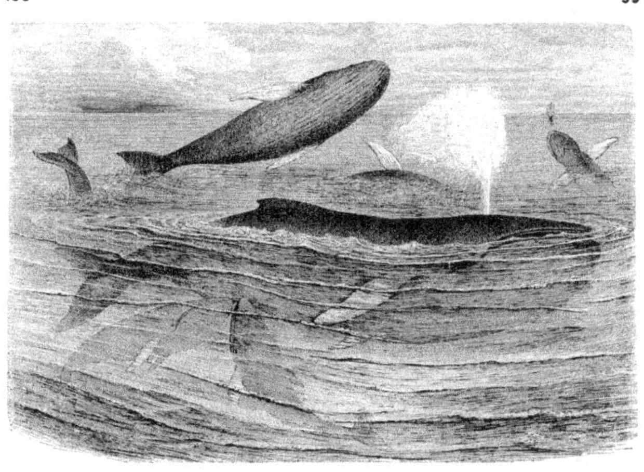

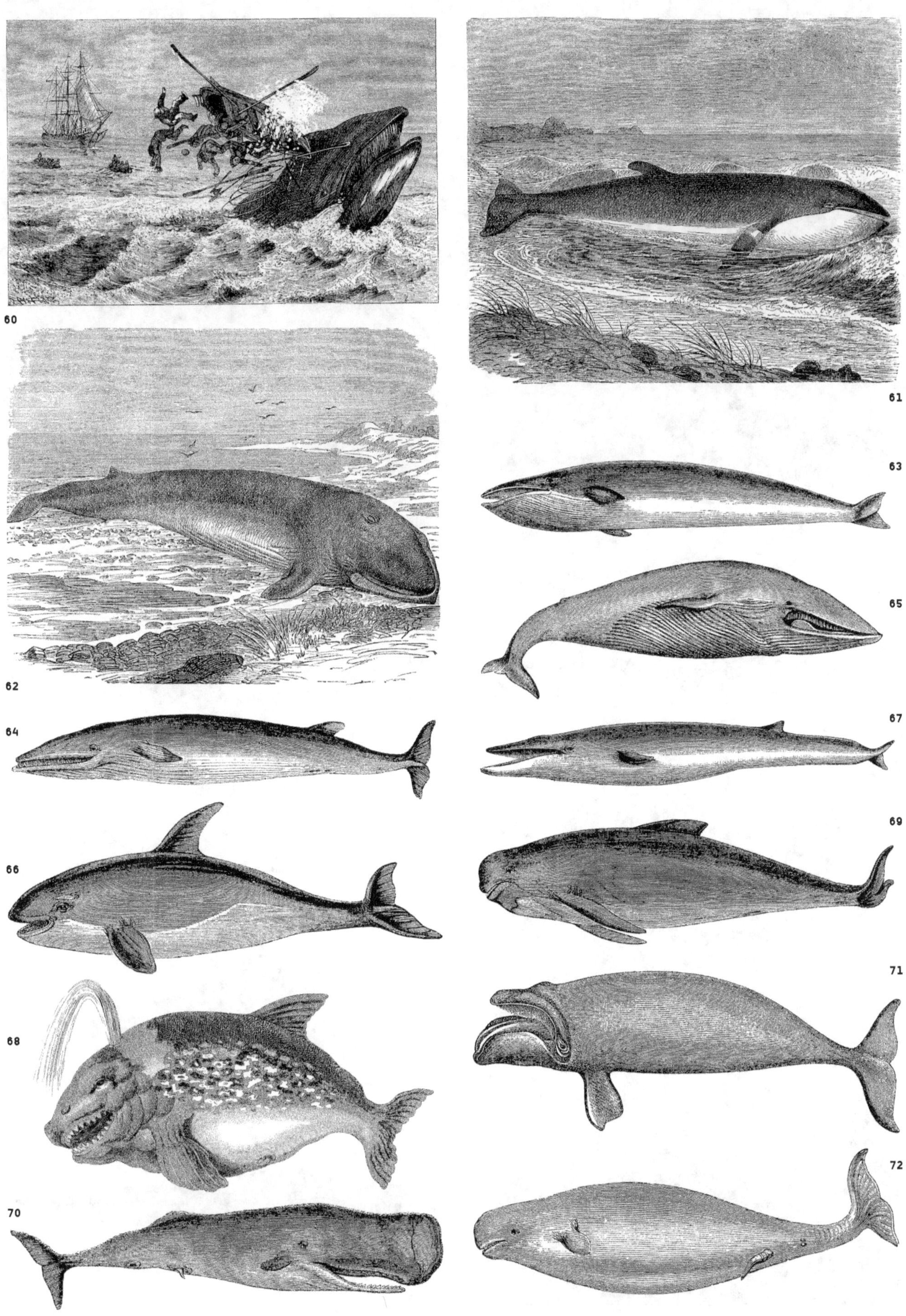

SEA-LIFE & MONSTERS OF THE DEEP

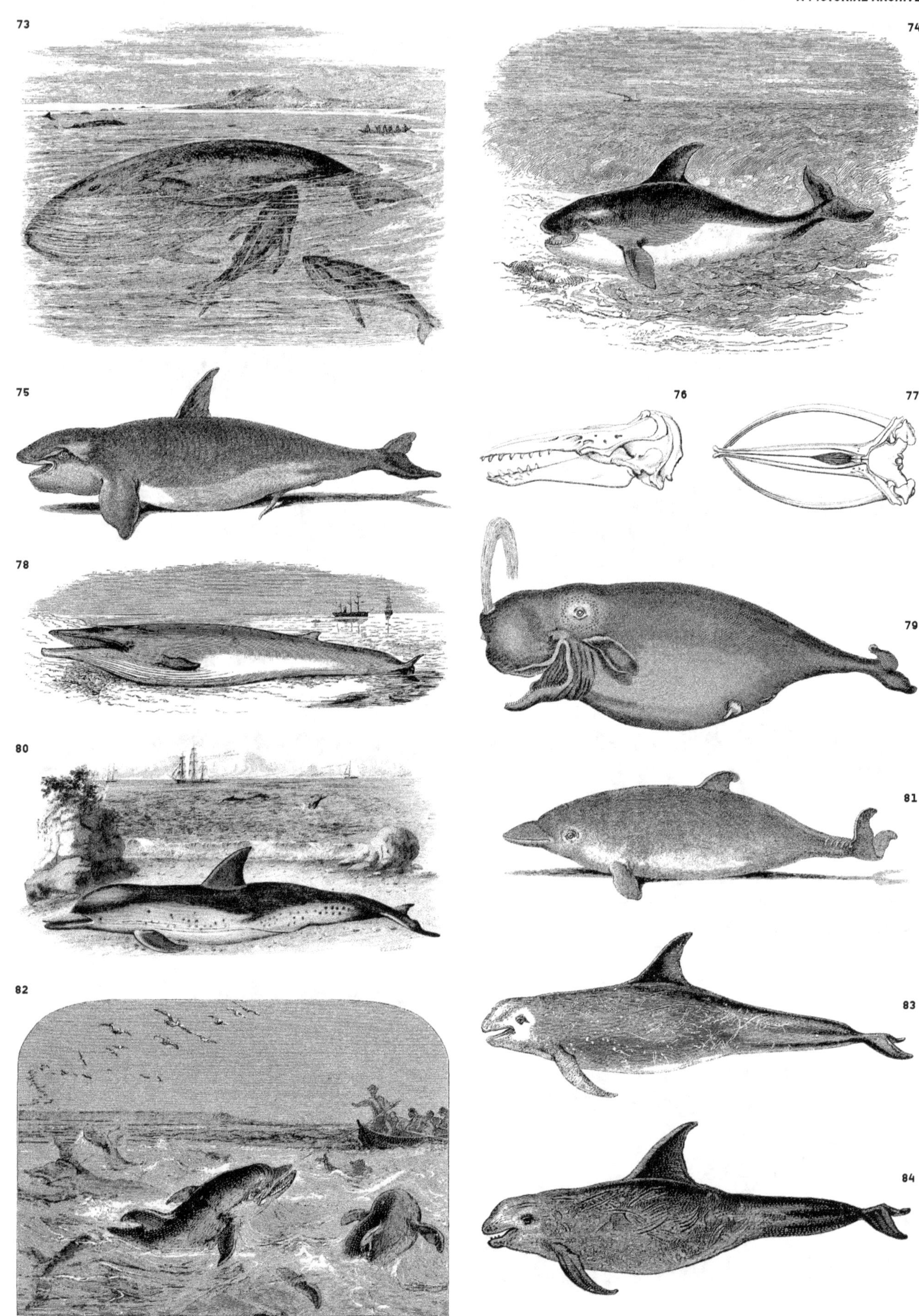

WHALES, DOLPHINS & PORPOISES

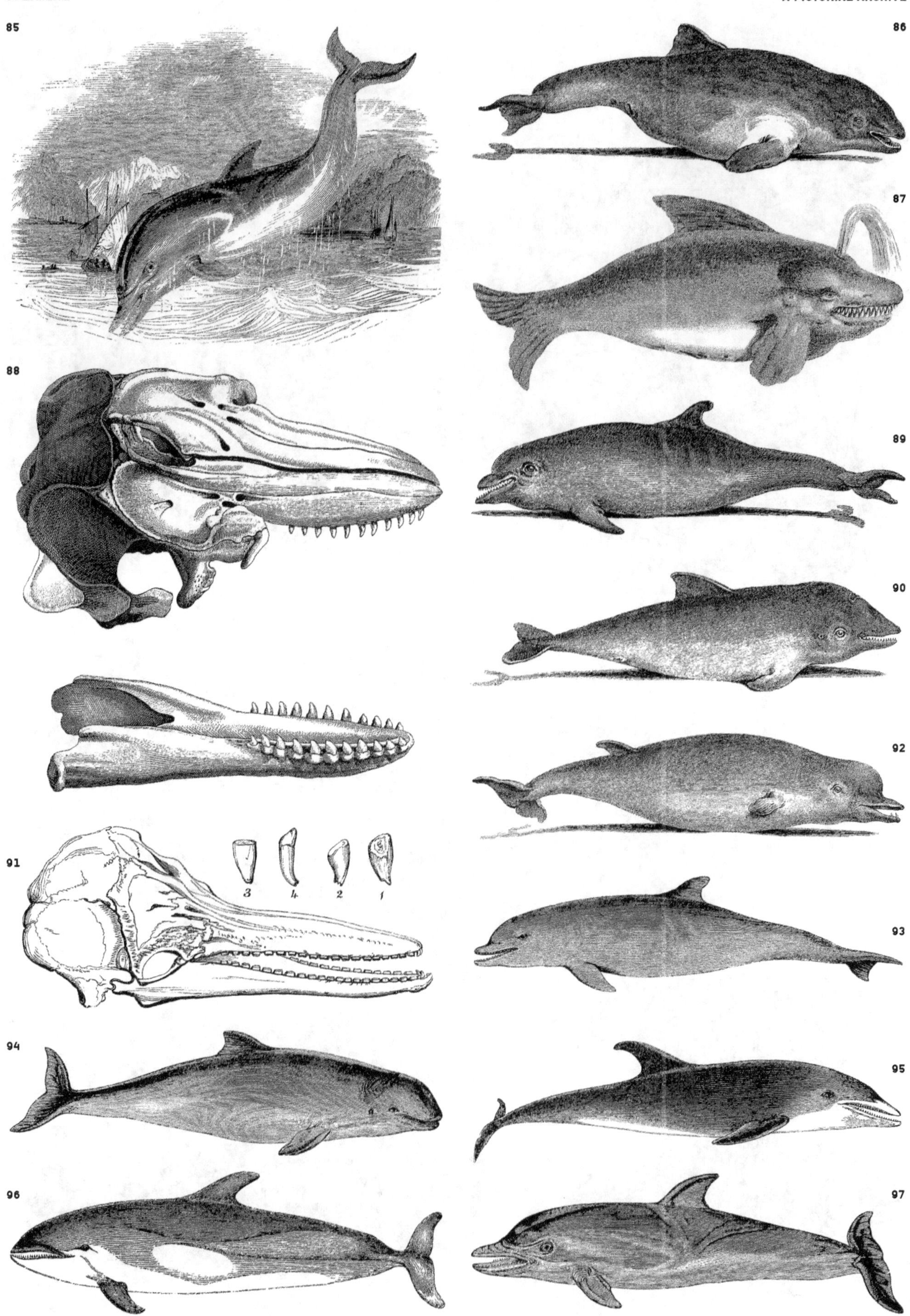

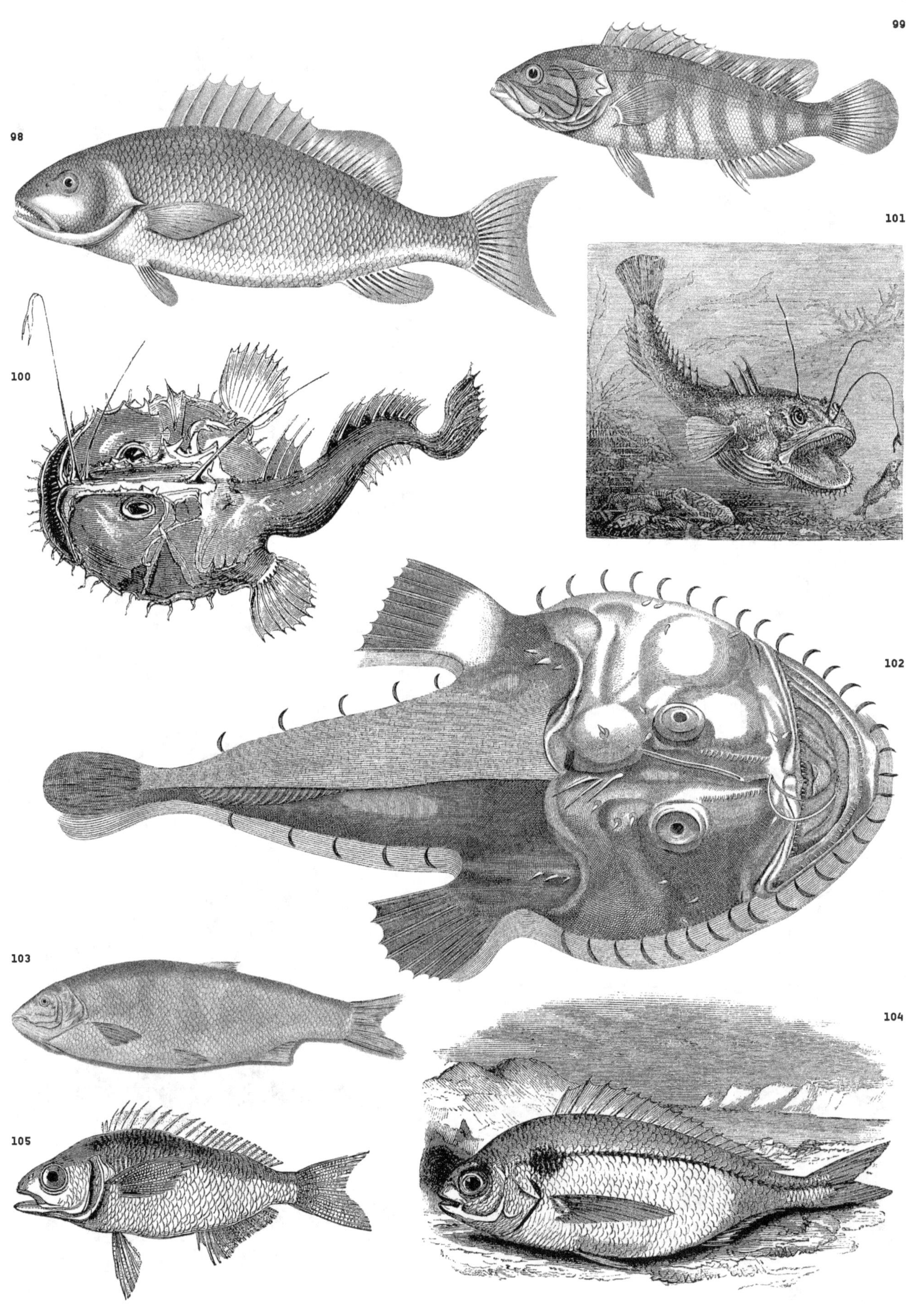

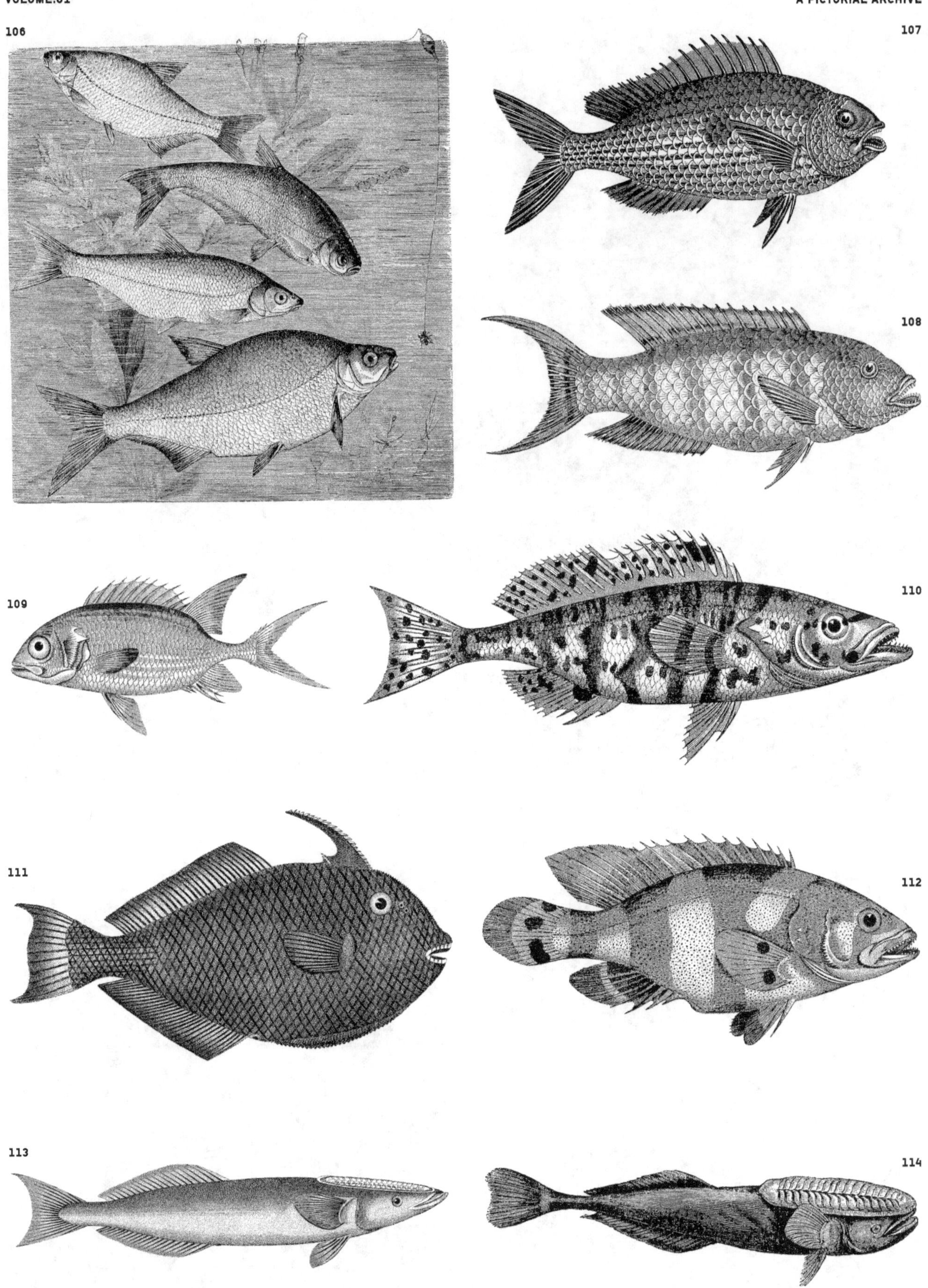
106
107
108
109
110
111
112
113
114

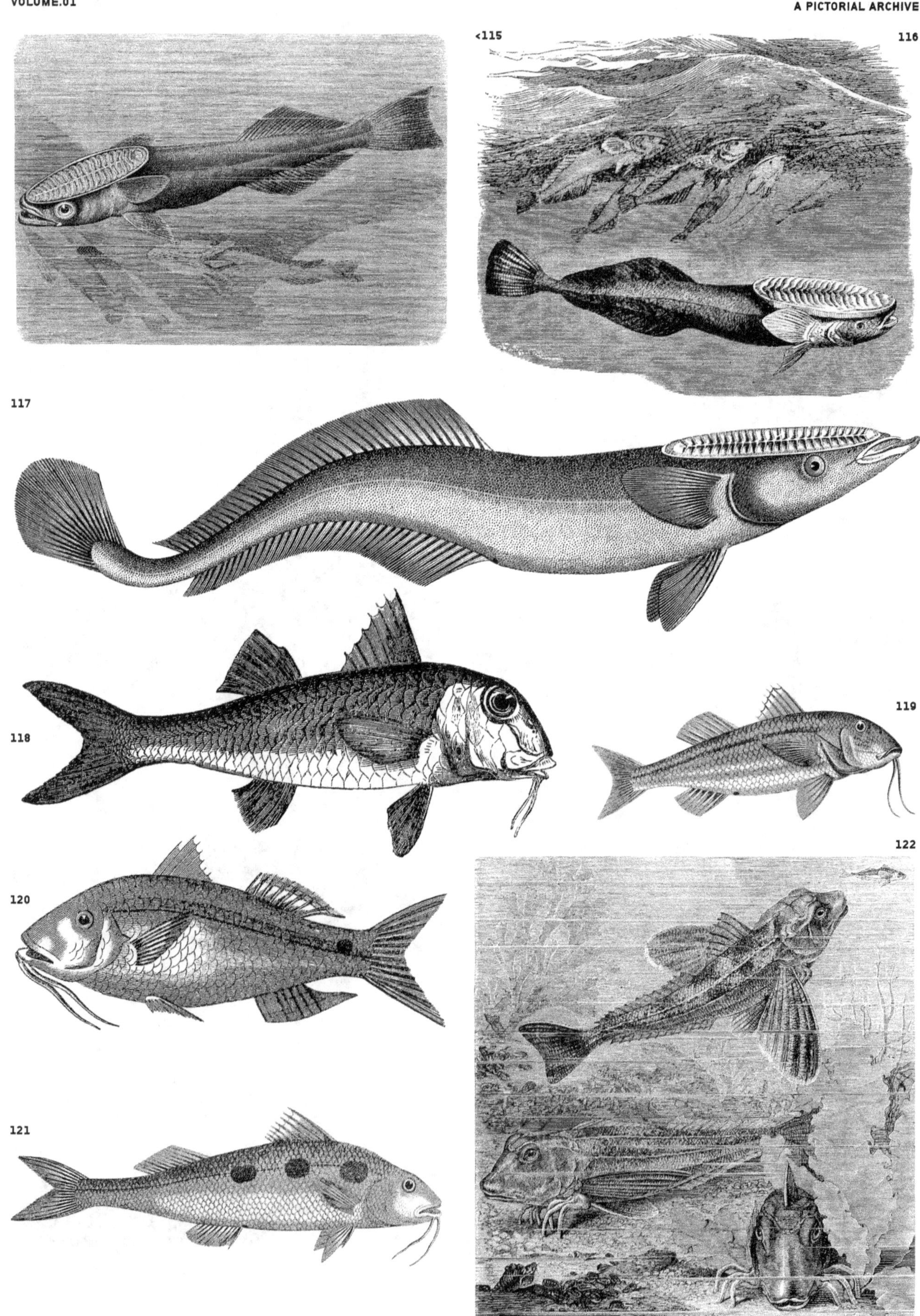

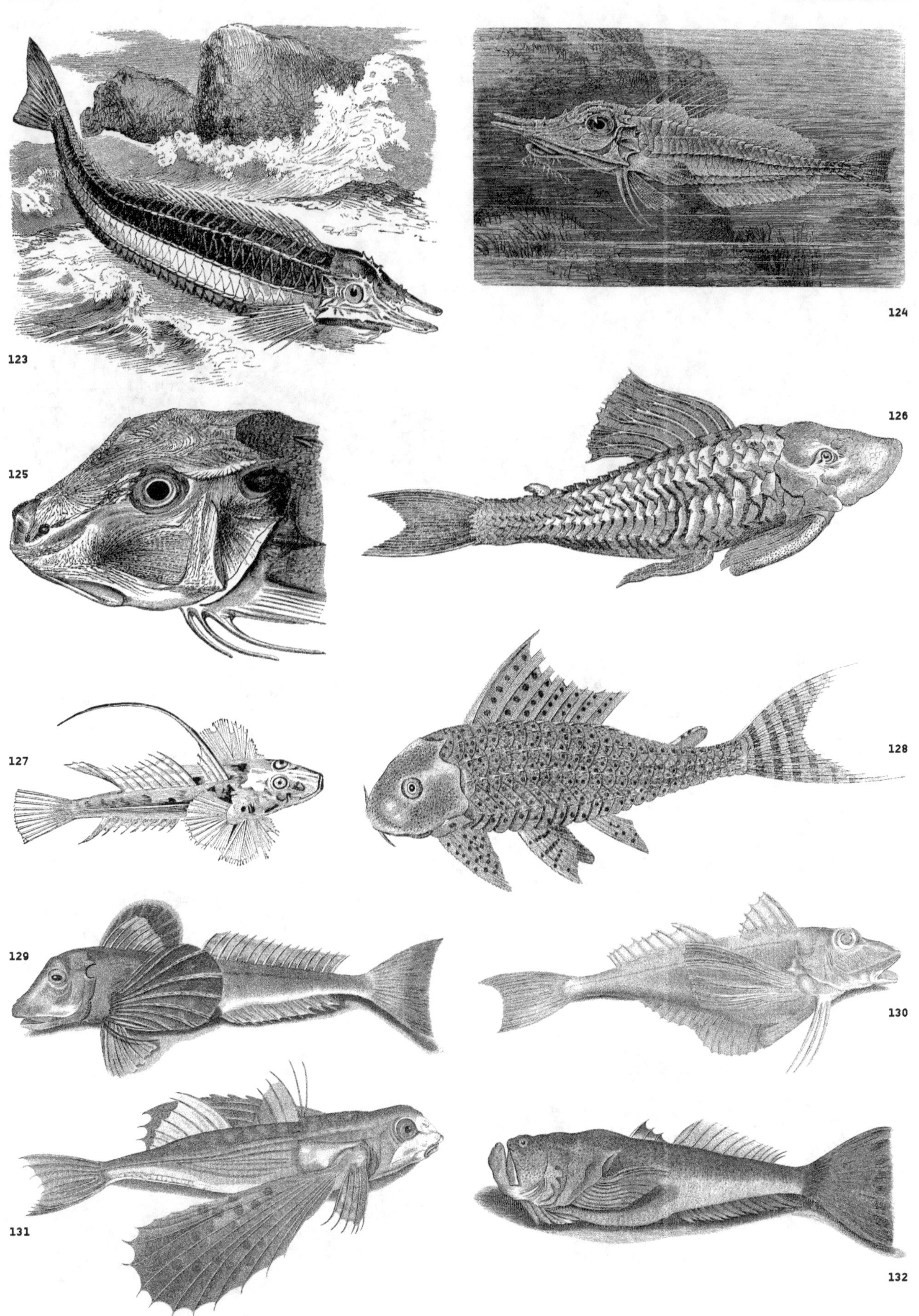

123

124

125

126

127

128

129

130

131

132

FISH

133

134

135

136

137

138

139

140

141

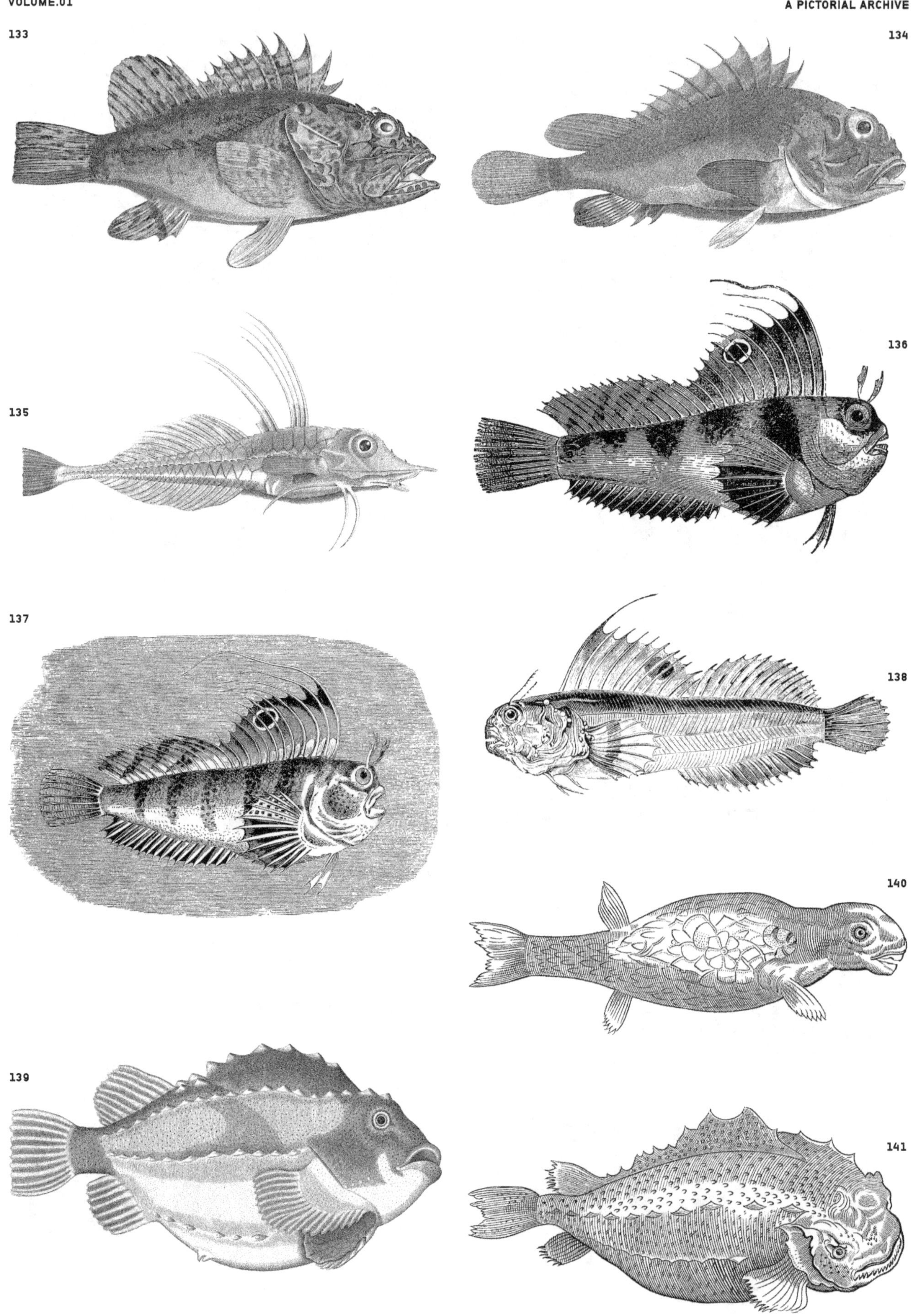

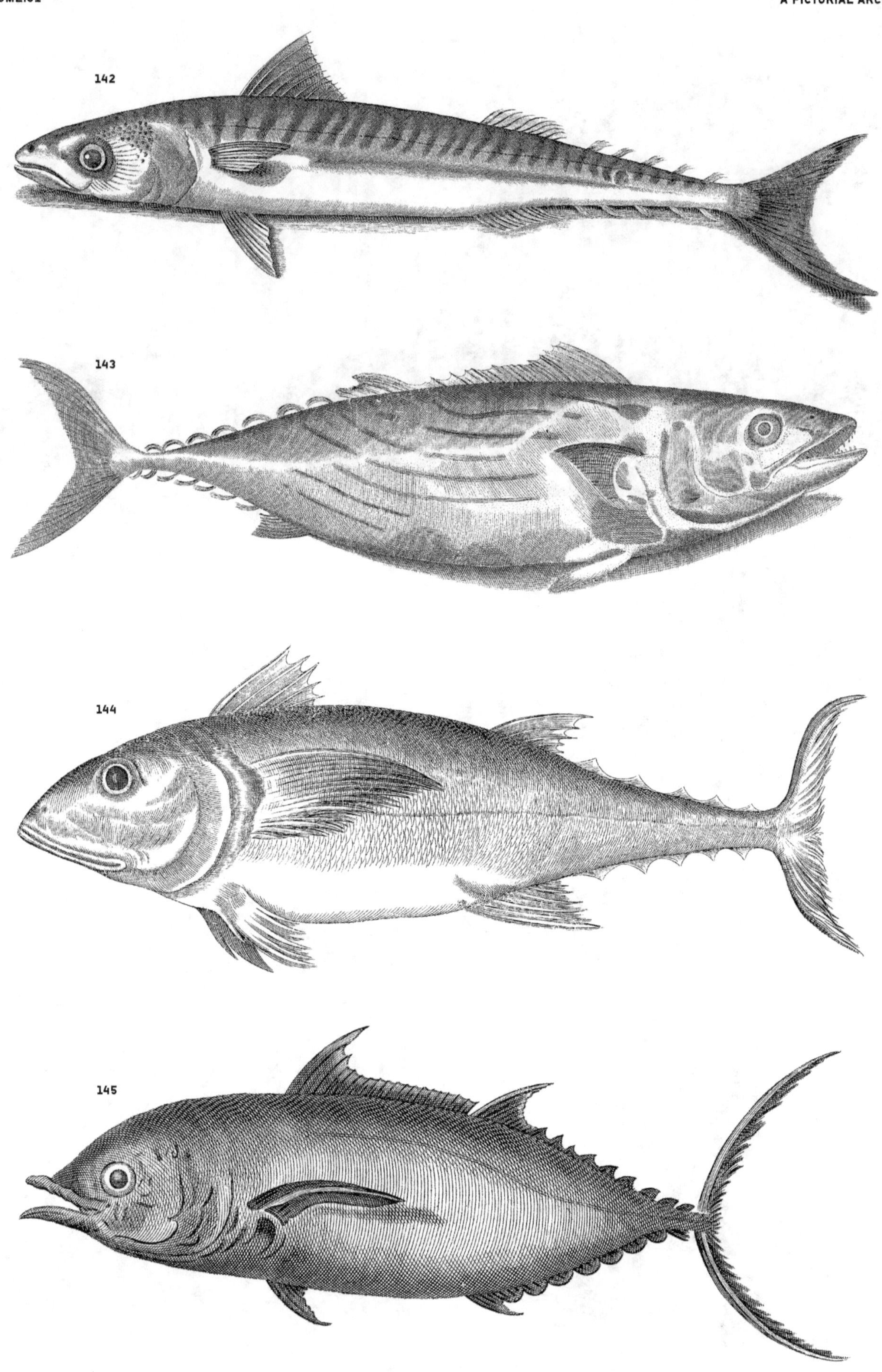

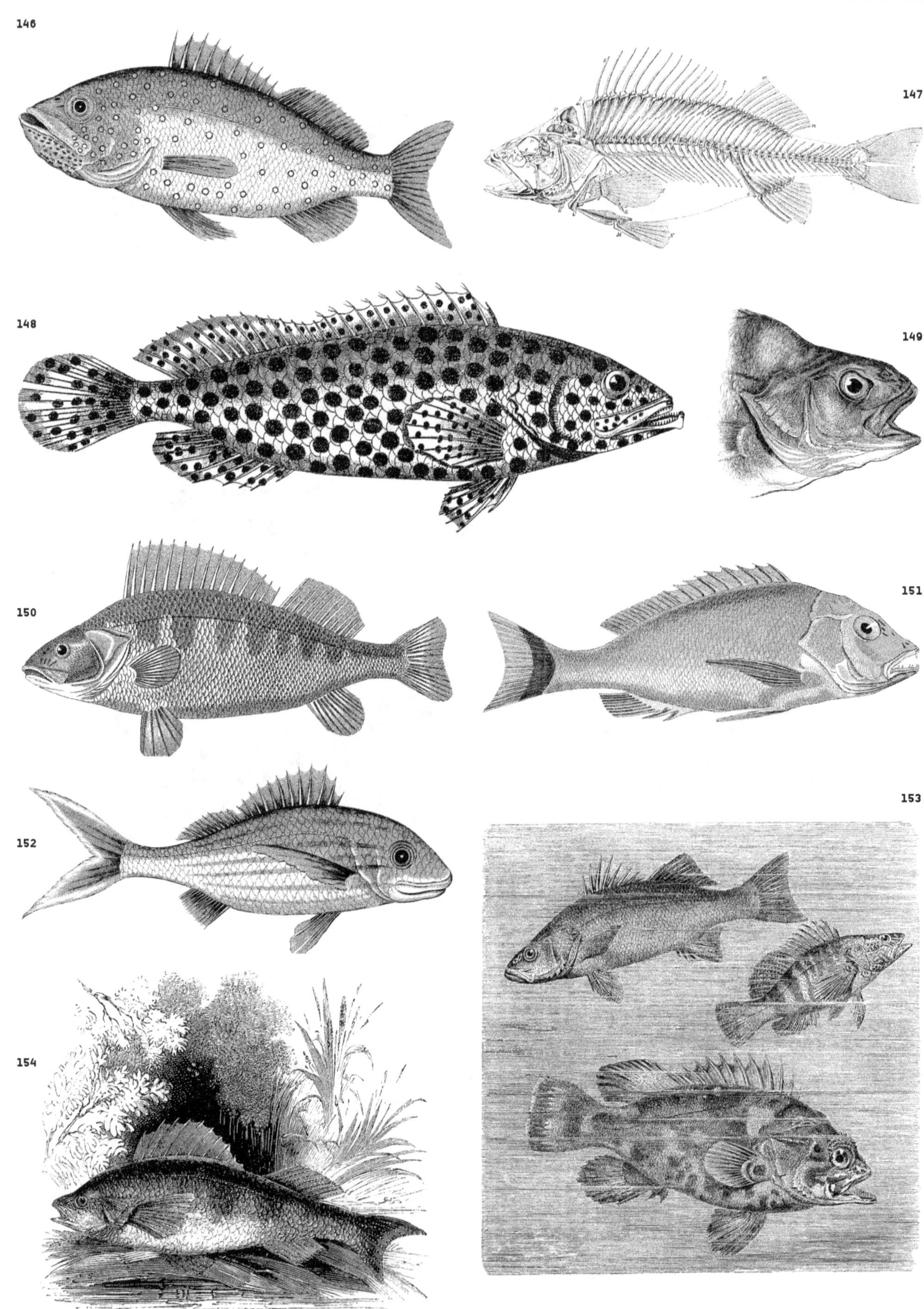

155

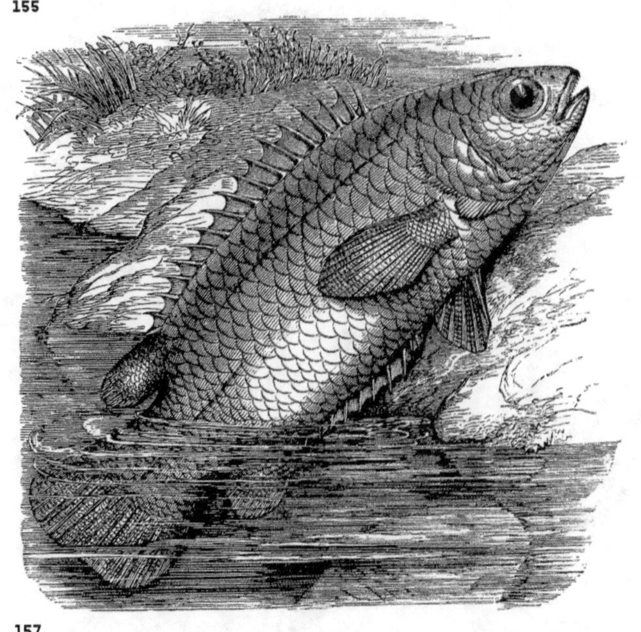

156

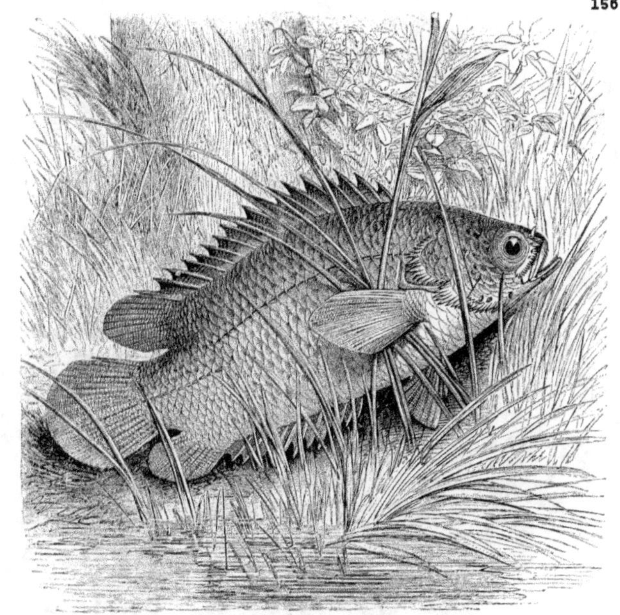

157

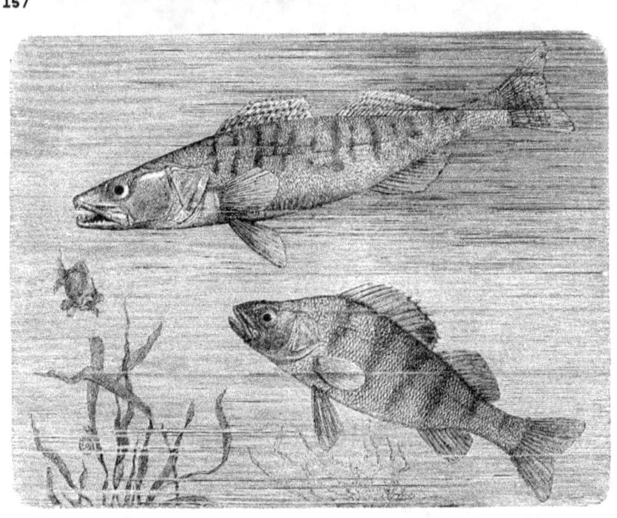

158

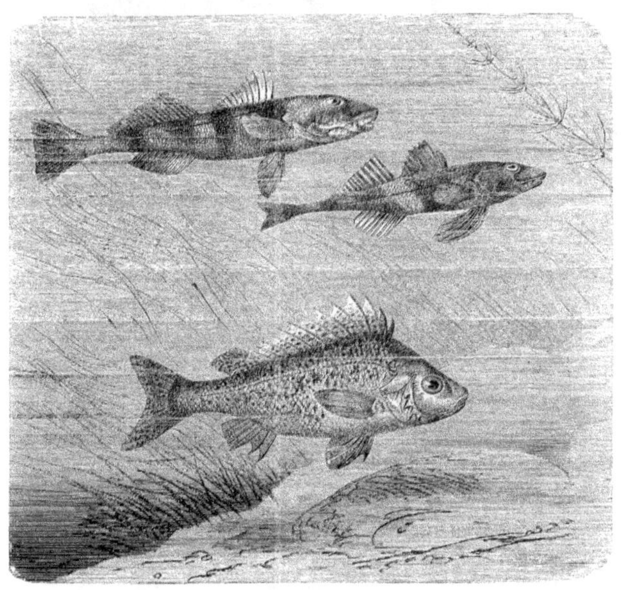

159

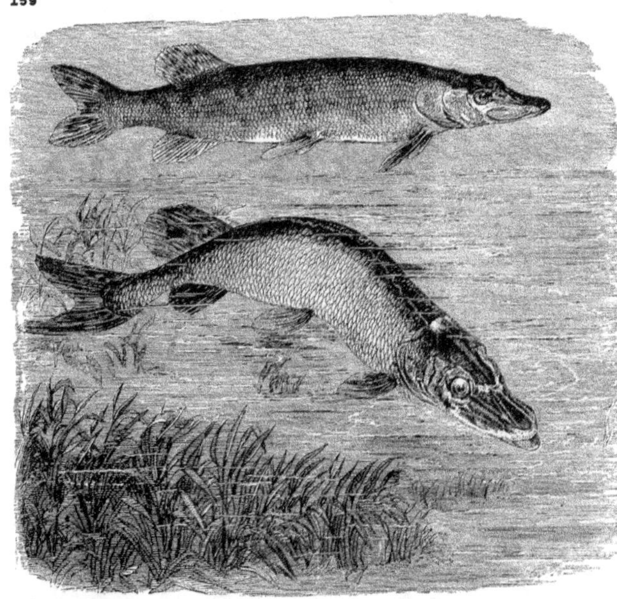

160

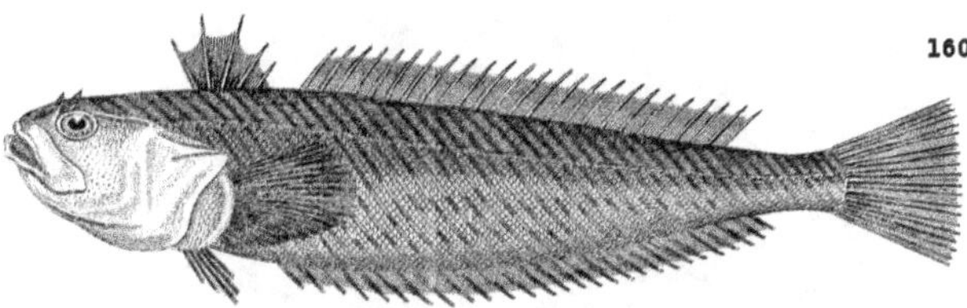

161

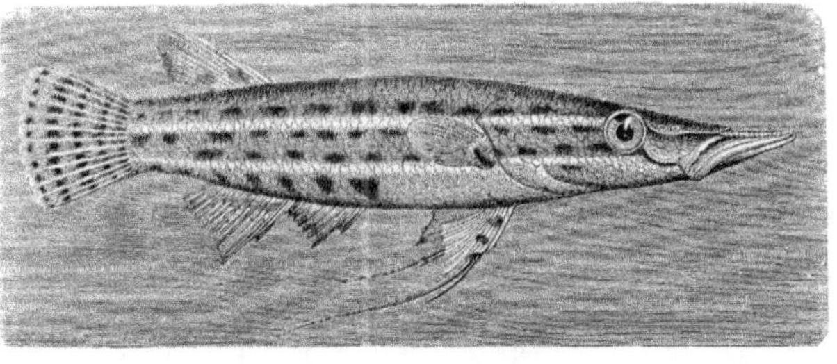

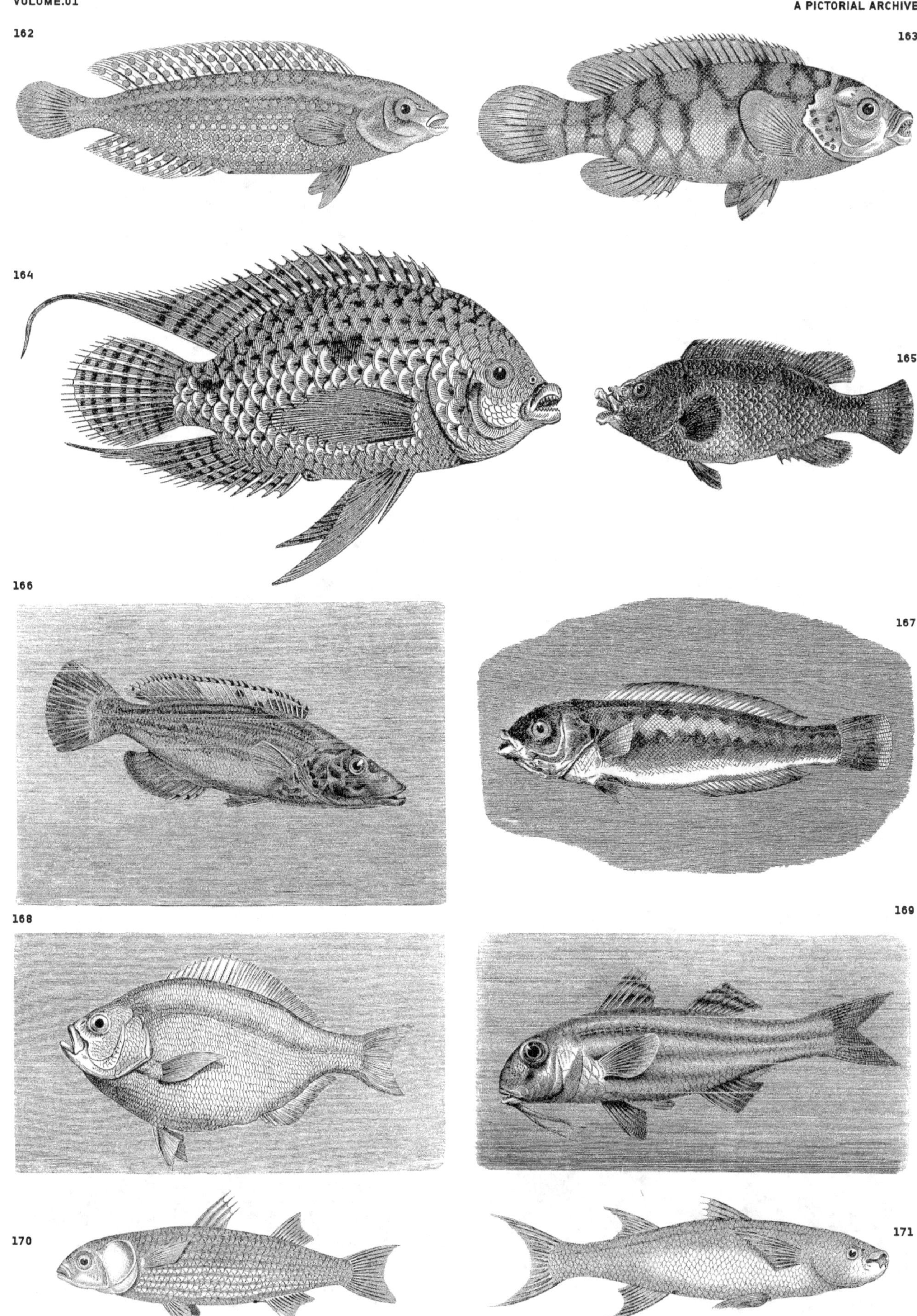

172

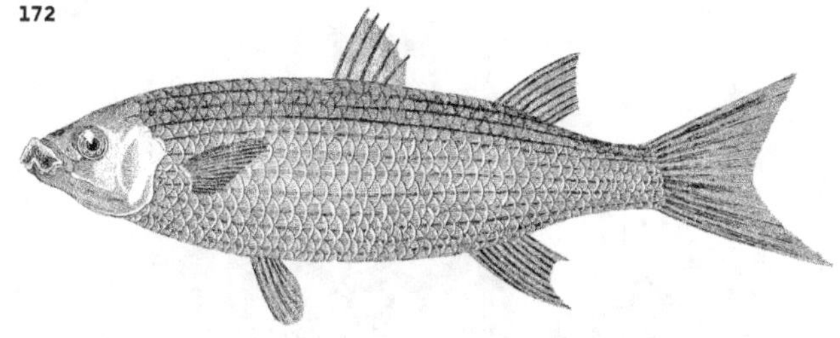

173

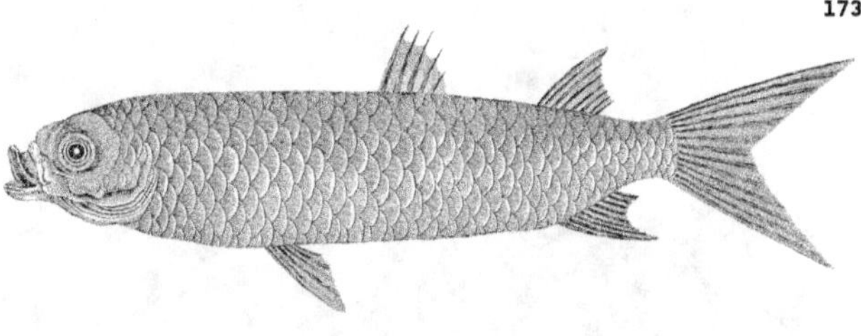

174

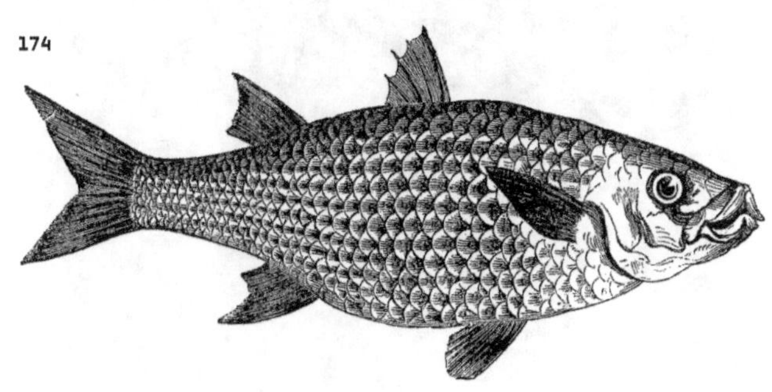

175

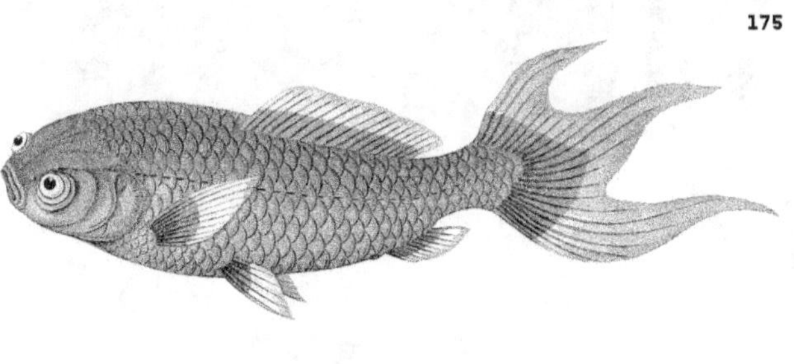

176

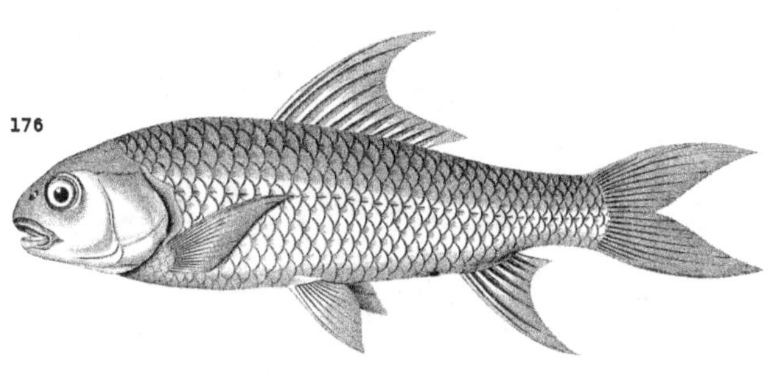

177

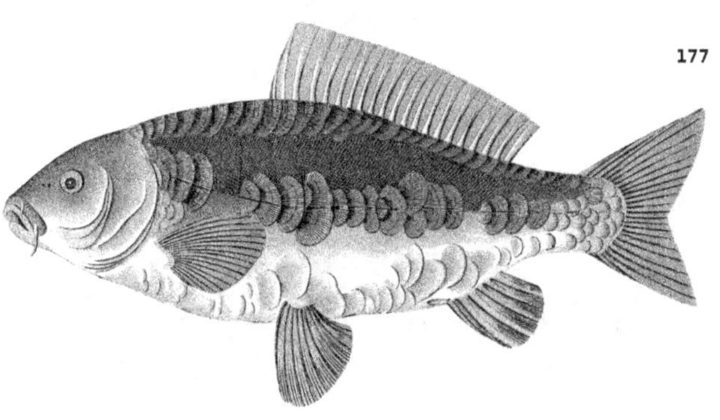

178

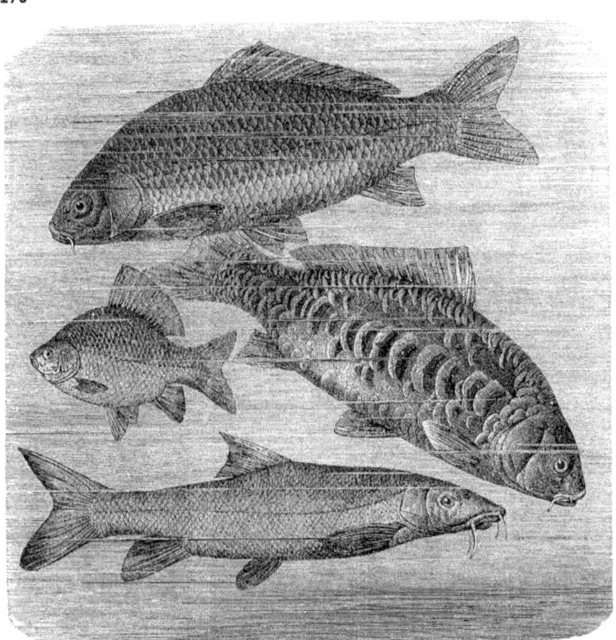

179

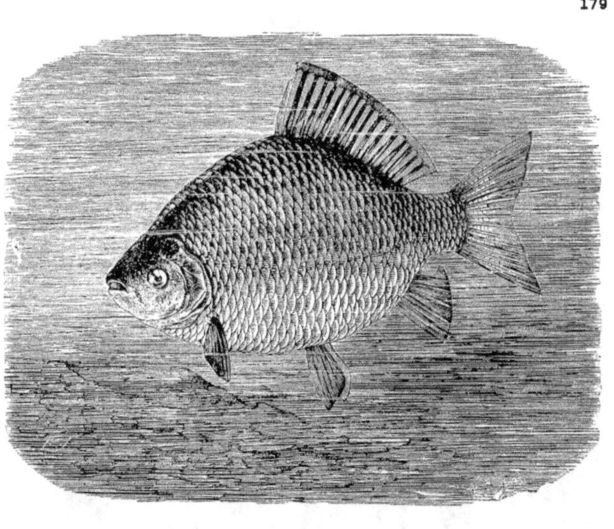

180

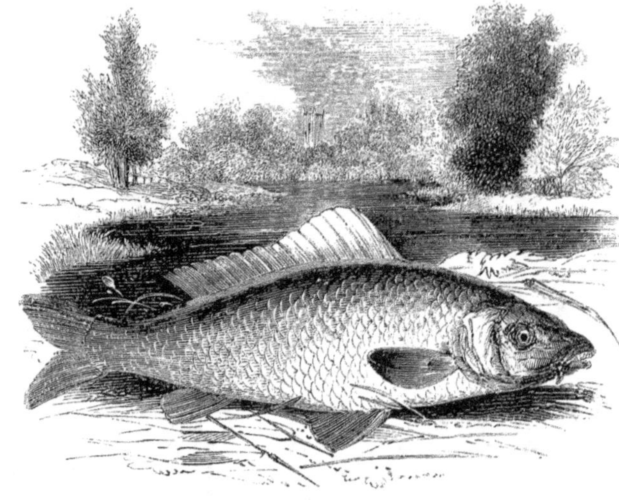

181

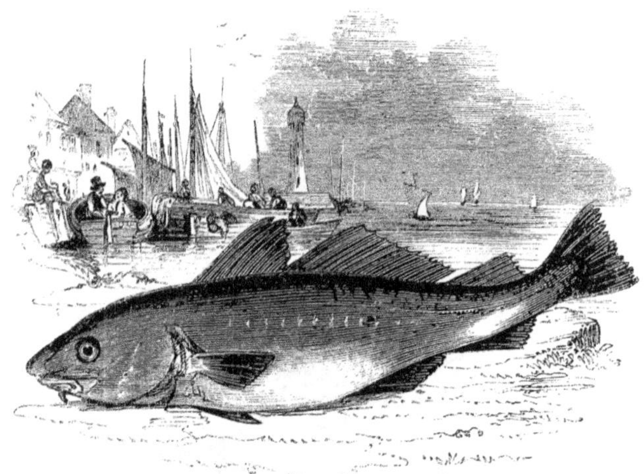

182

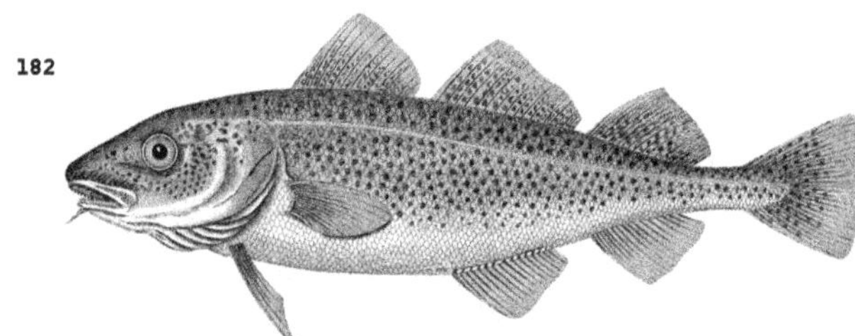

183

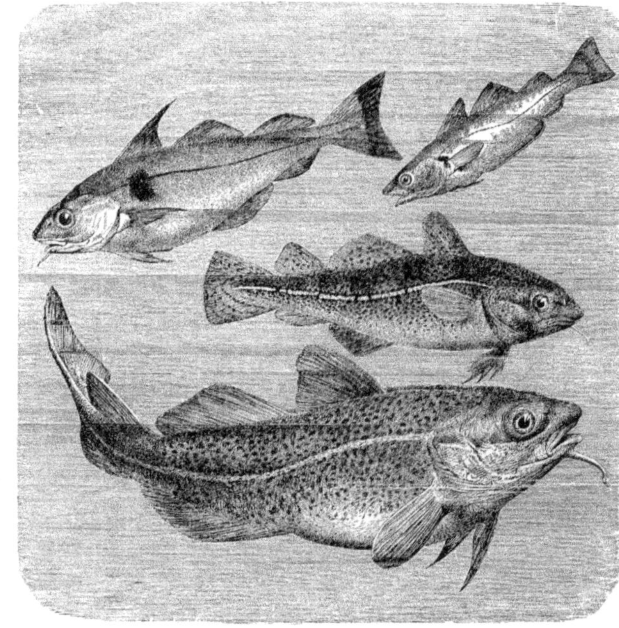

184

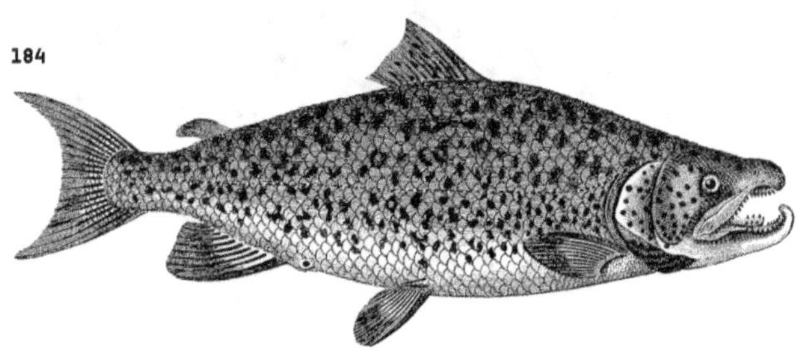

185

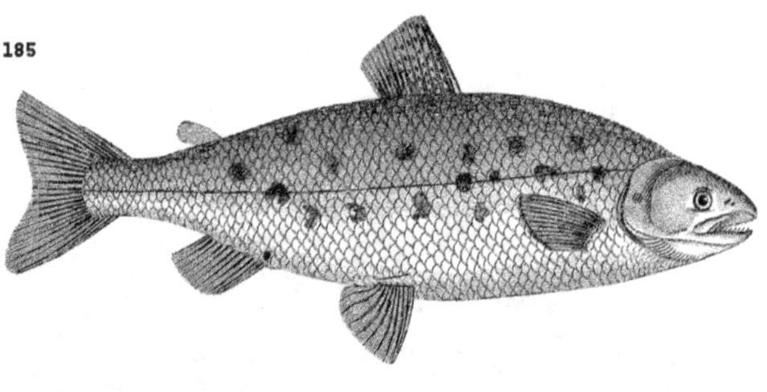

187

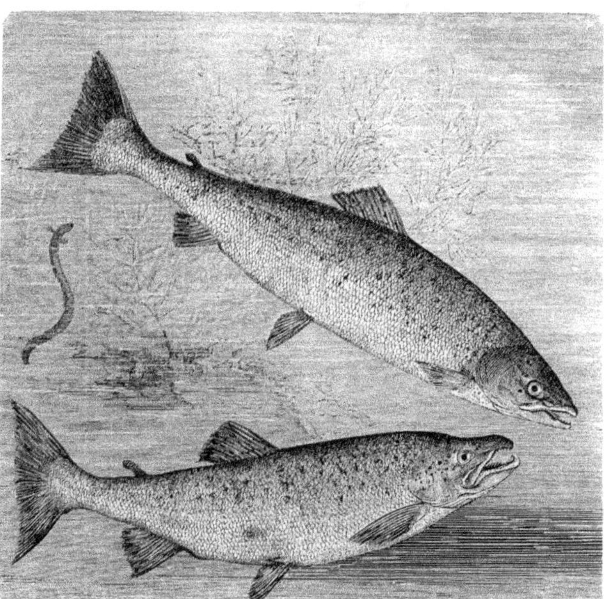

186

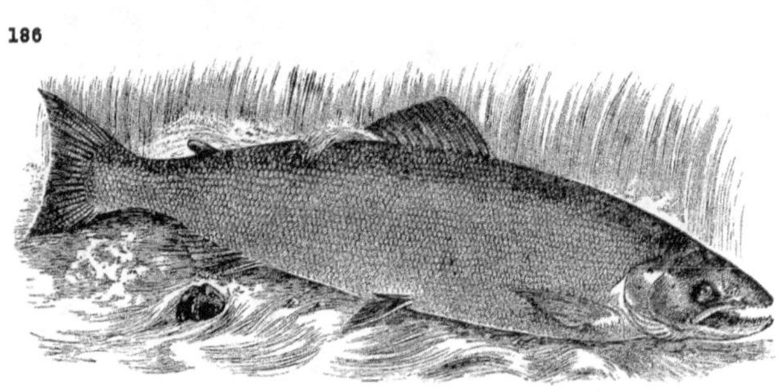

188
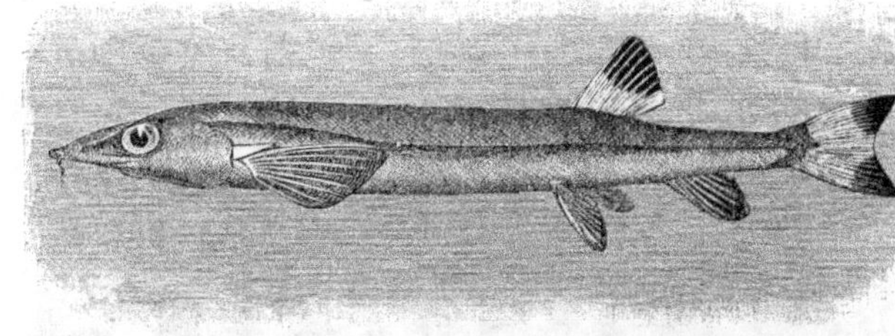

190
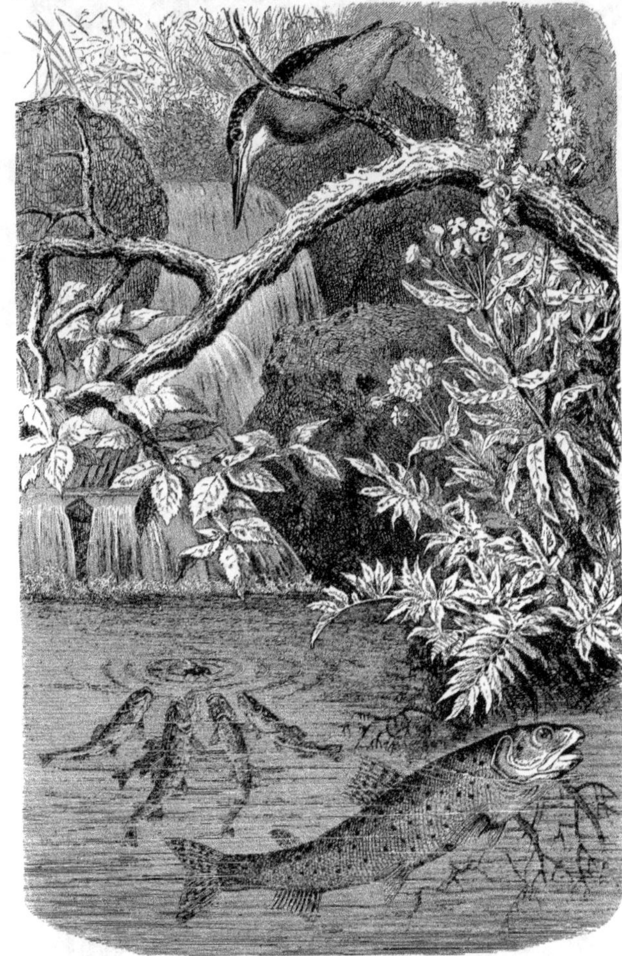

189
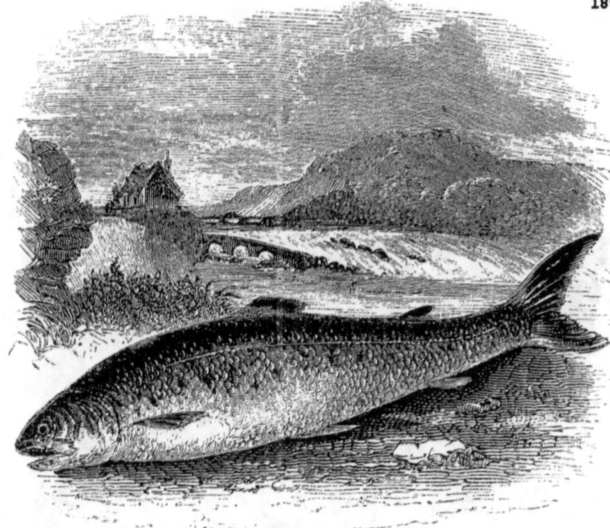

191
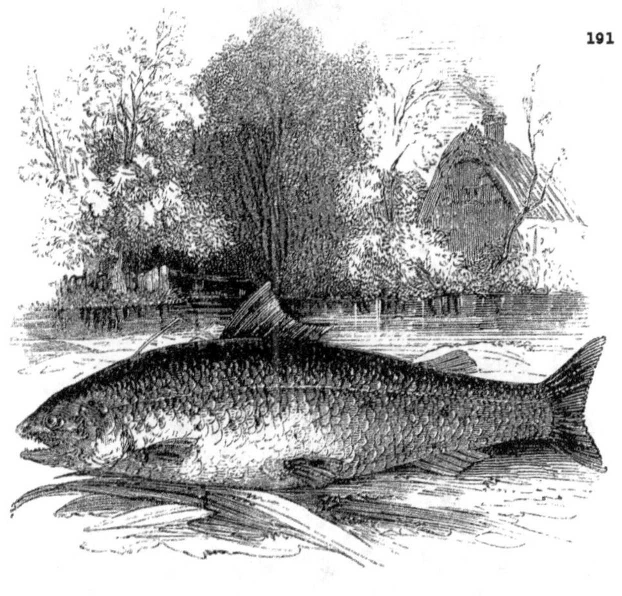

192
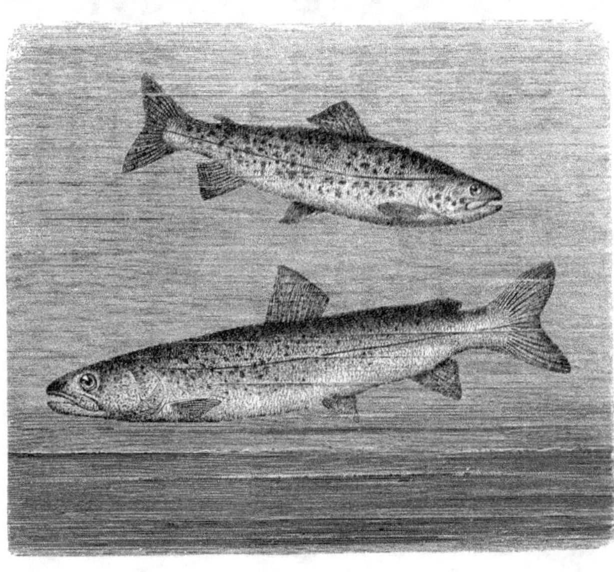

193
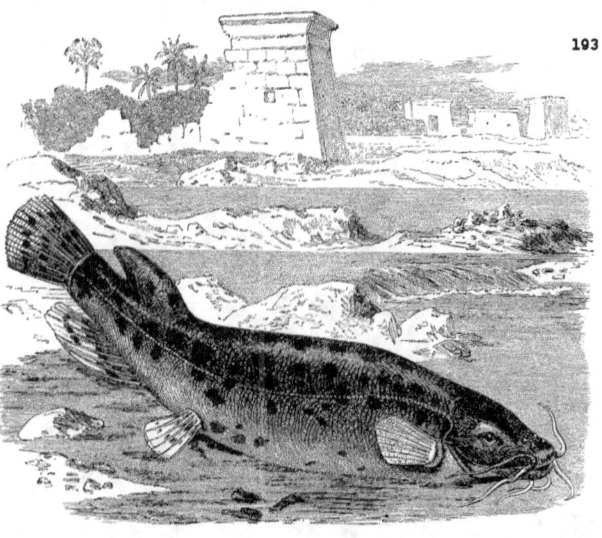

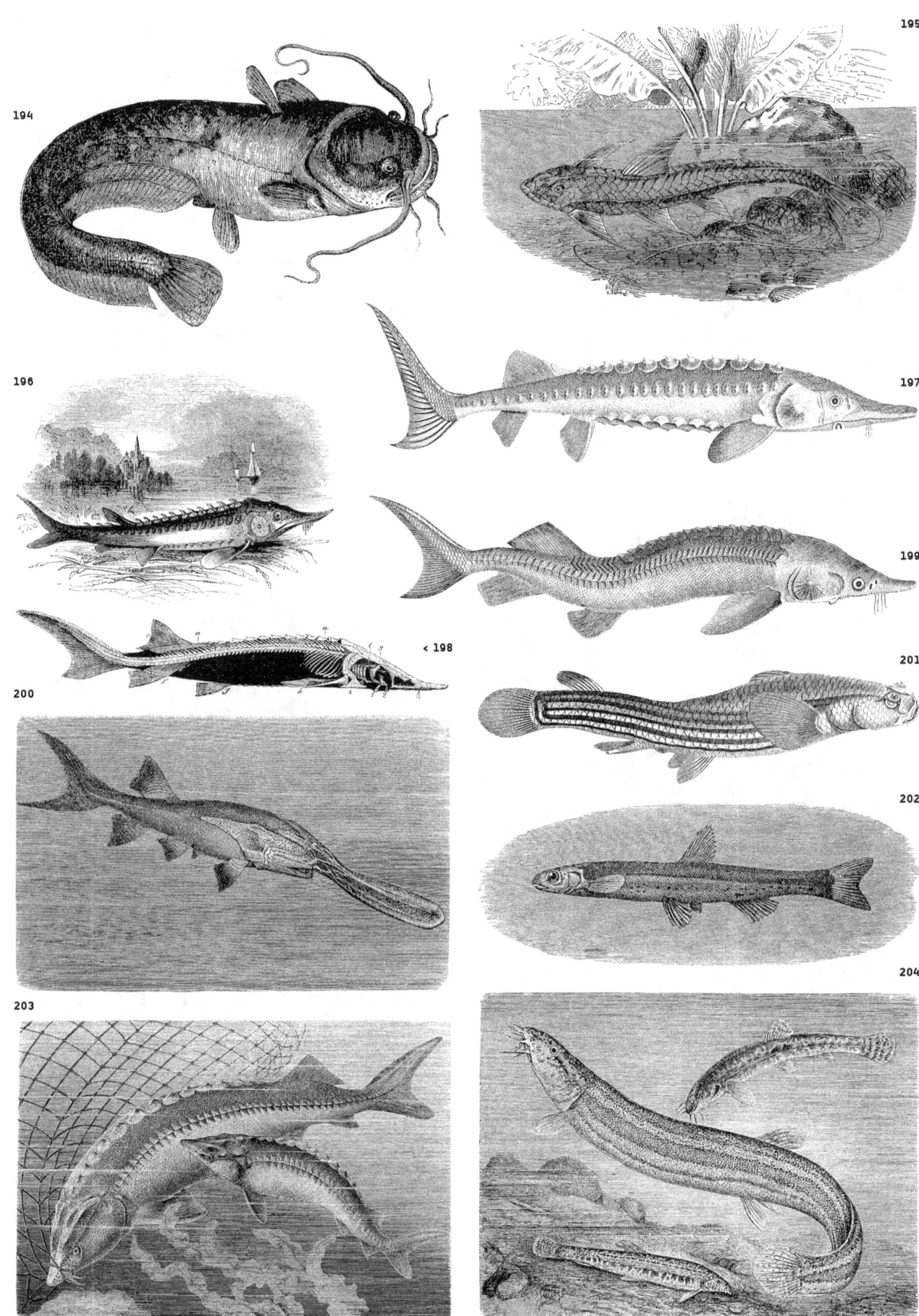

195

194

196

197

199

< 198

200

201

202

204

203

205

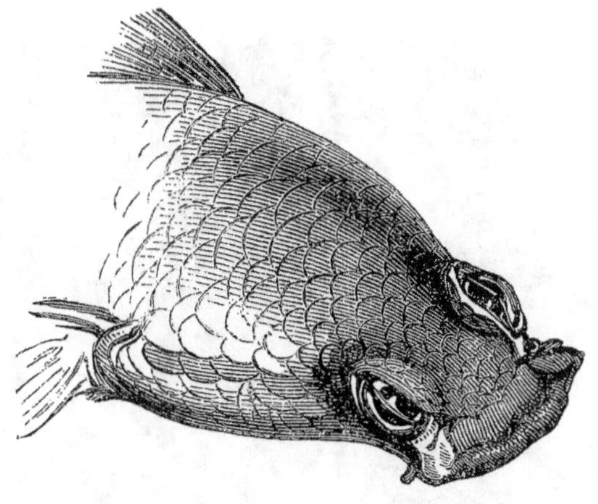

206

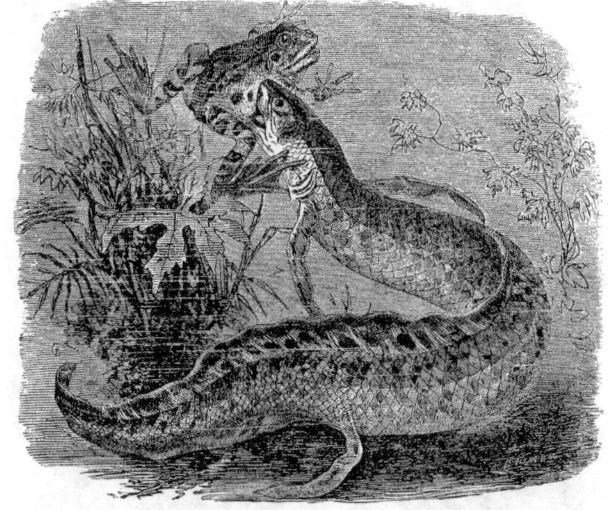

207

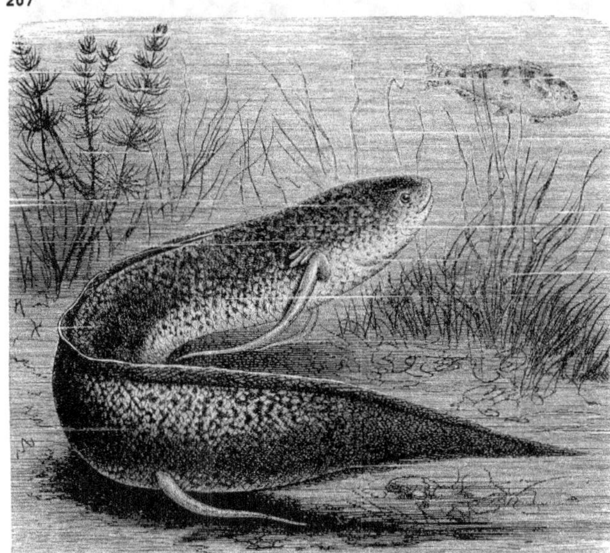

208

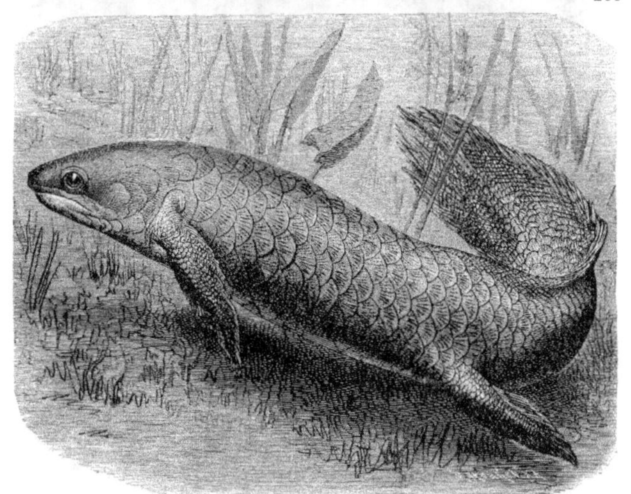

209

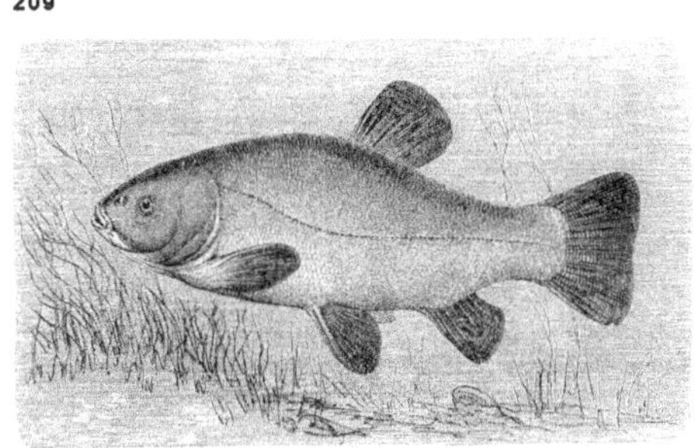

210

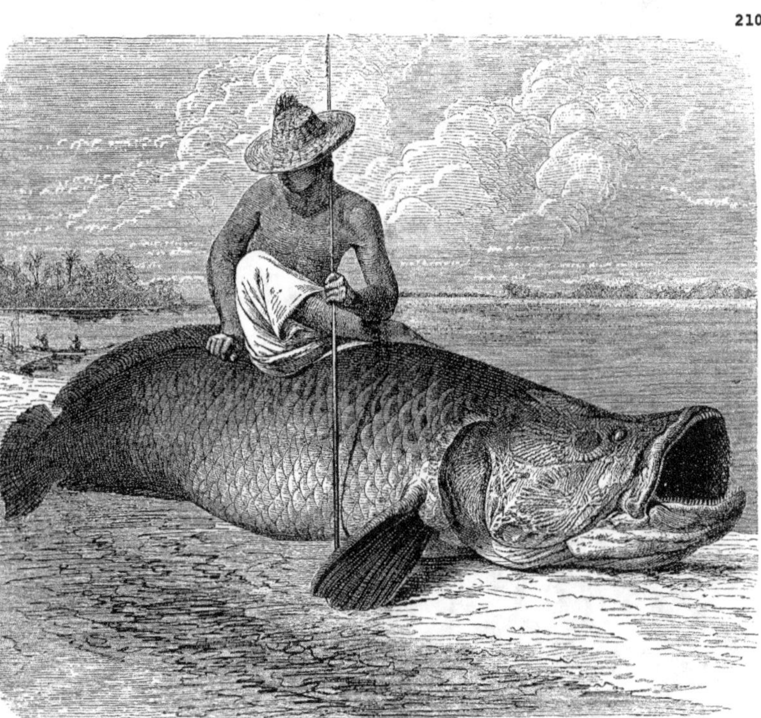

211

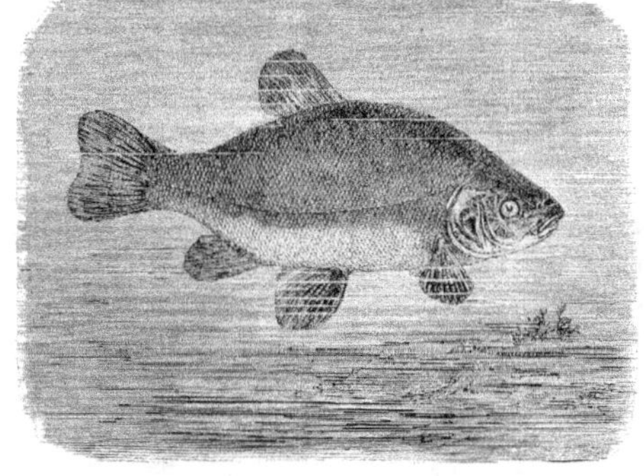

212

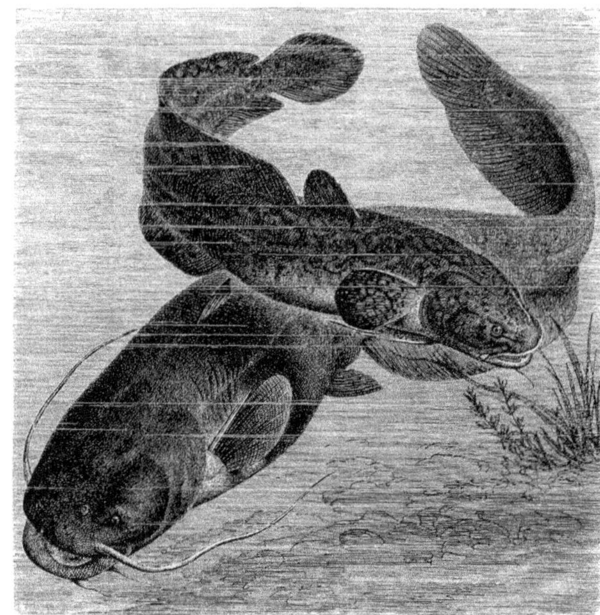

213

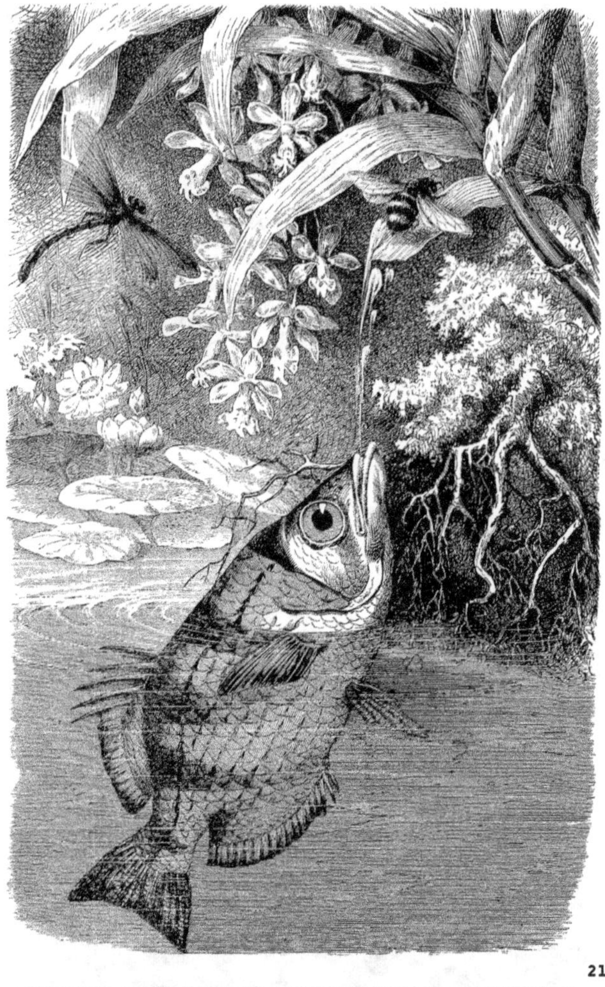

214

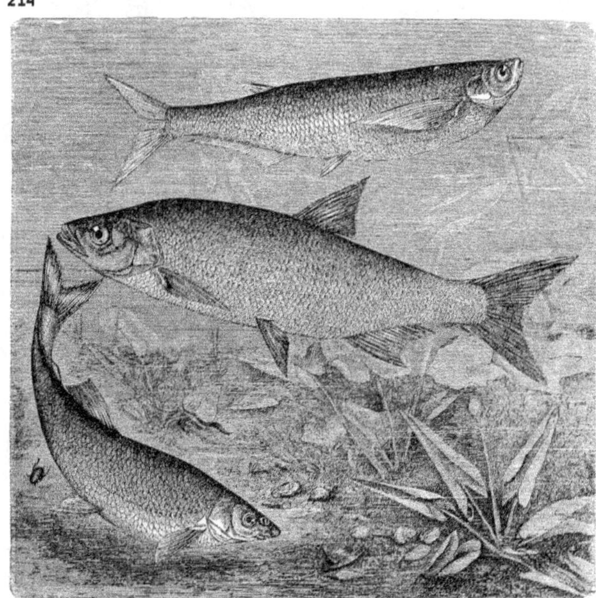

215

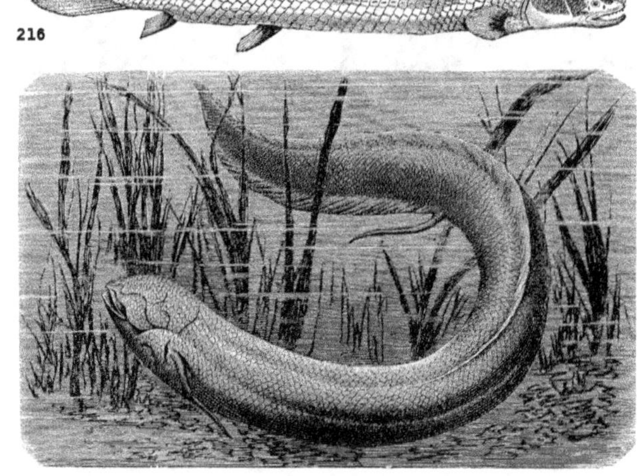

216

217

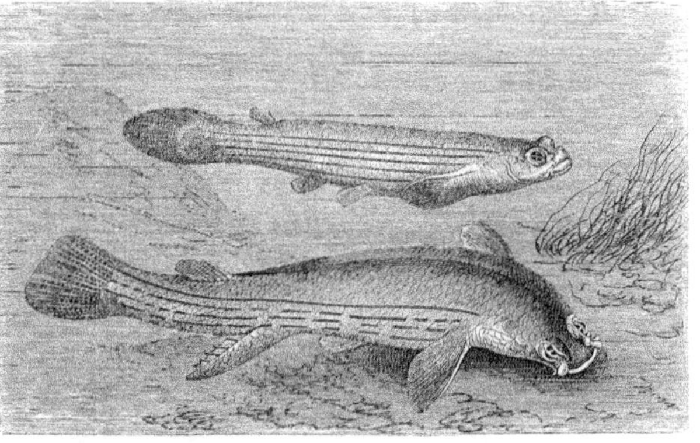

218

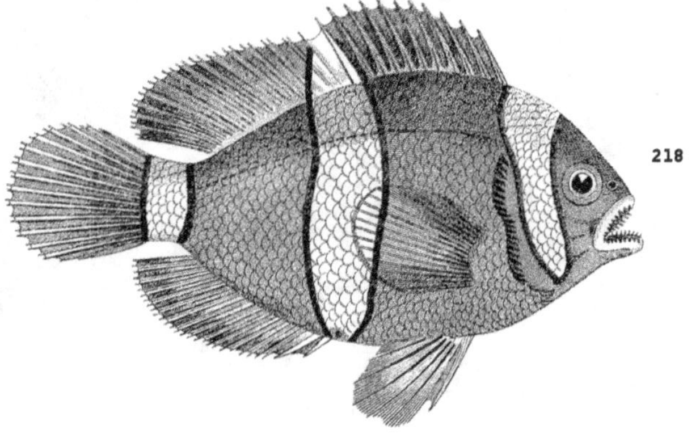

219

220

221

222

223

224

225

226

227

228

229

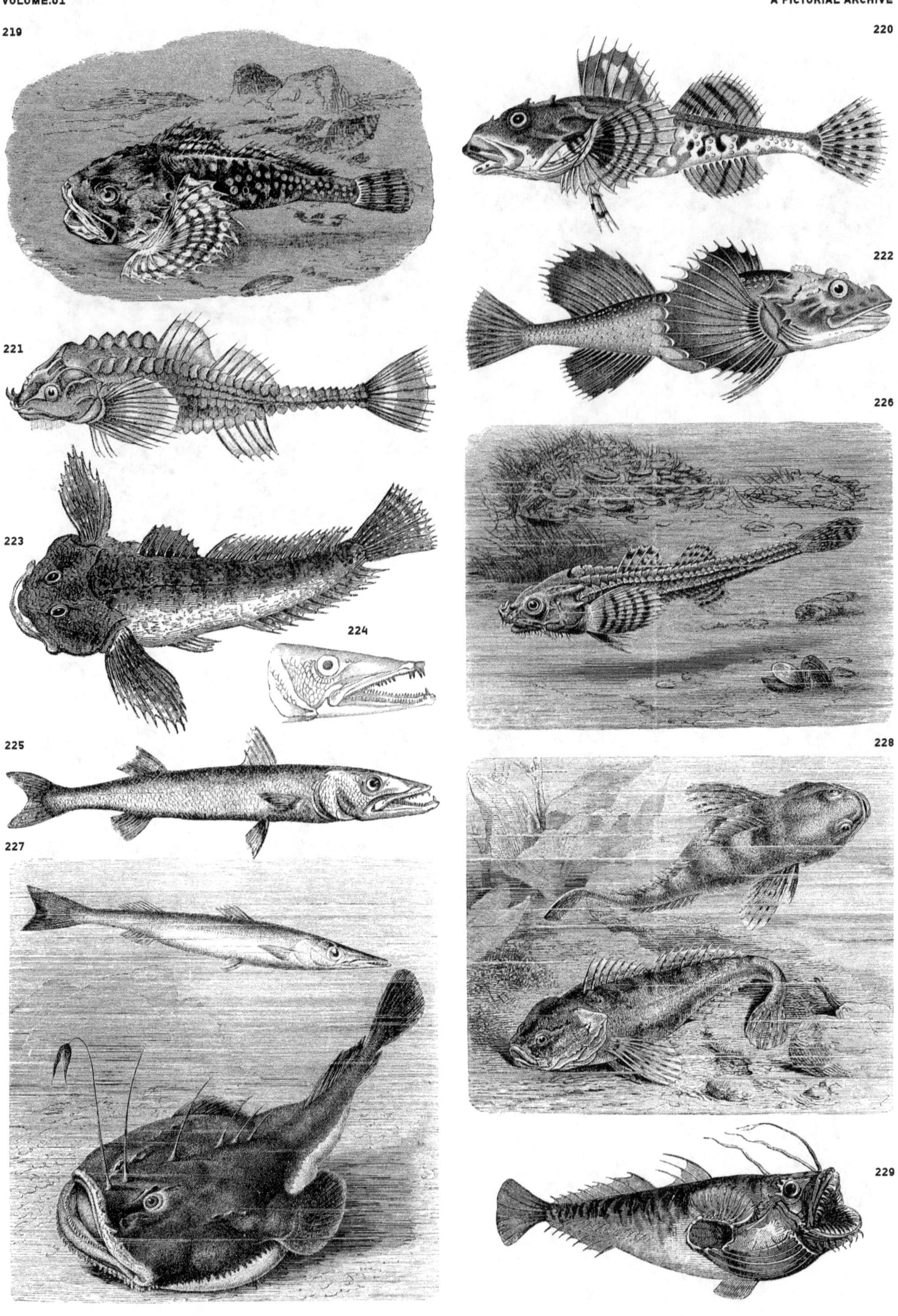

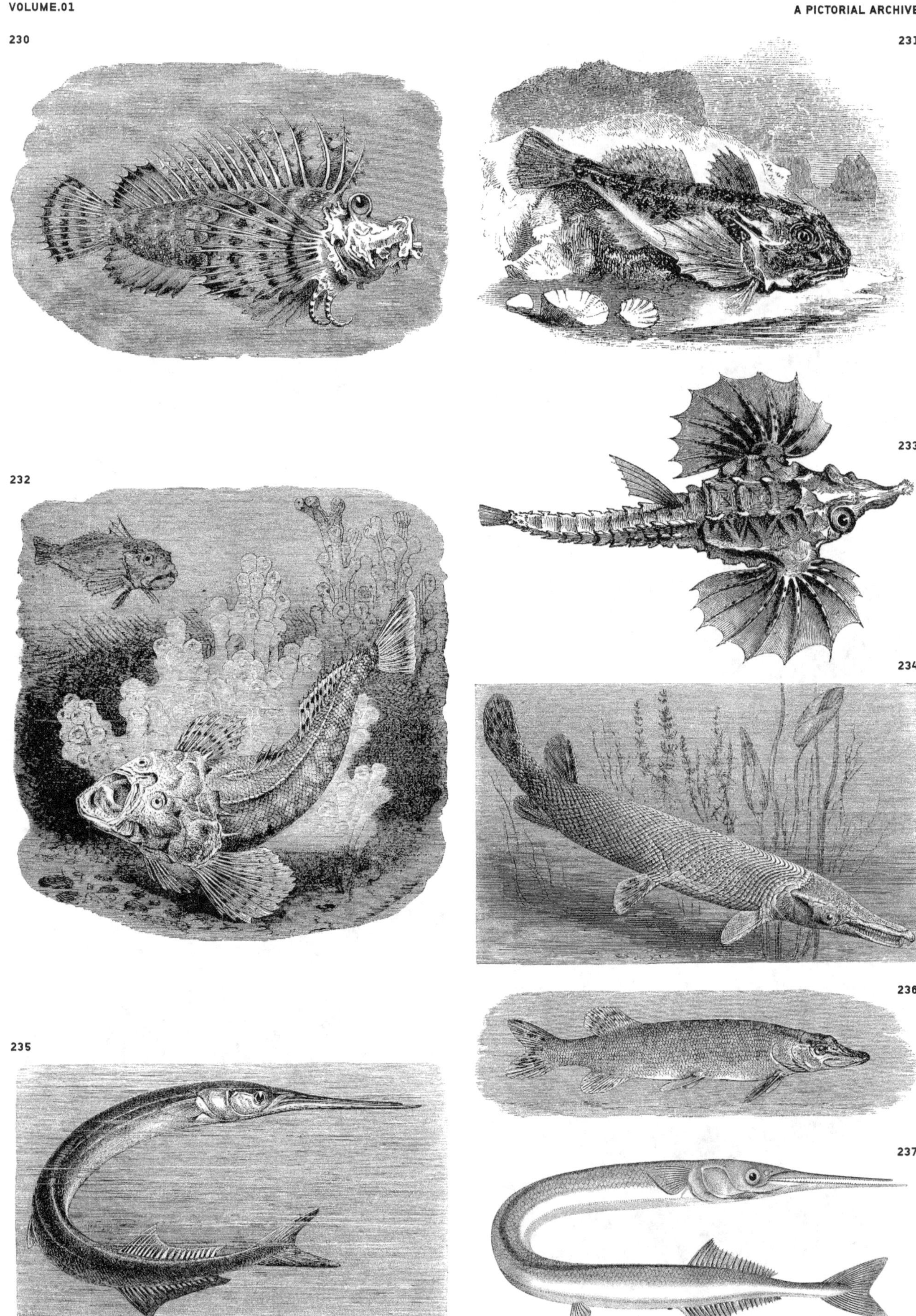

230

231

232

233

234

235

236

237

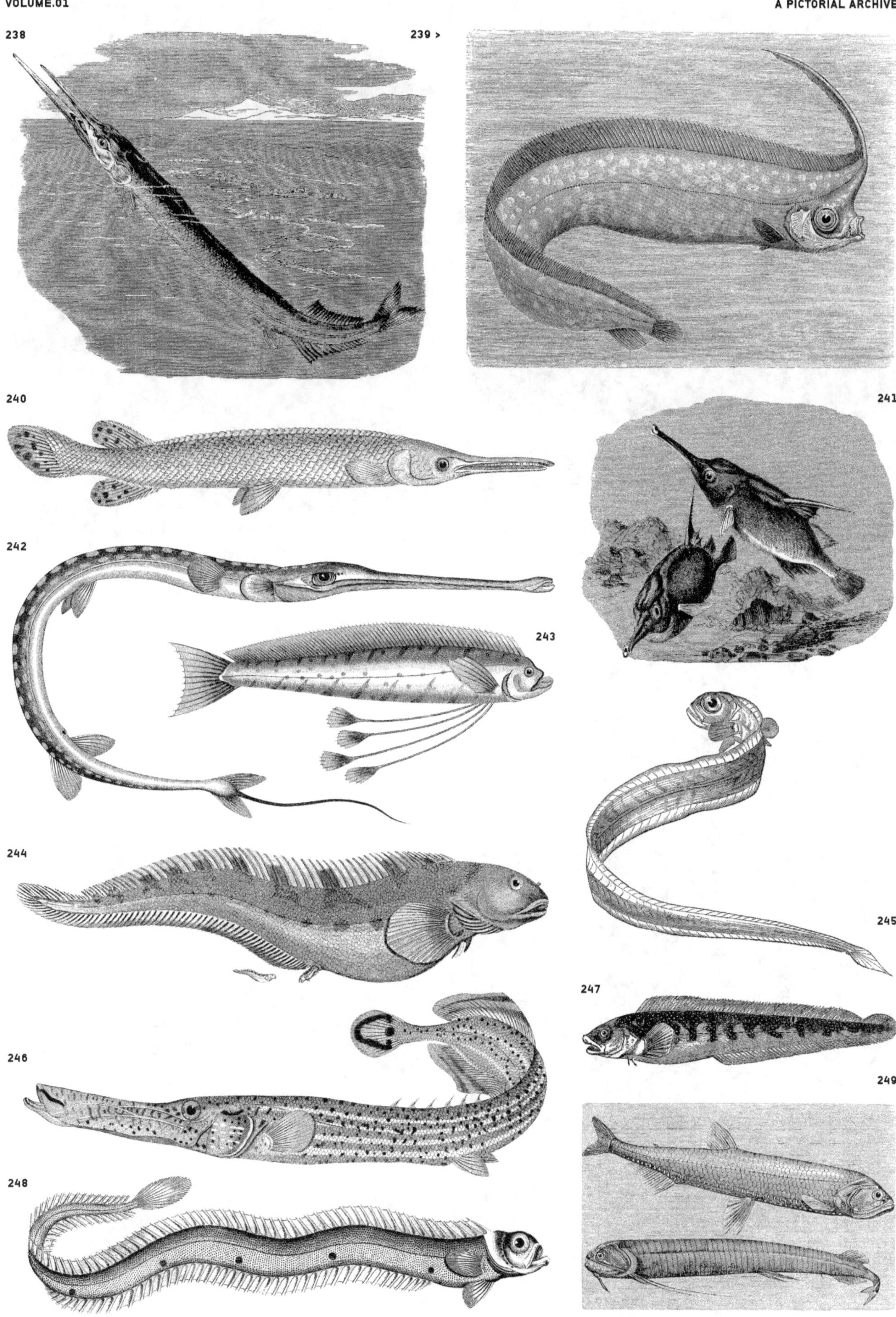

250

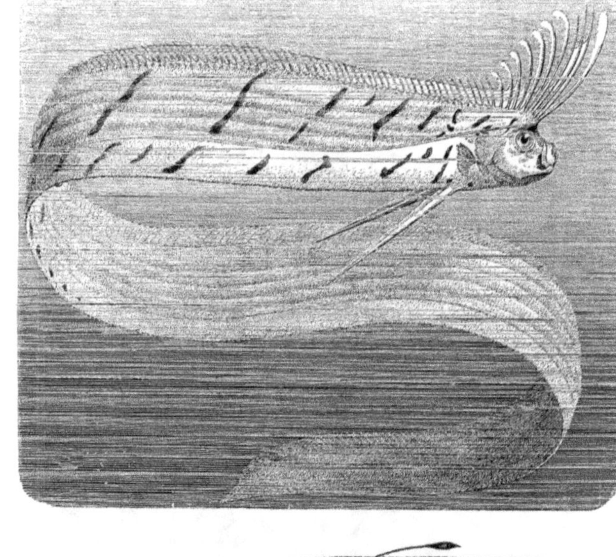

251

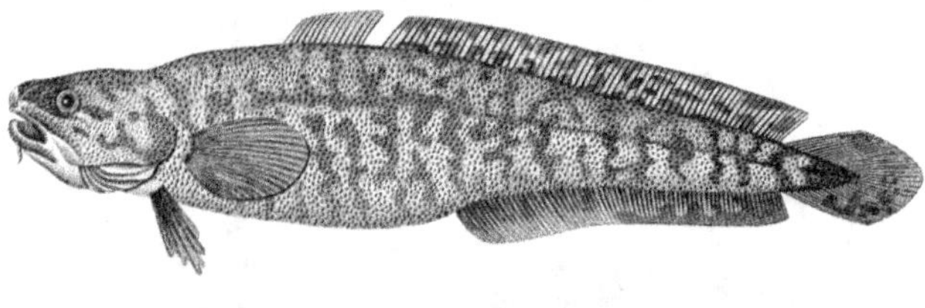

252

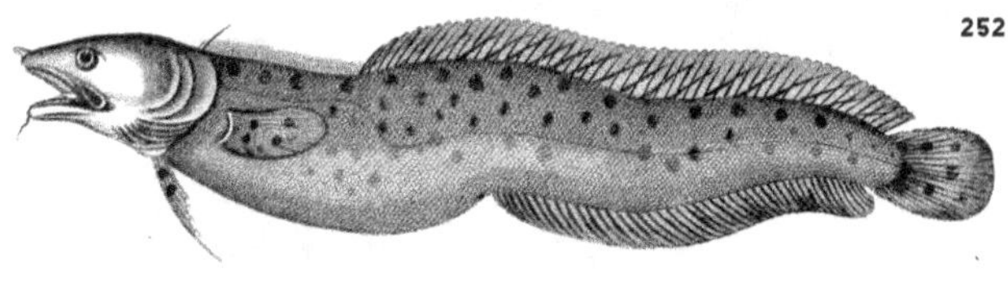

253

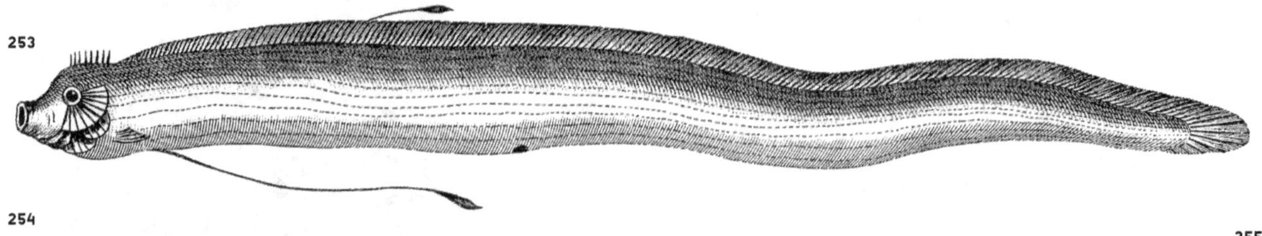

254

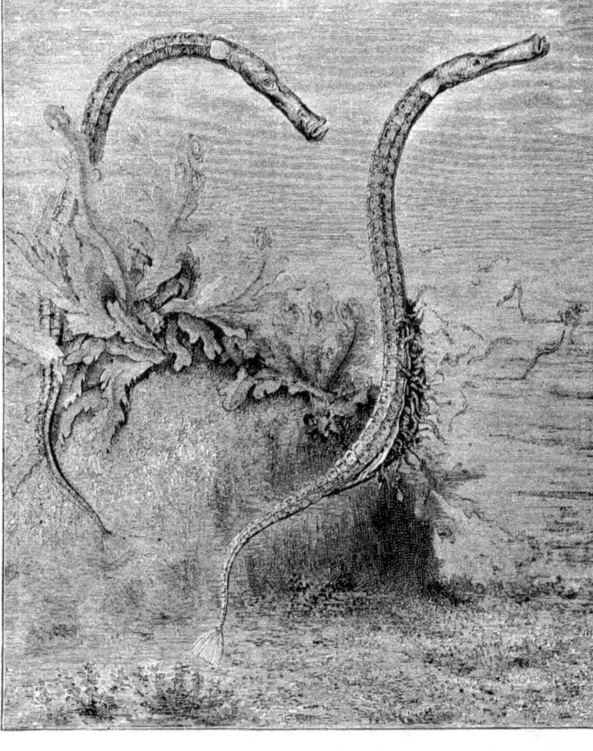

255

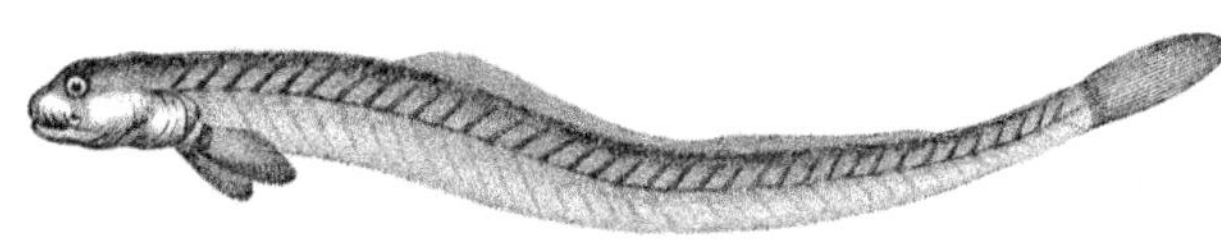

256

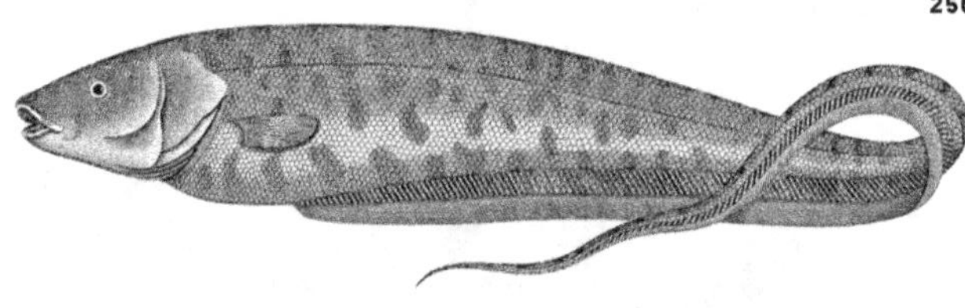

257

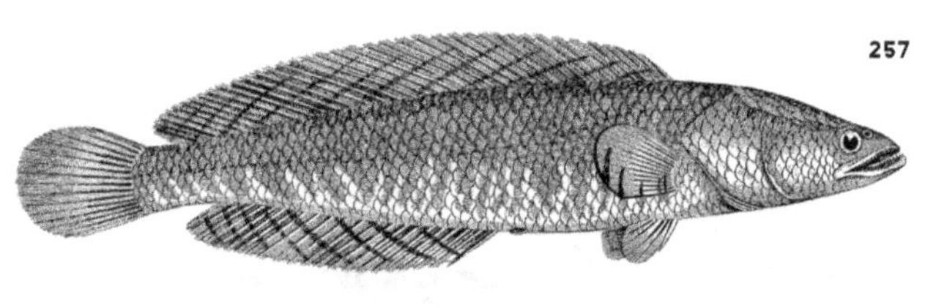

258

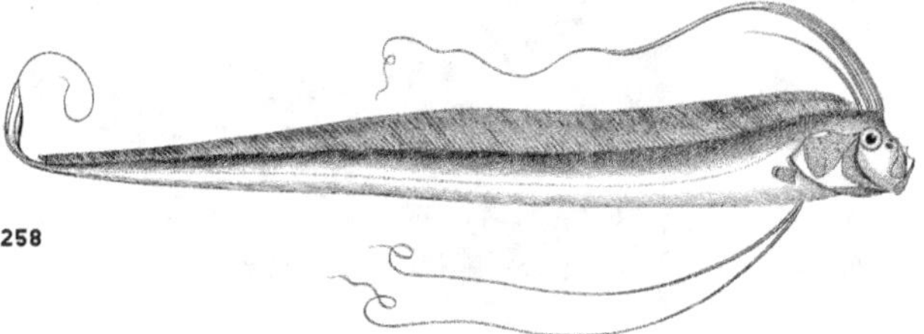

259

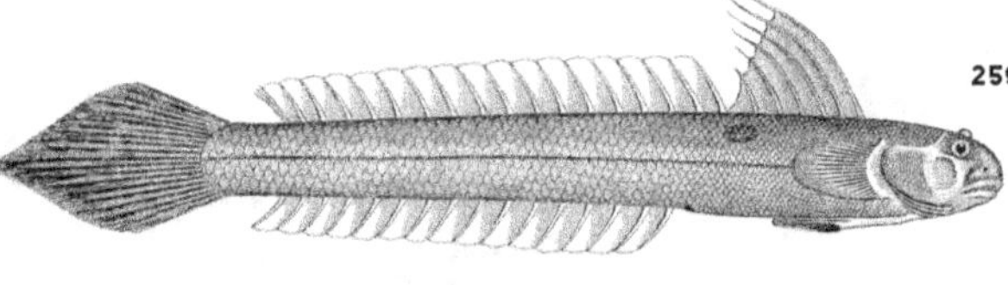

260
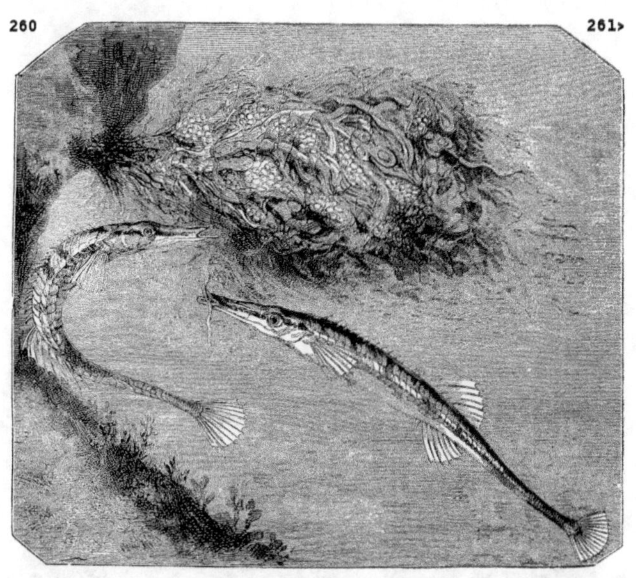

261
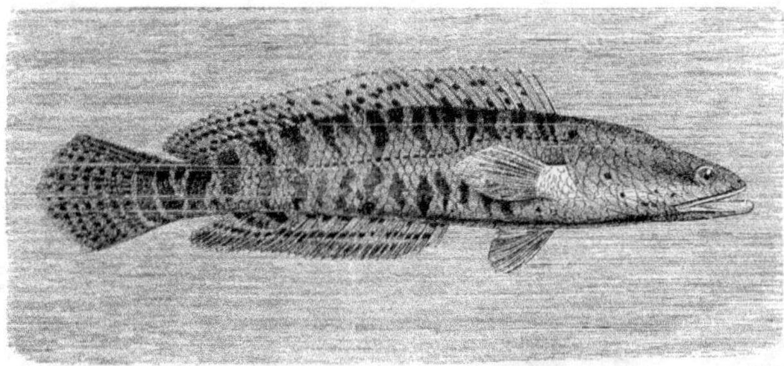

262
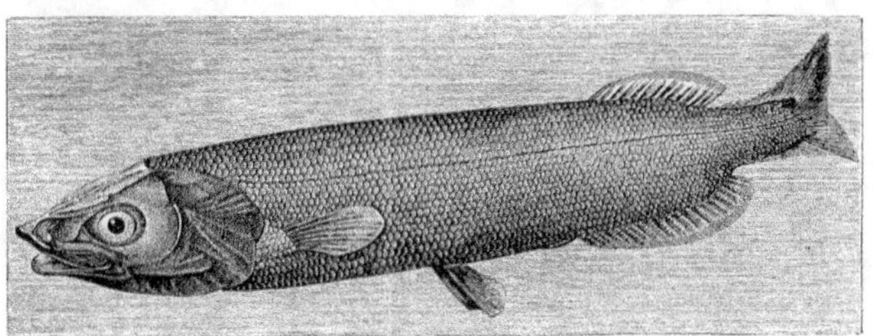

263
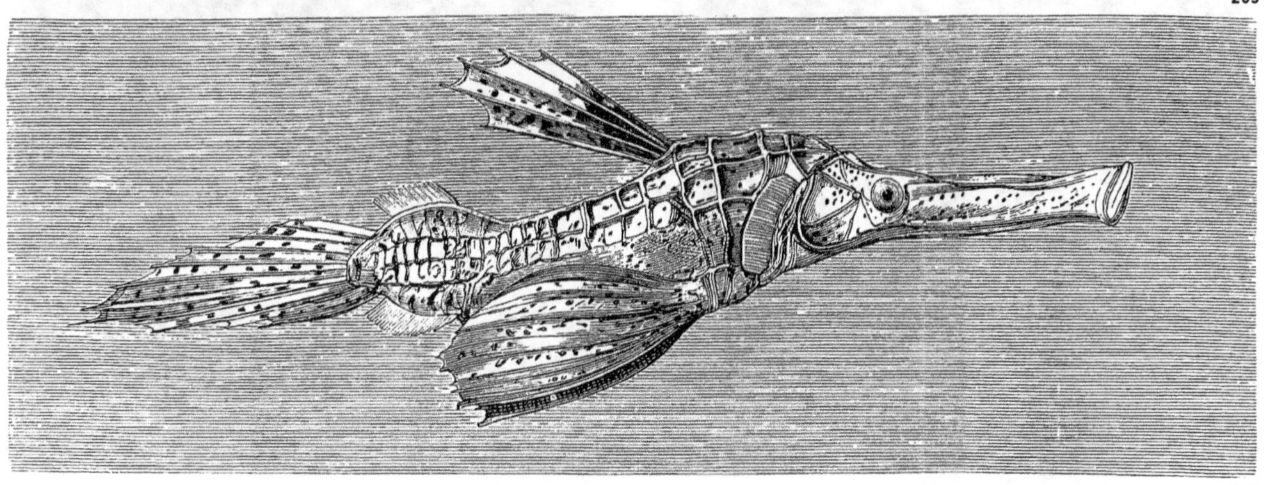

264
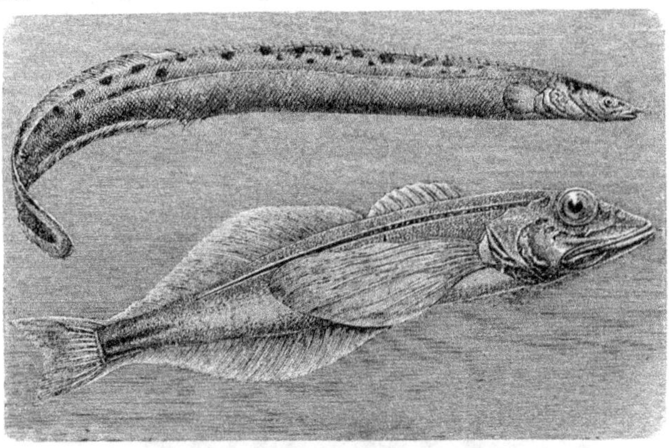

265
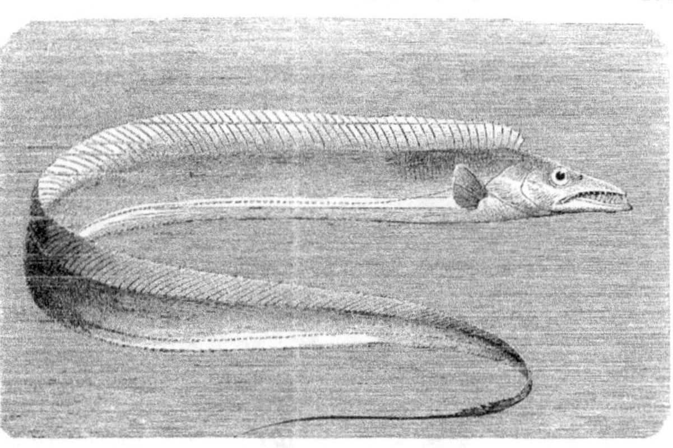

266
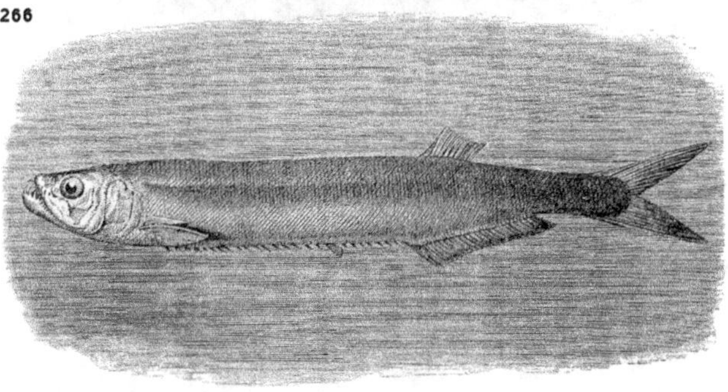

267
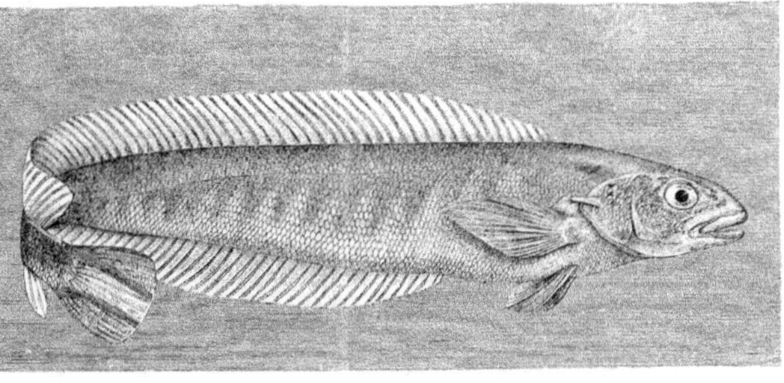

268

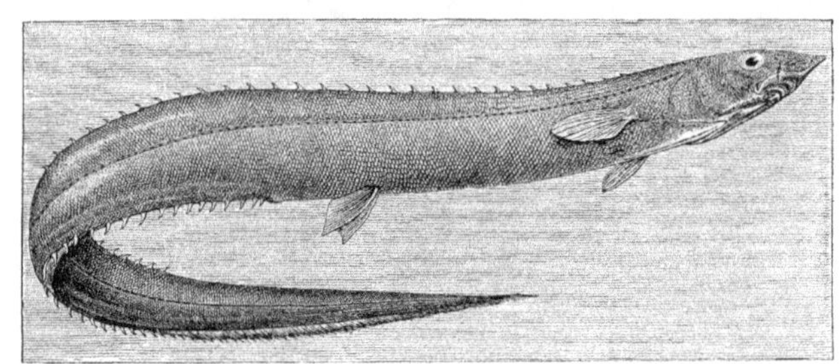

269>

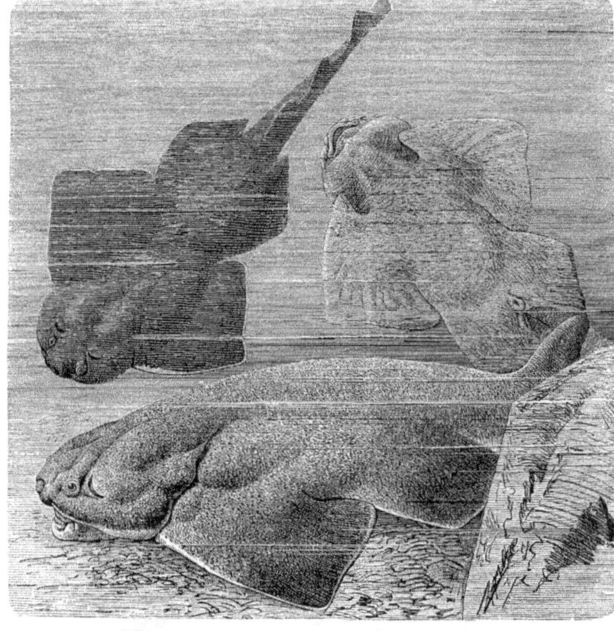

270

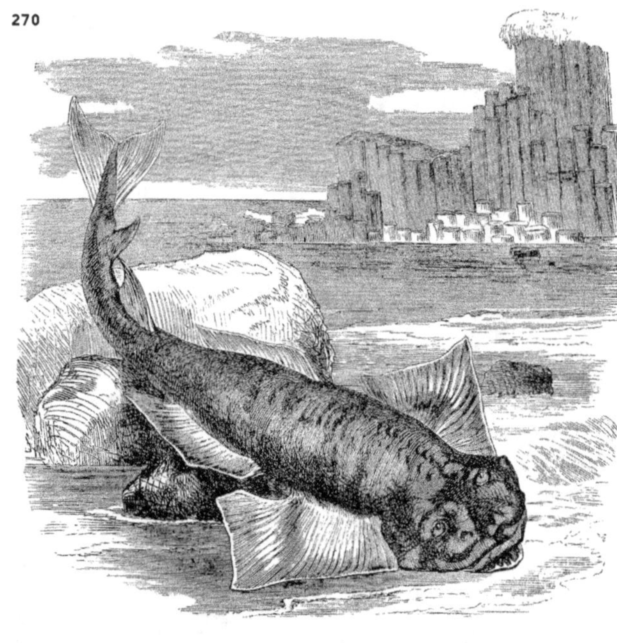

271

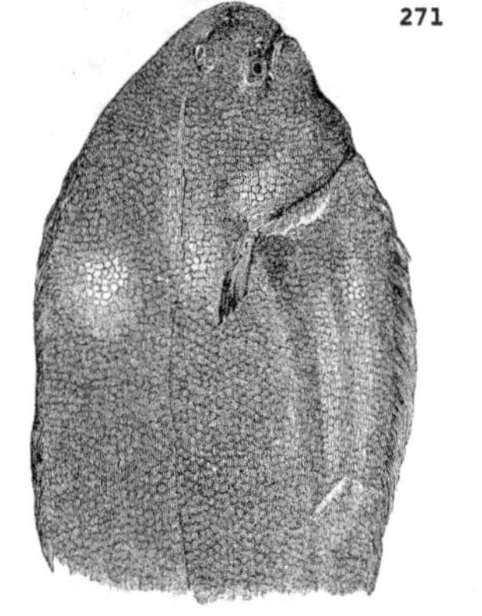

272

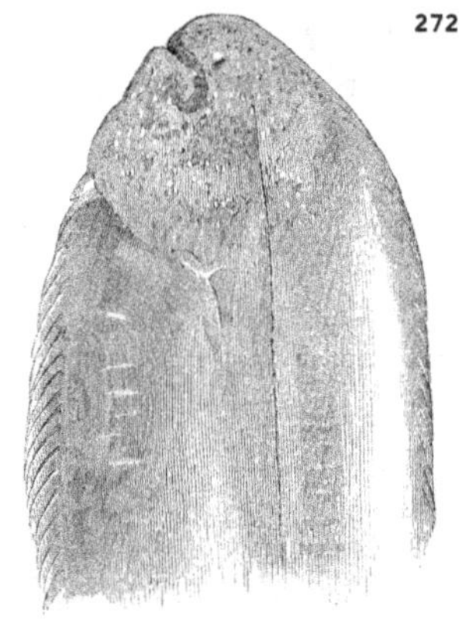

273

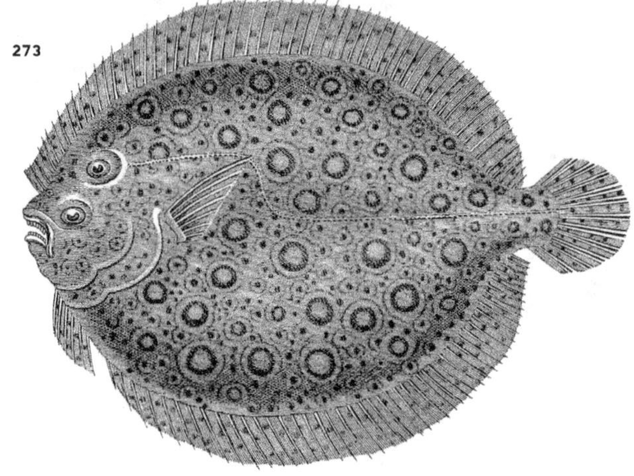

274

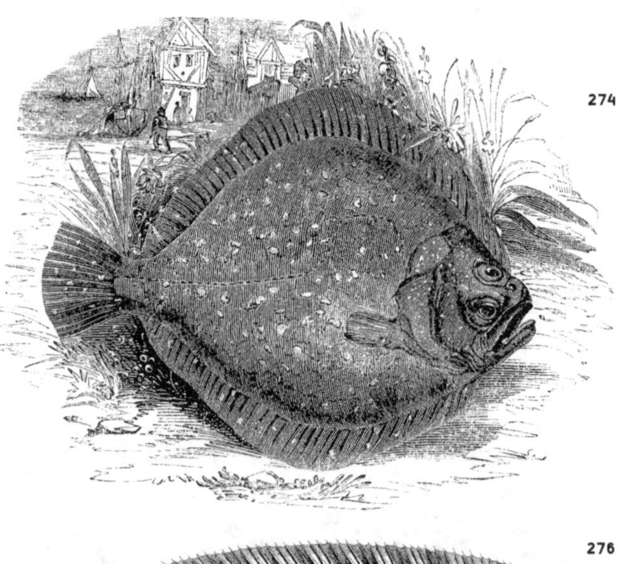

275

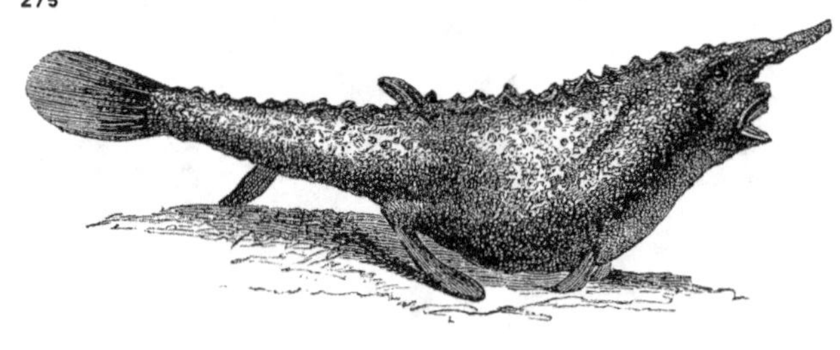

276

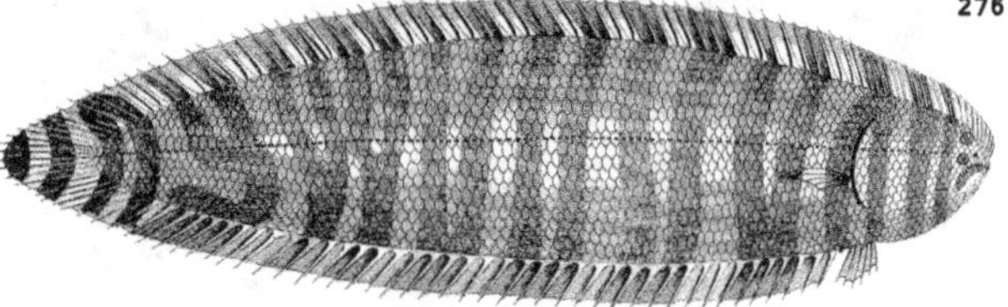

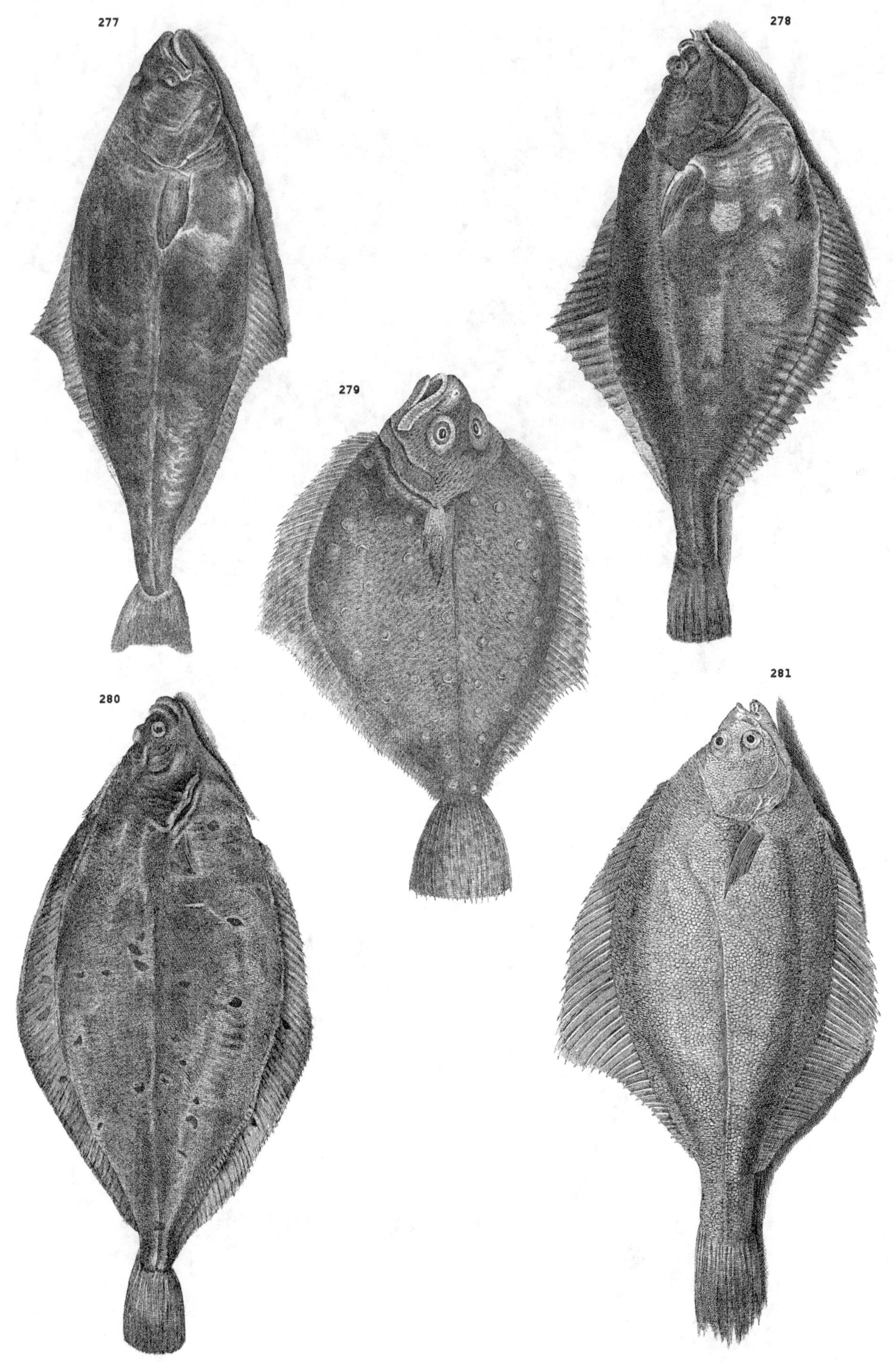
277
278
279
280
281

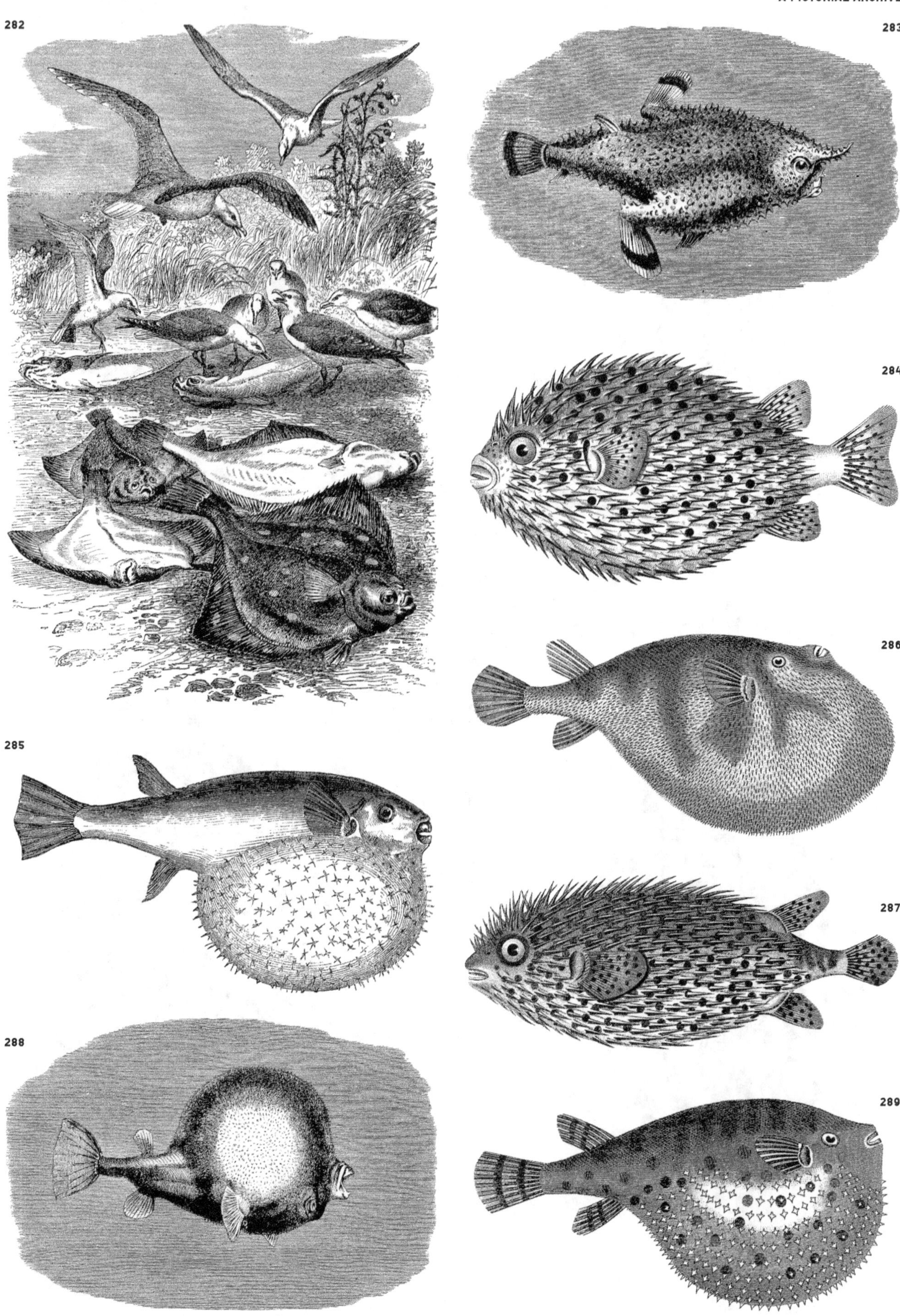

282

283

284

285

286

287

288

289

290

291

292

293

294

295

296

297

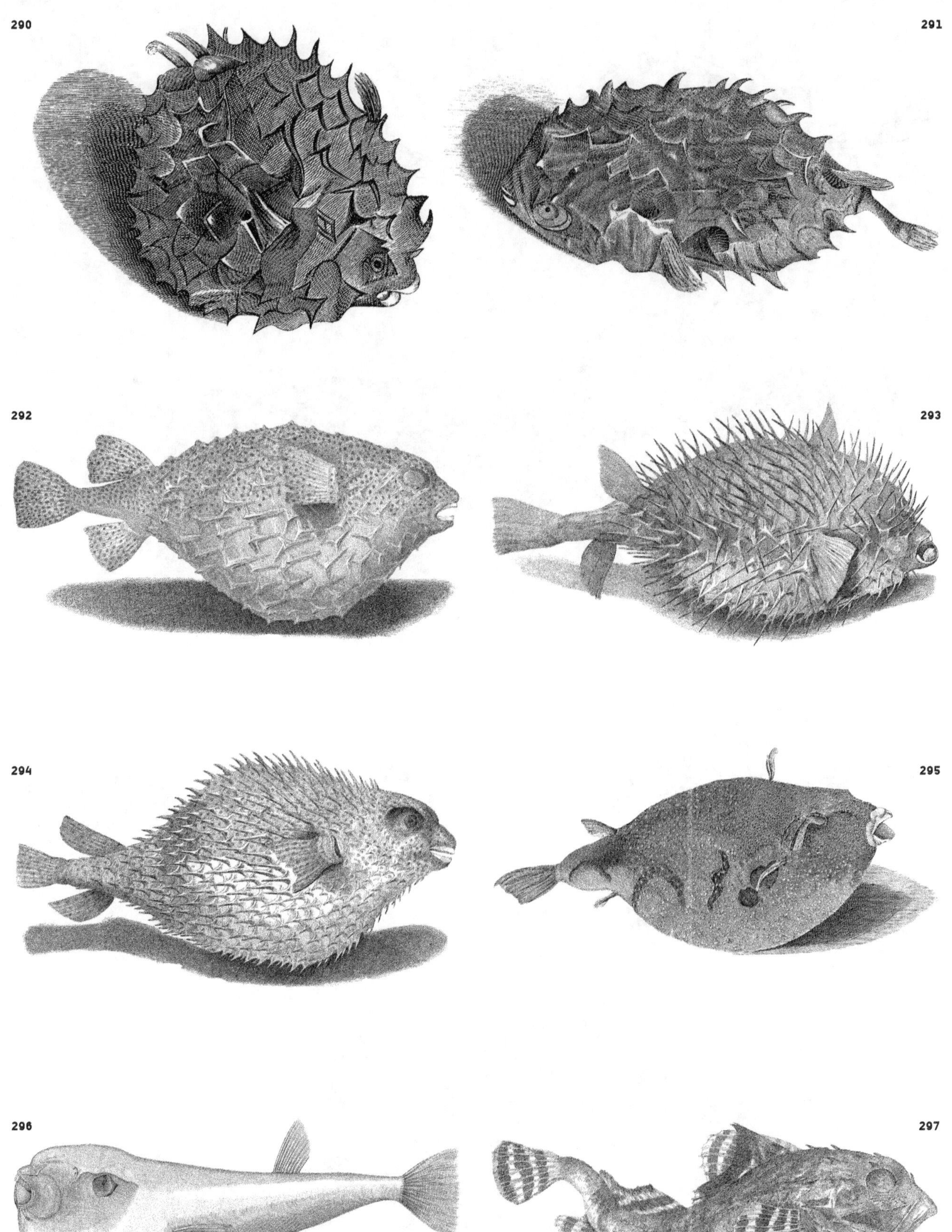

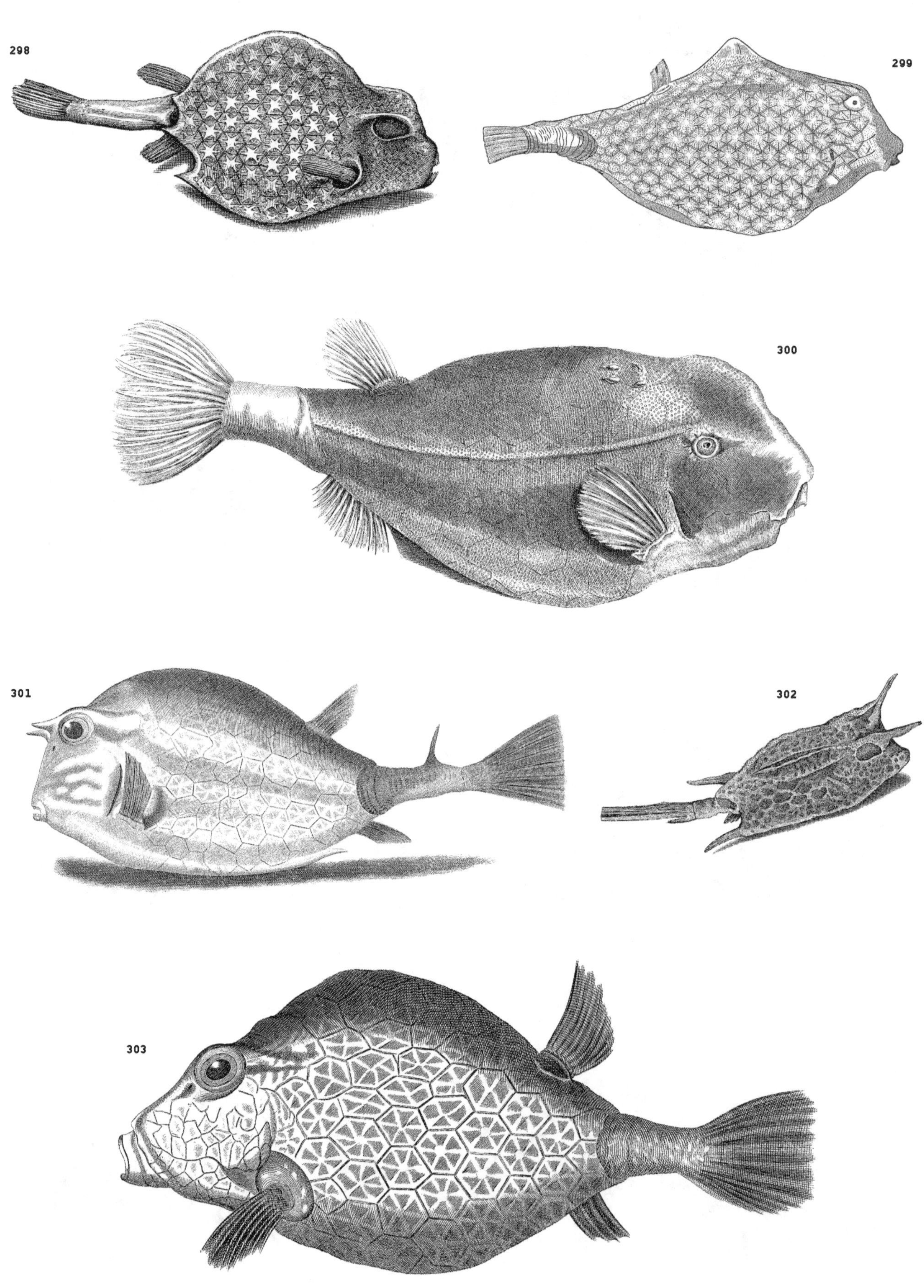
298
299
300
301
302
303

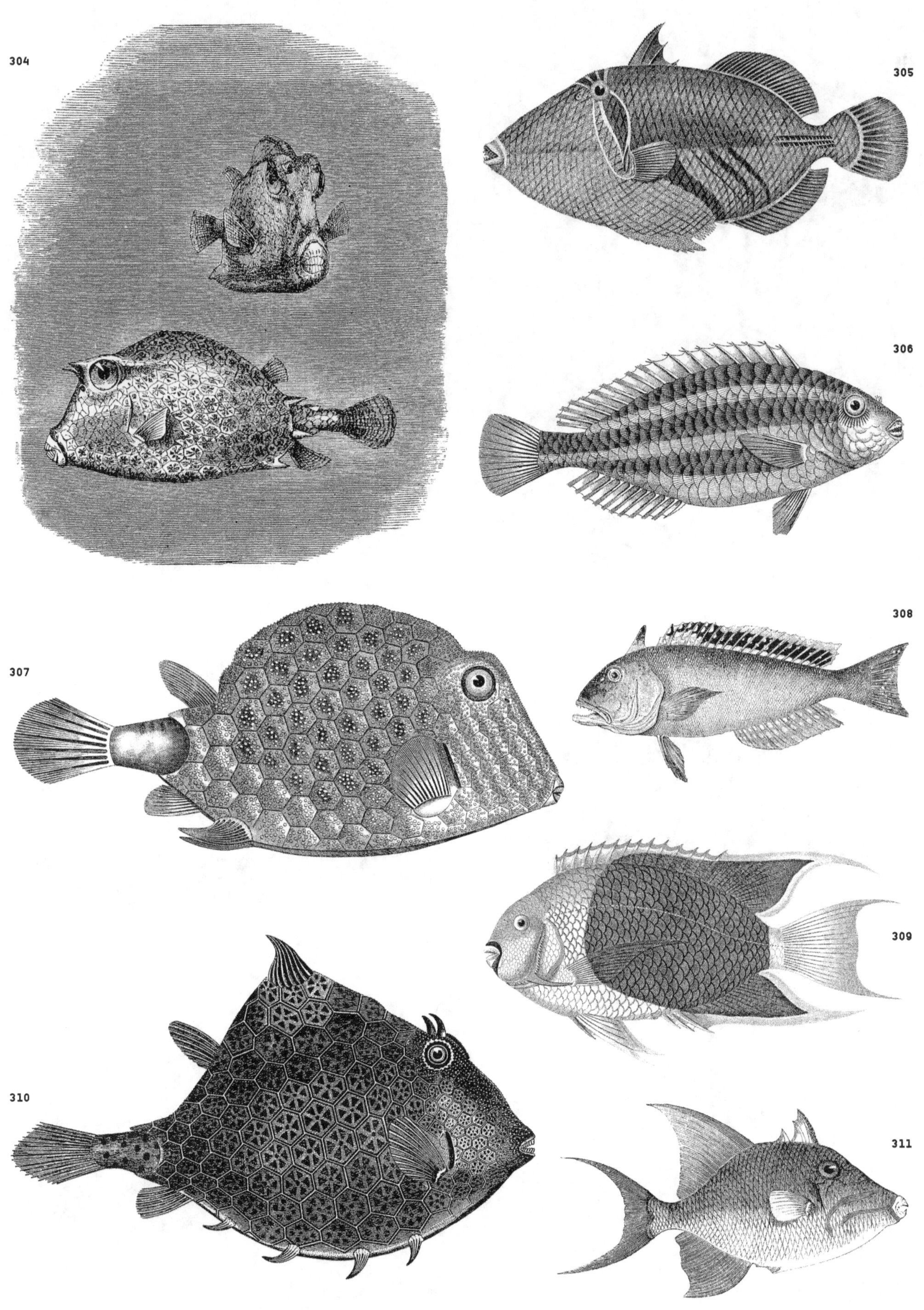

304
305
306
307
308
309
310
311

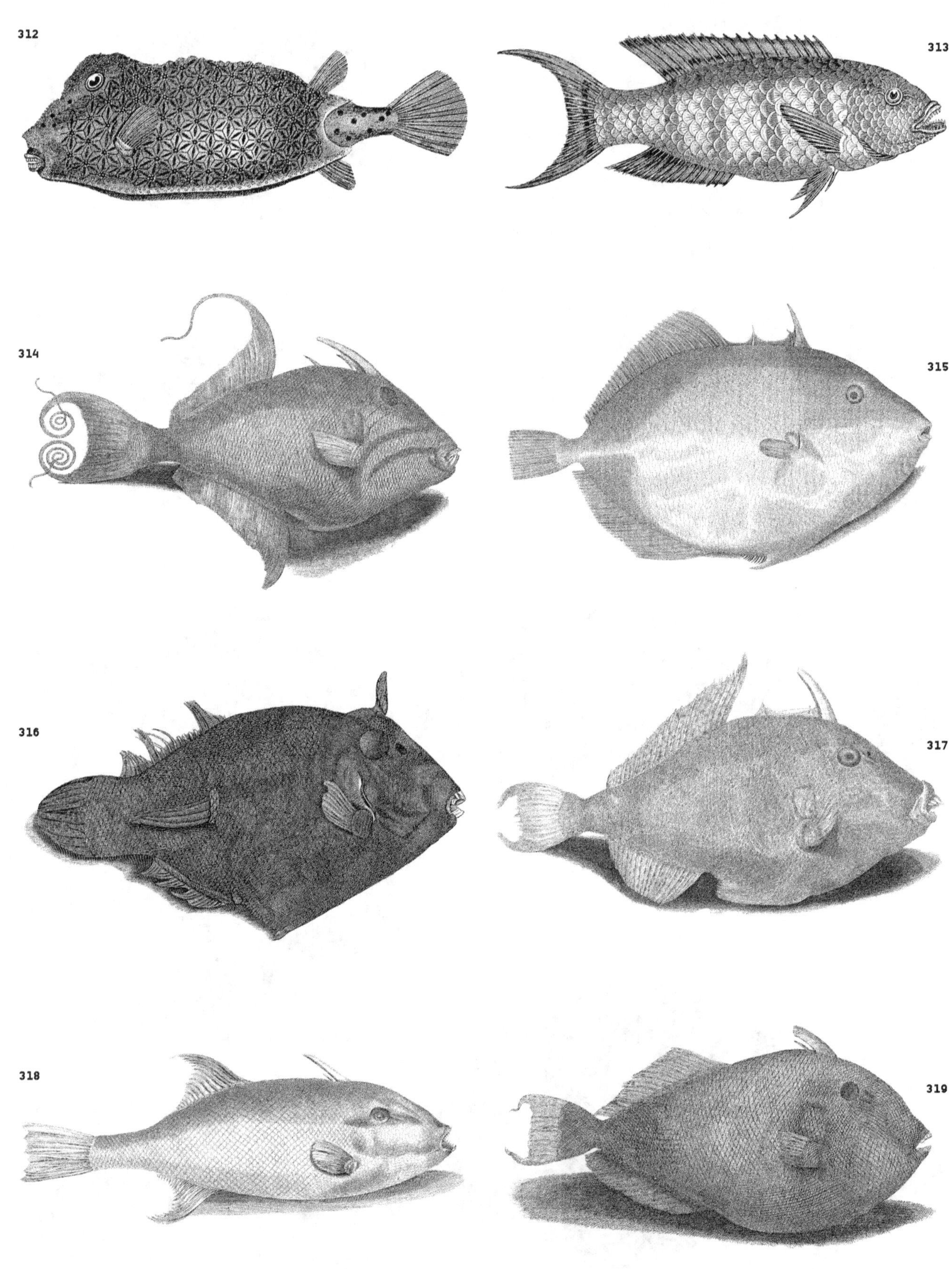

312
313
314
315
316
317
318
319

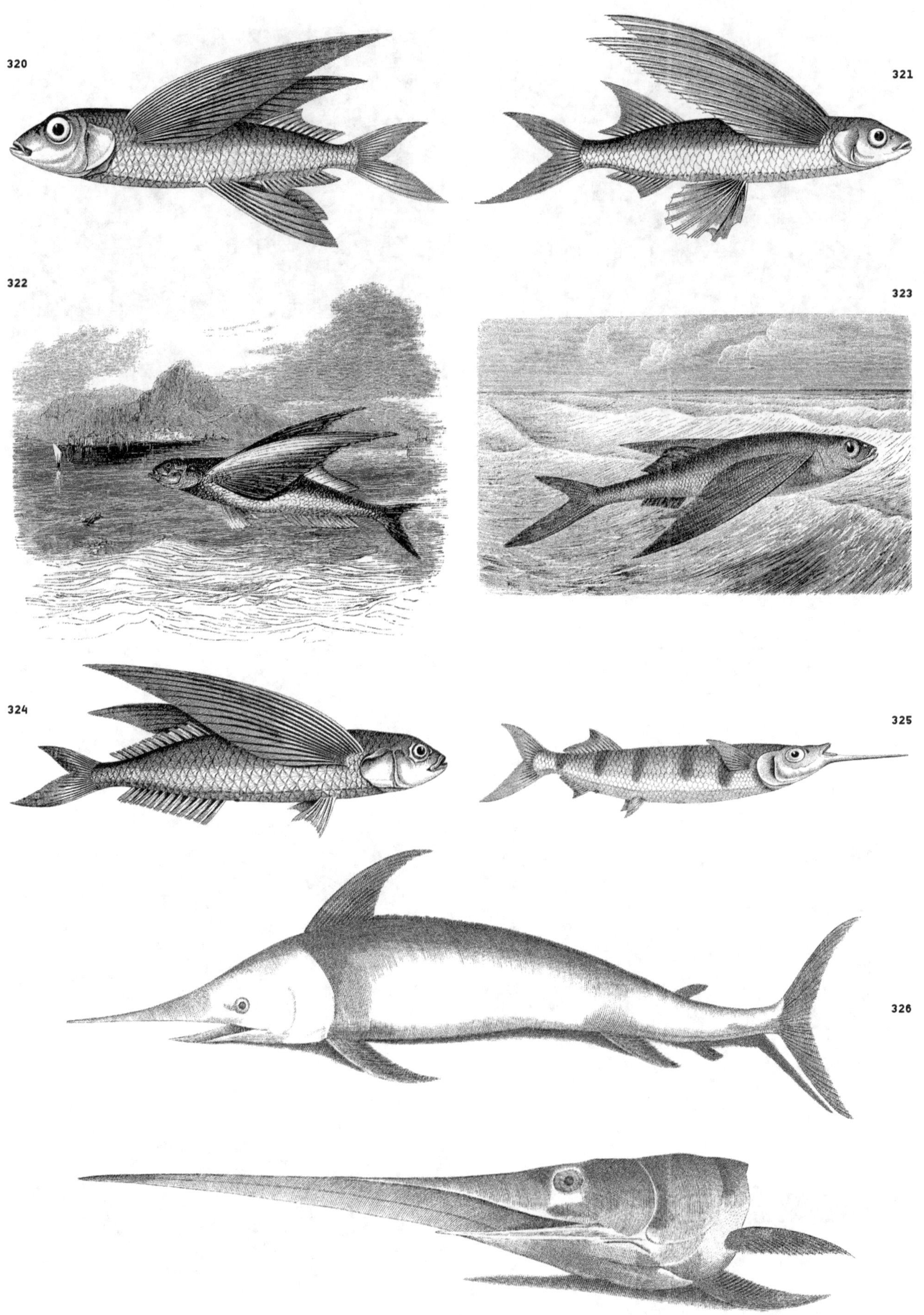

FISH

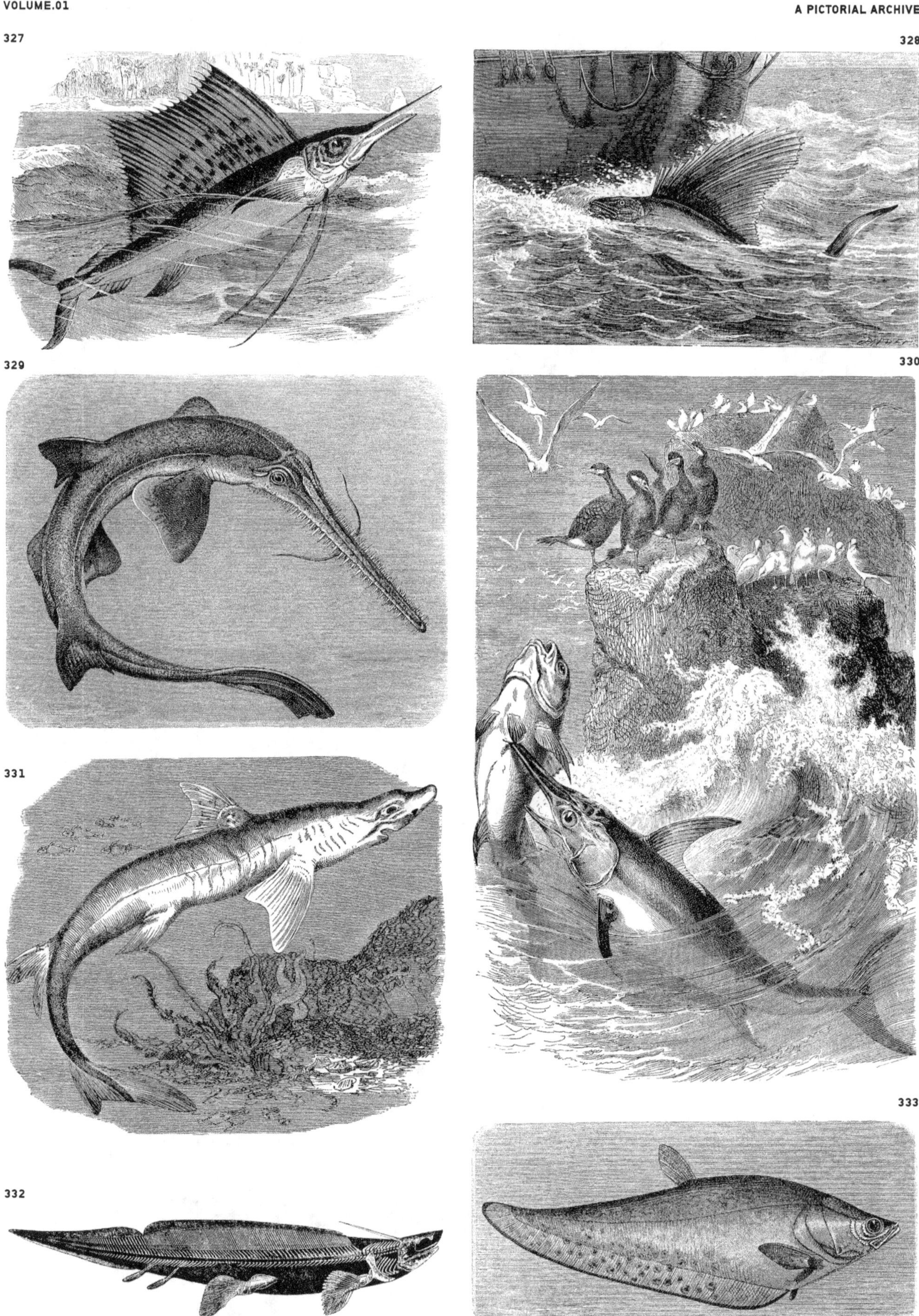

327

328

329

330

331

332

333

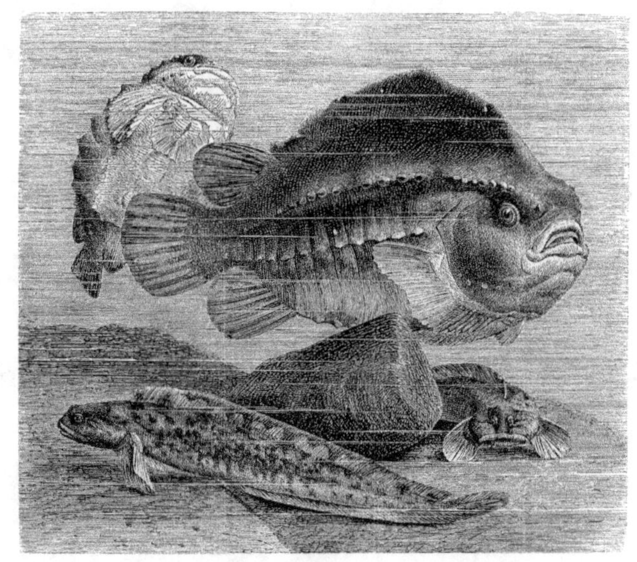

334

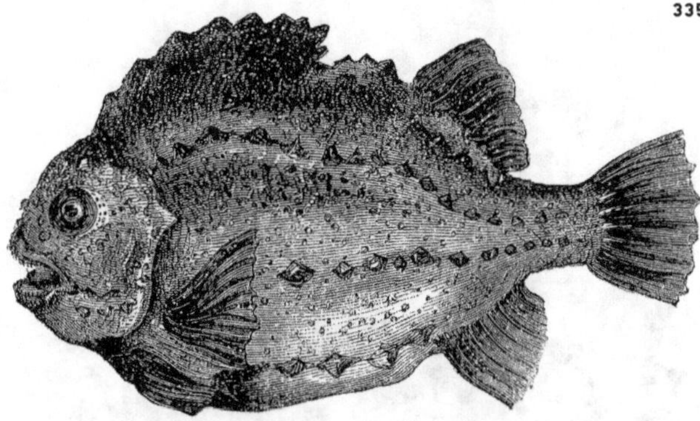

335

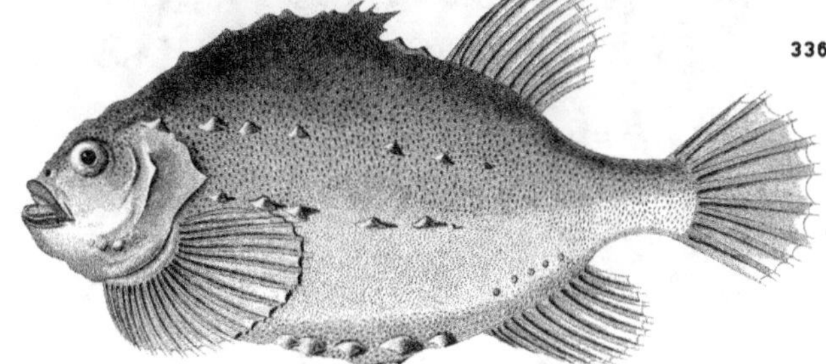

336

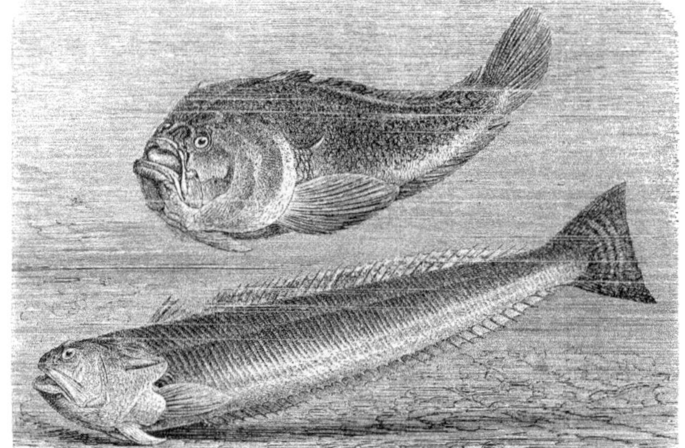

337

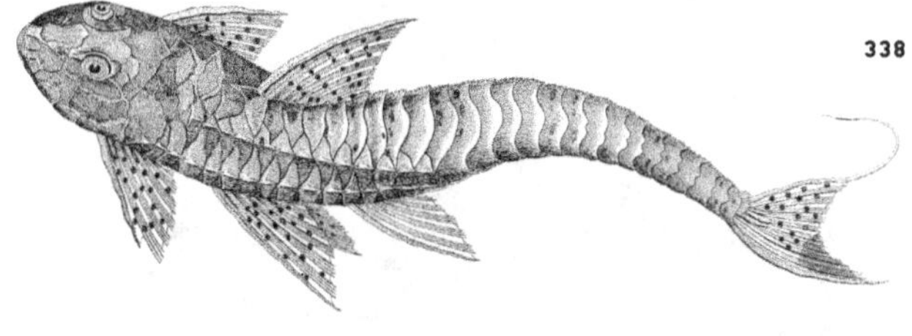

338

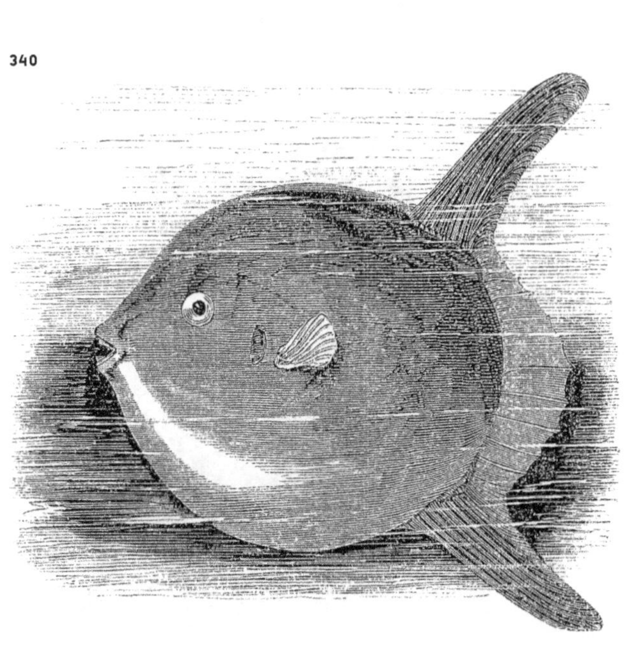

340

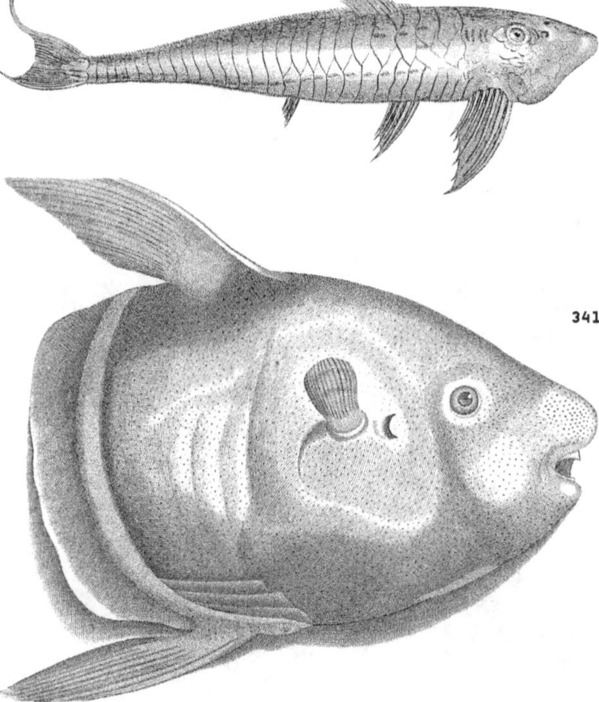

339

341

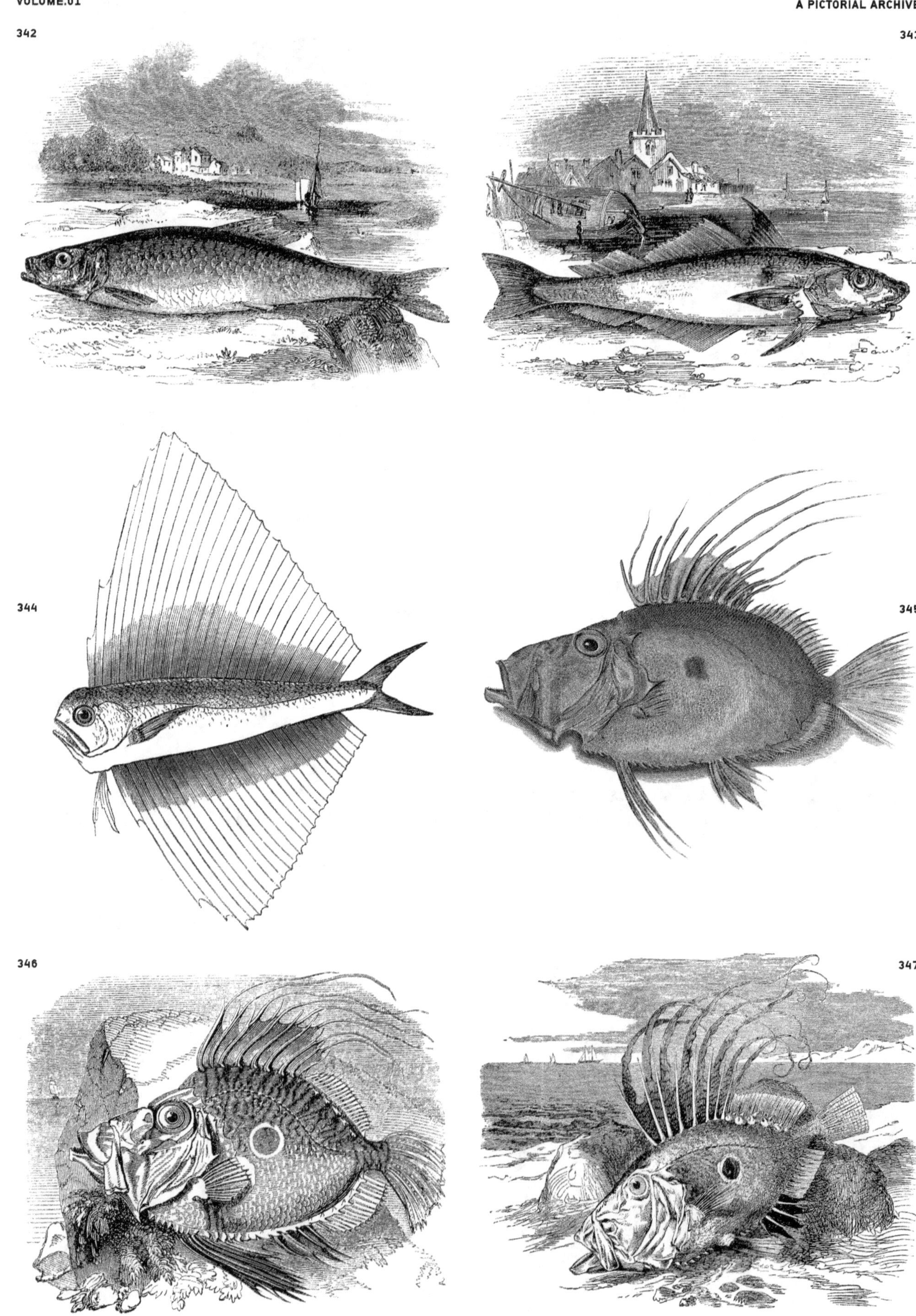

342

343

344

345

346

347

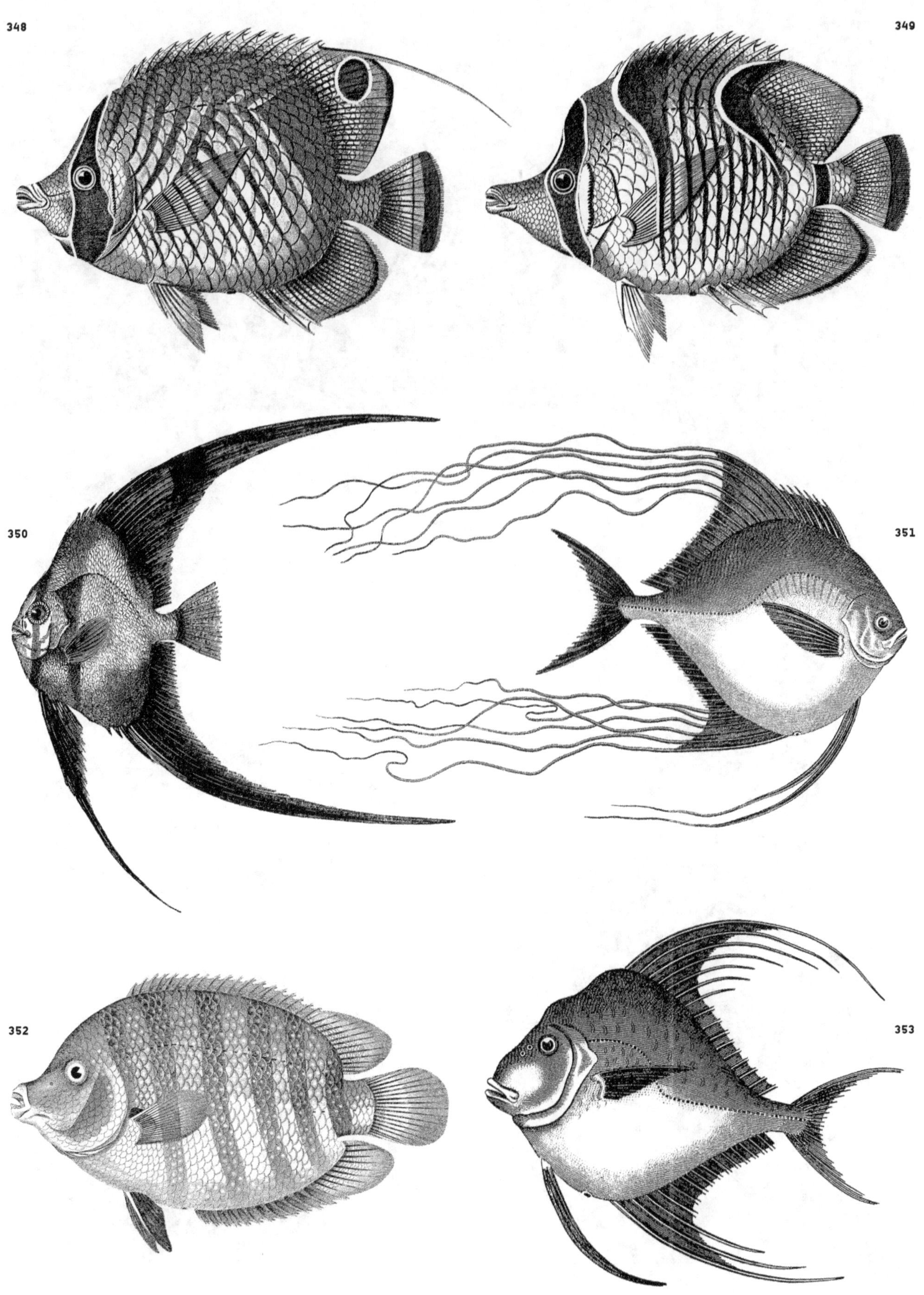

348
349
350
351
352
353

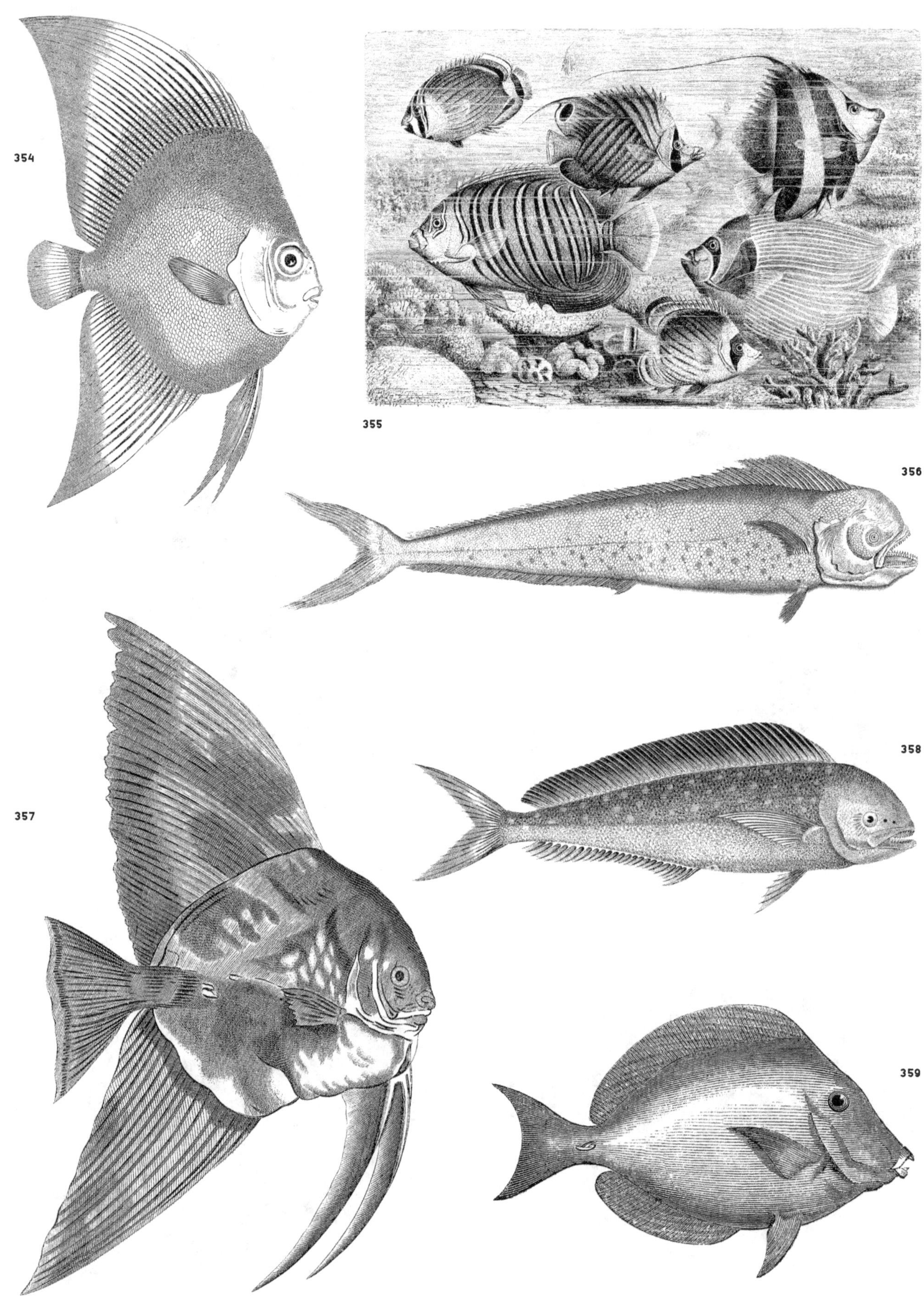

354

355

356

357

358

359

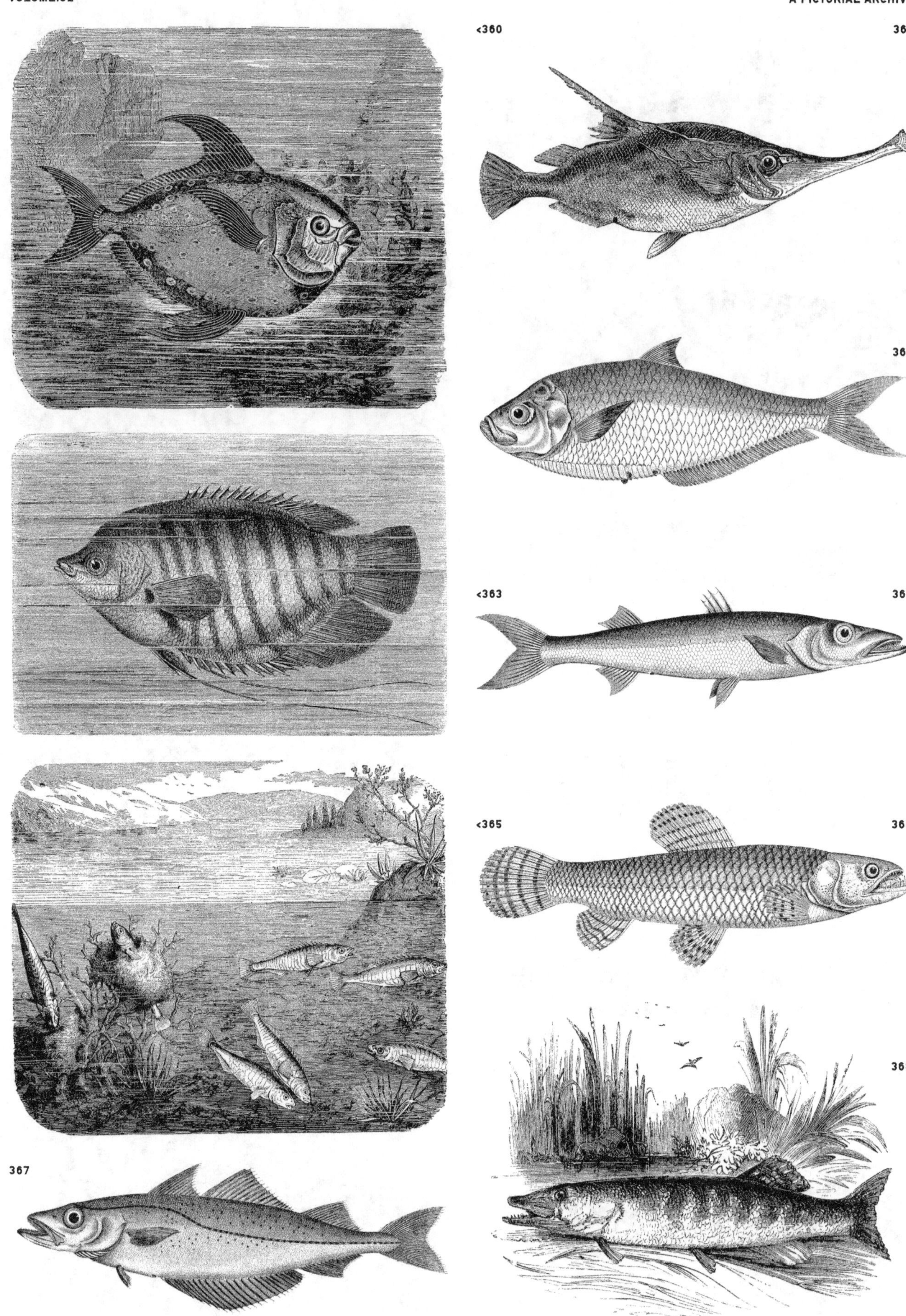
<360
361
362
<363
364
<365
366
368
367

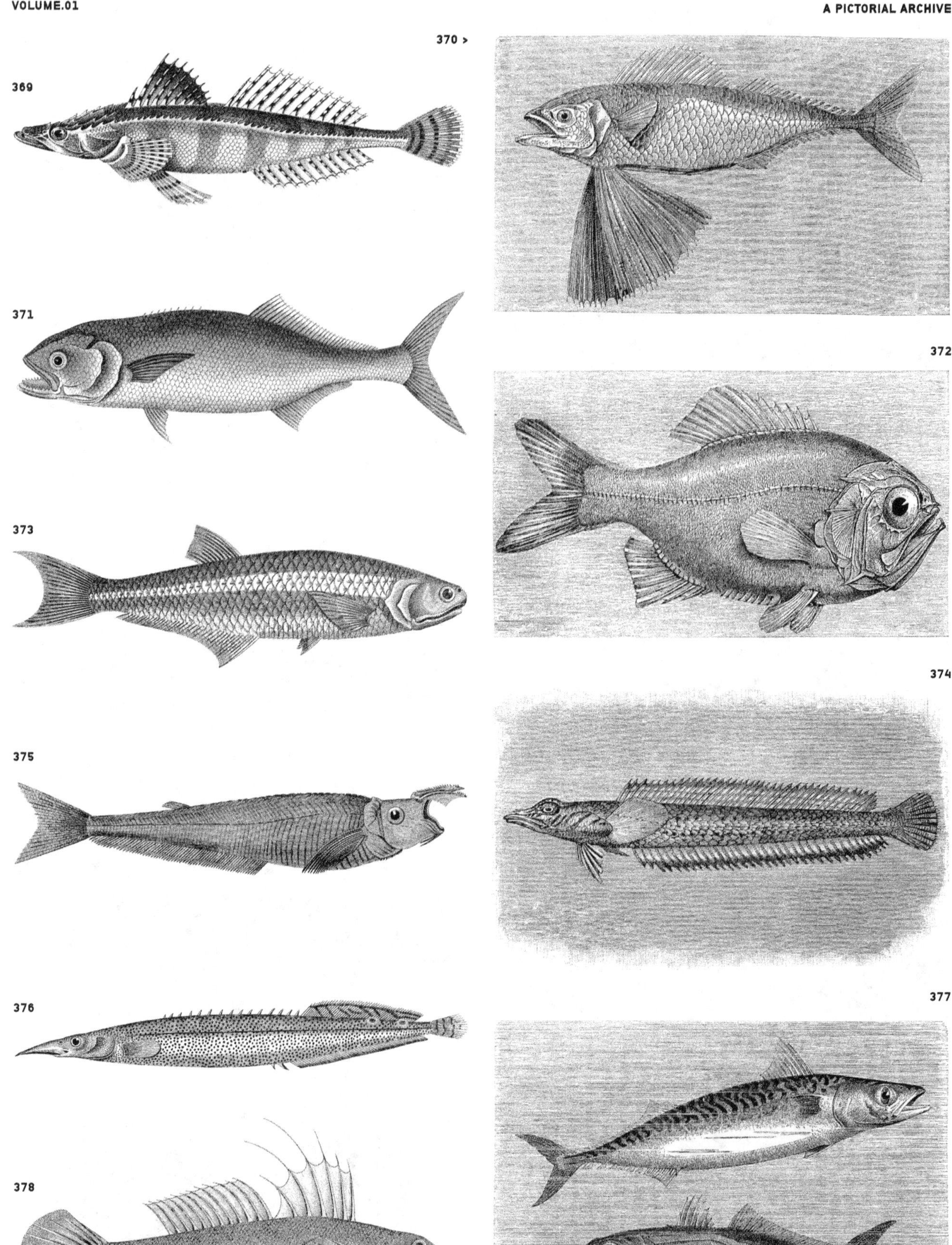

370 >

369

371

372

373

374

375

376

377

378

379

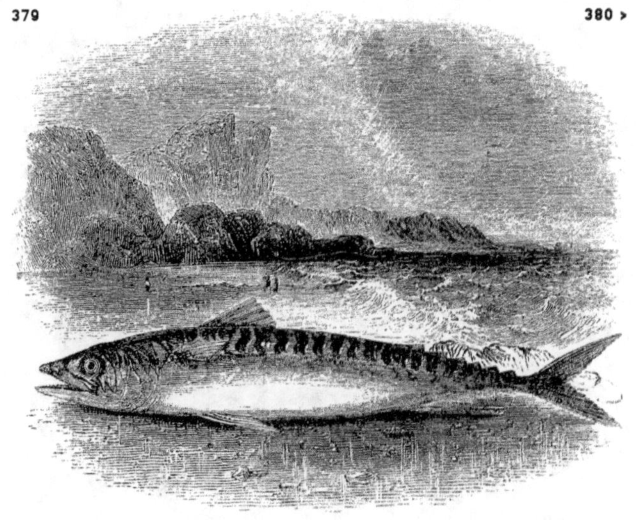

380 >

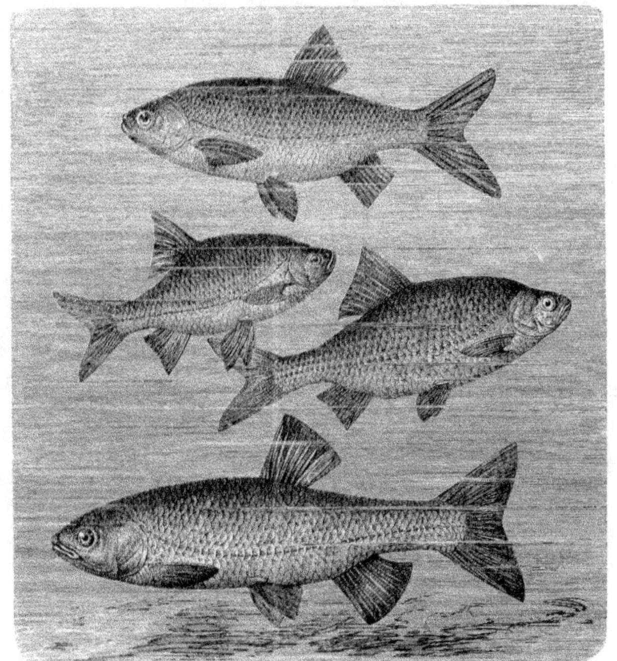

381

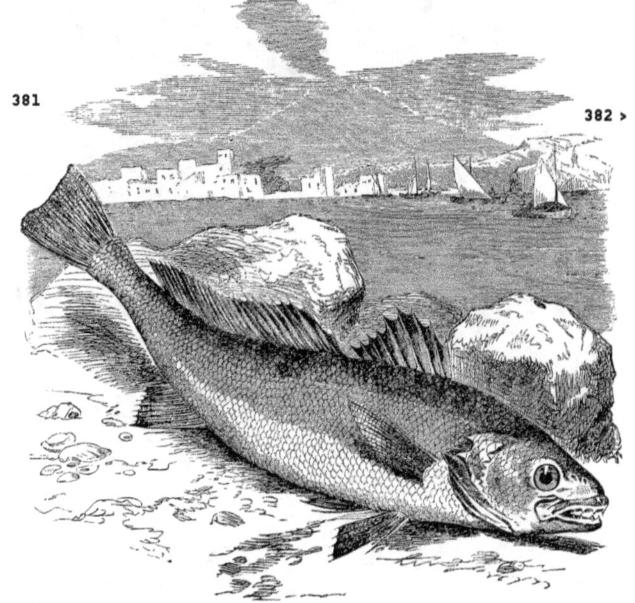

382 >

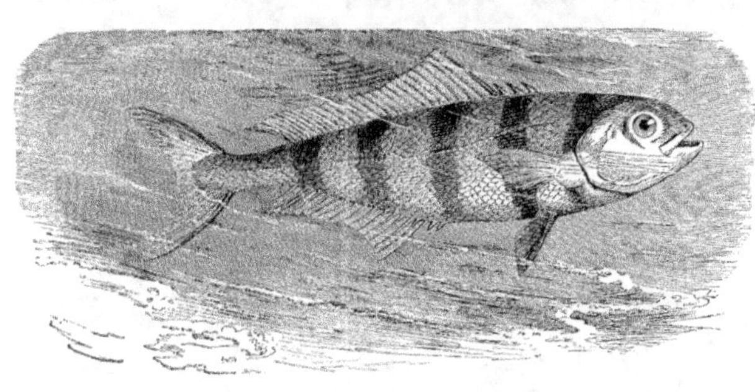

383

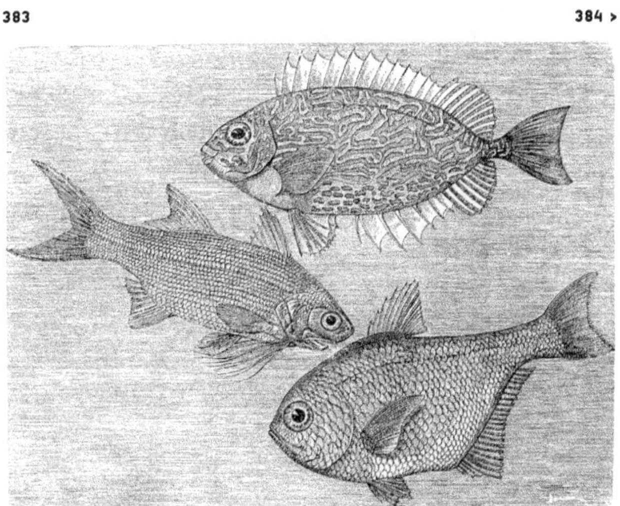

384 >

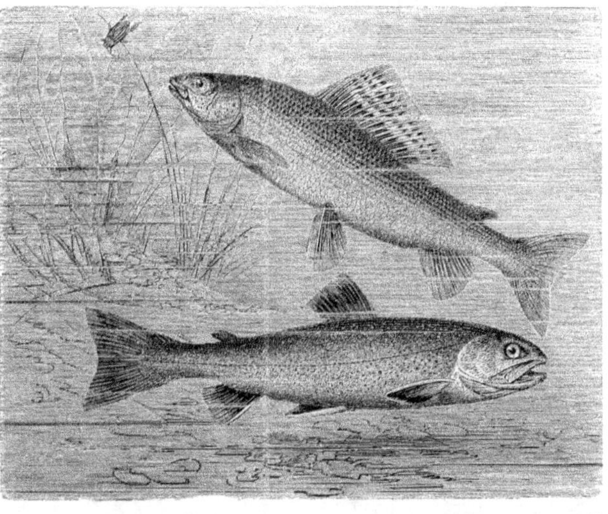

385

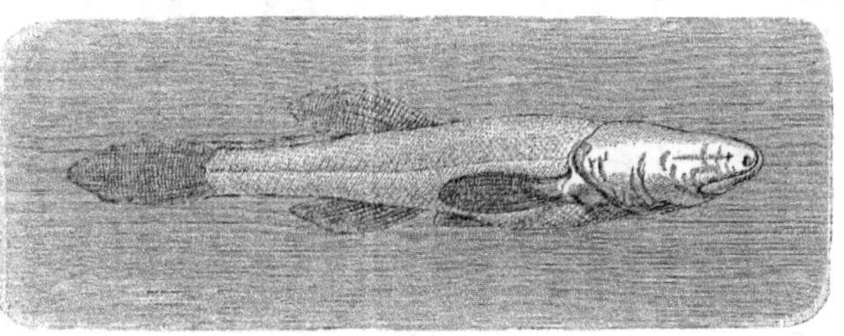

386

387 >

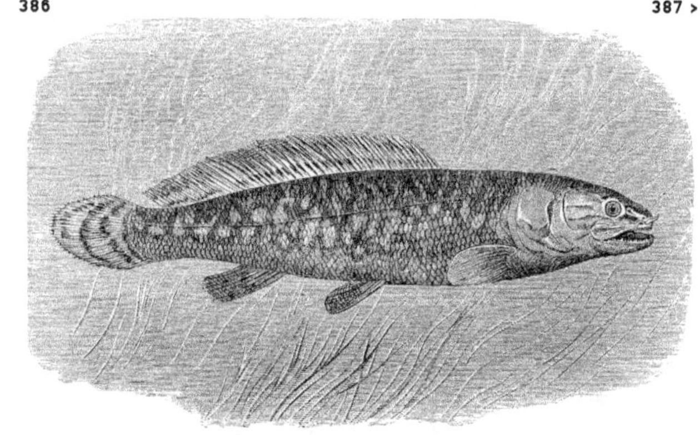

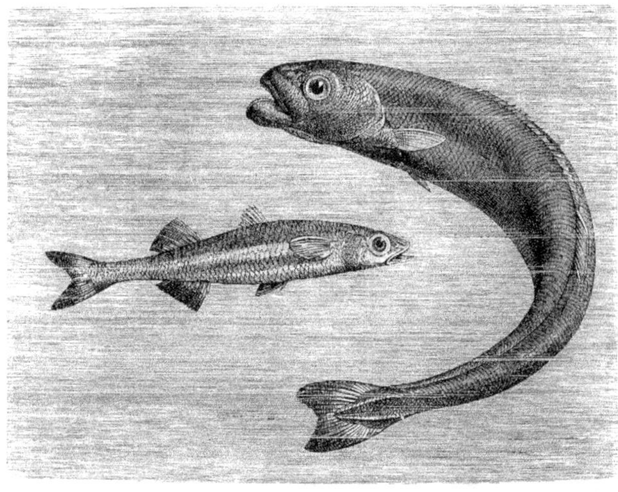

388

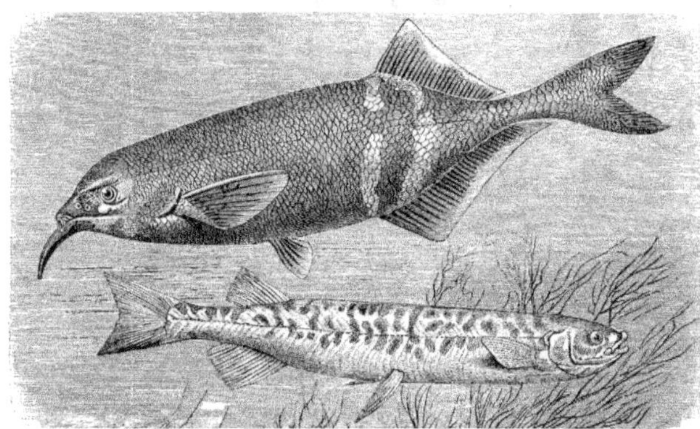

389

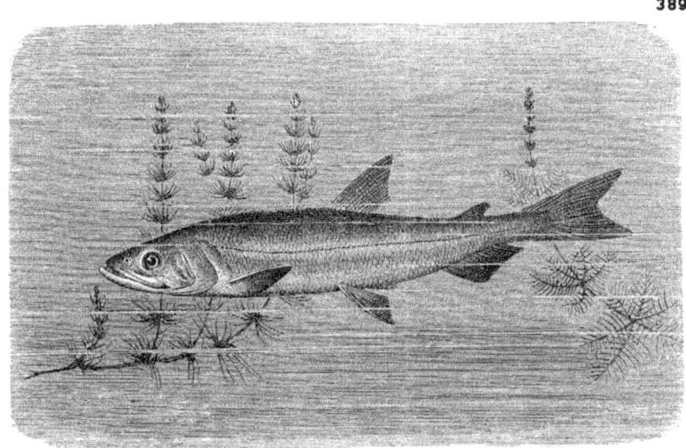

390

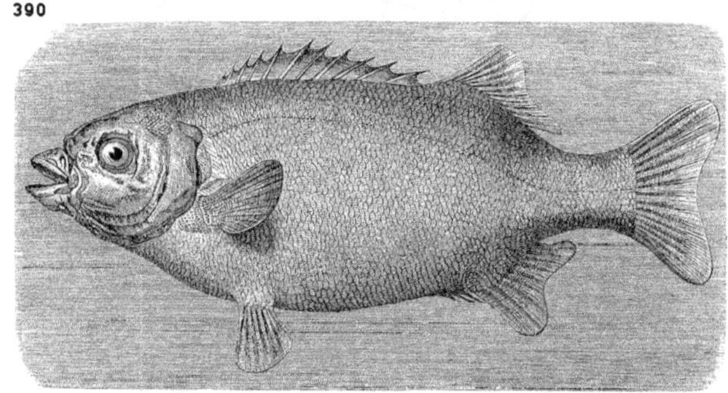

391

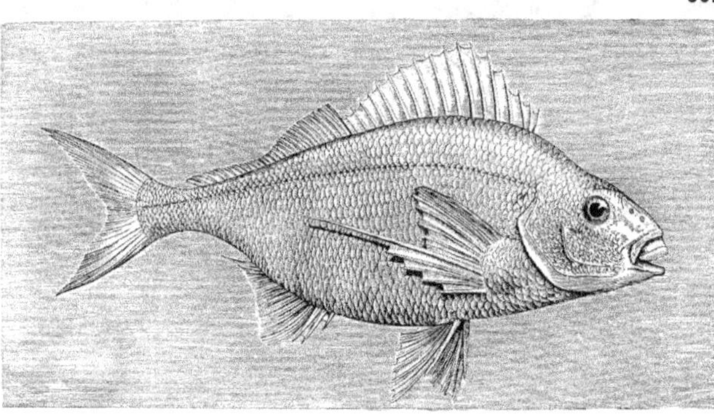

392

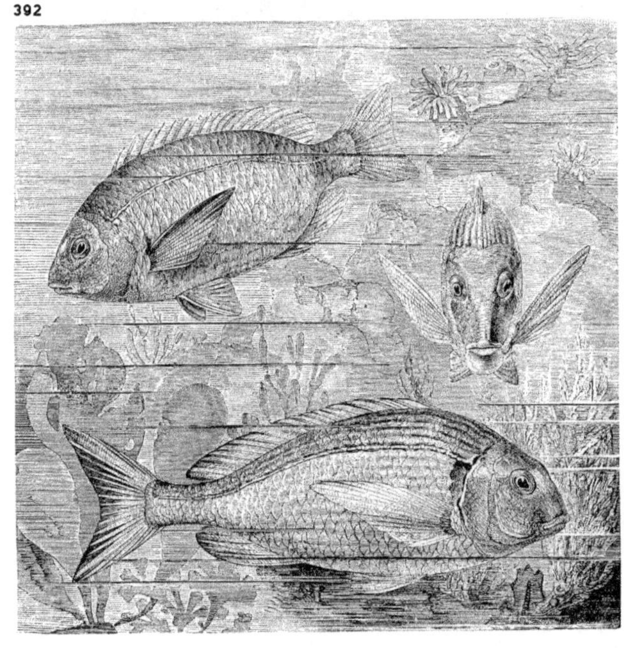

393

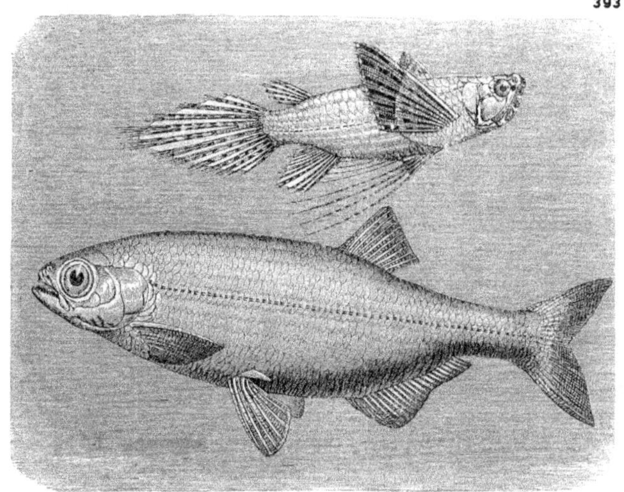

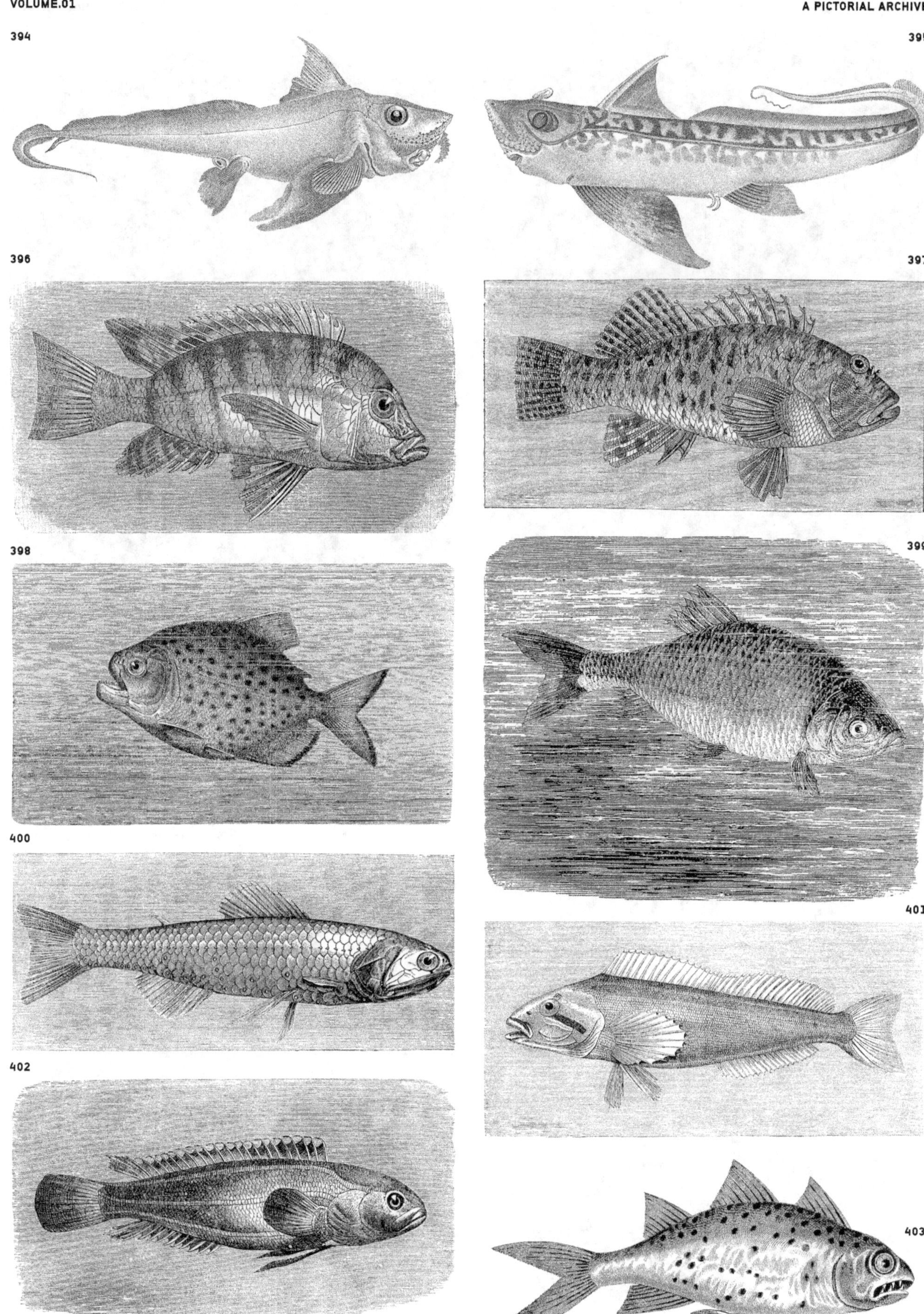

404
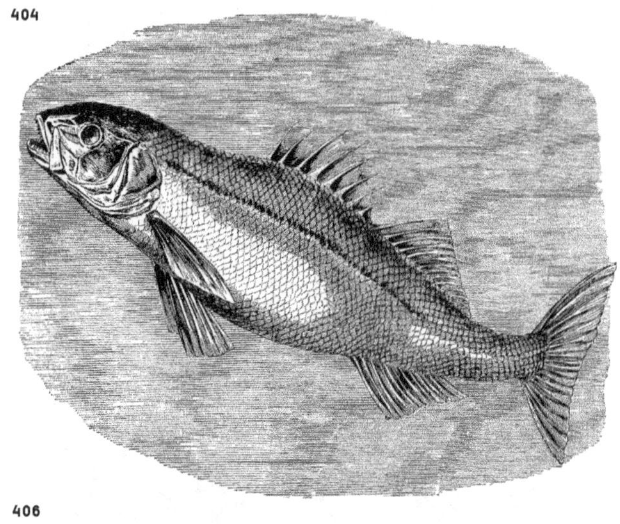

405
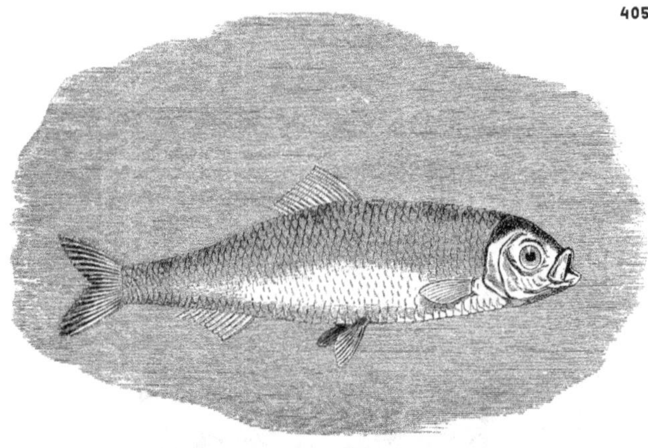

406
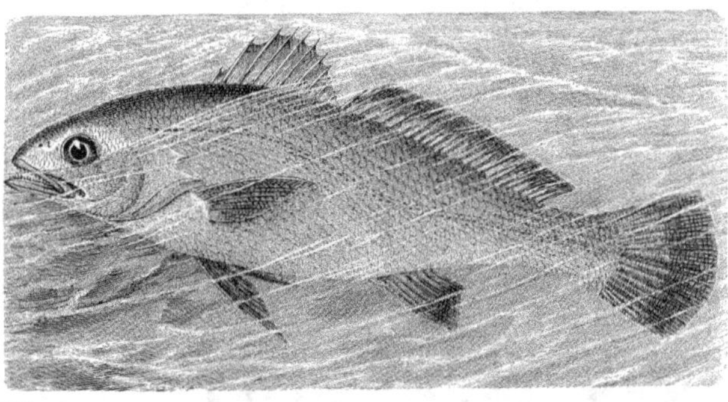

407
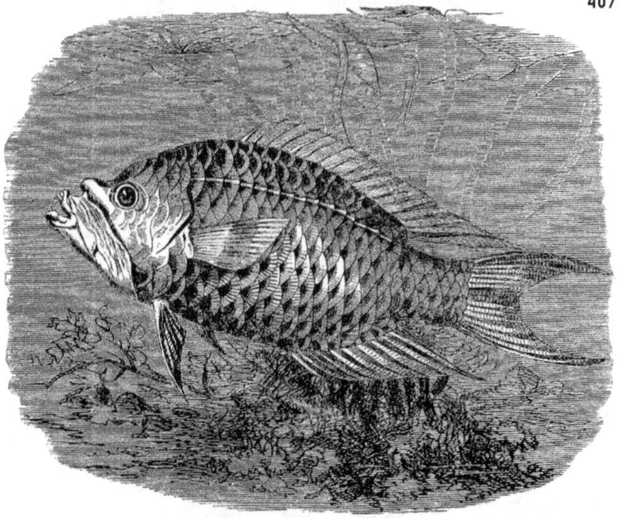

408
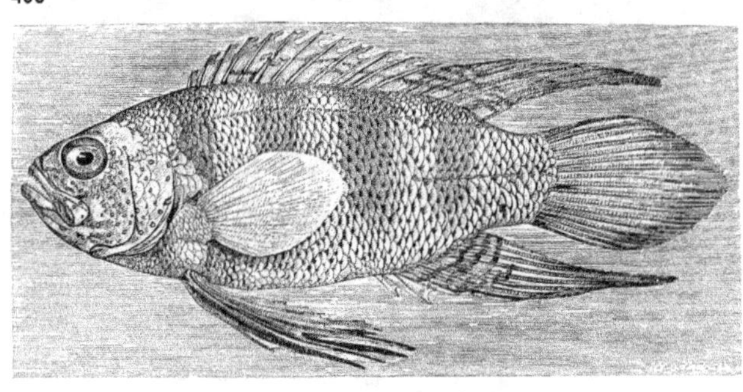

409
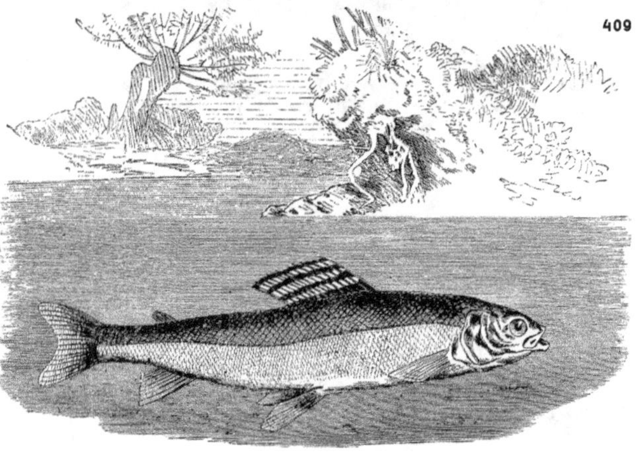

410
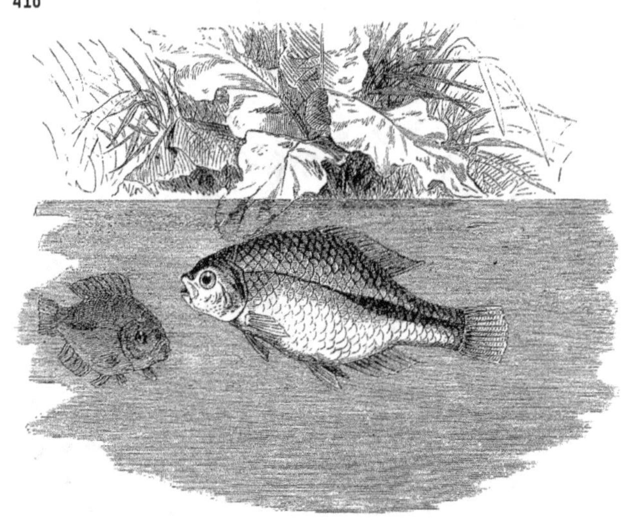

411
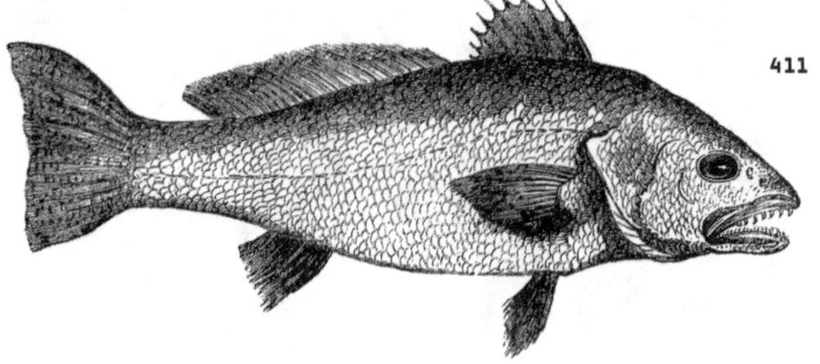

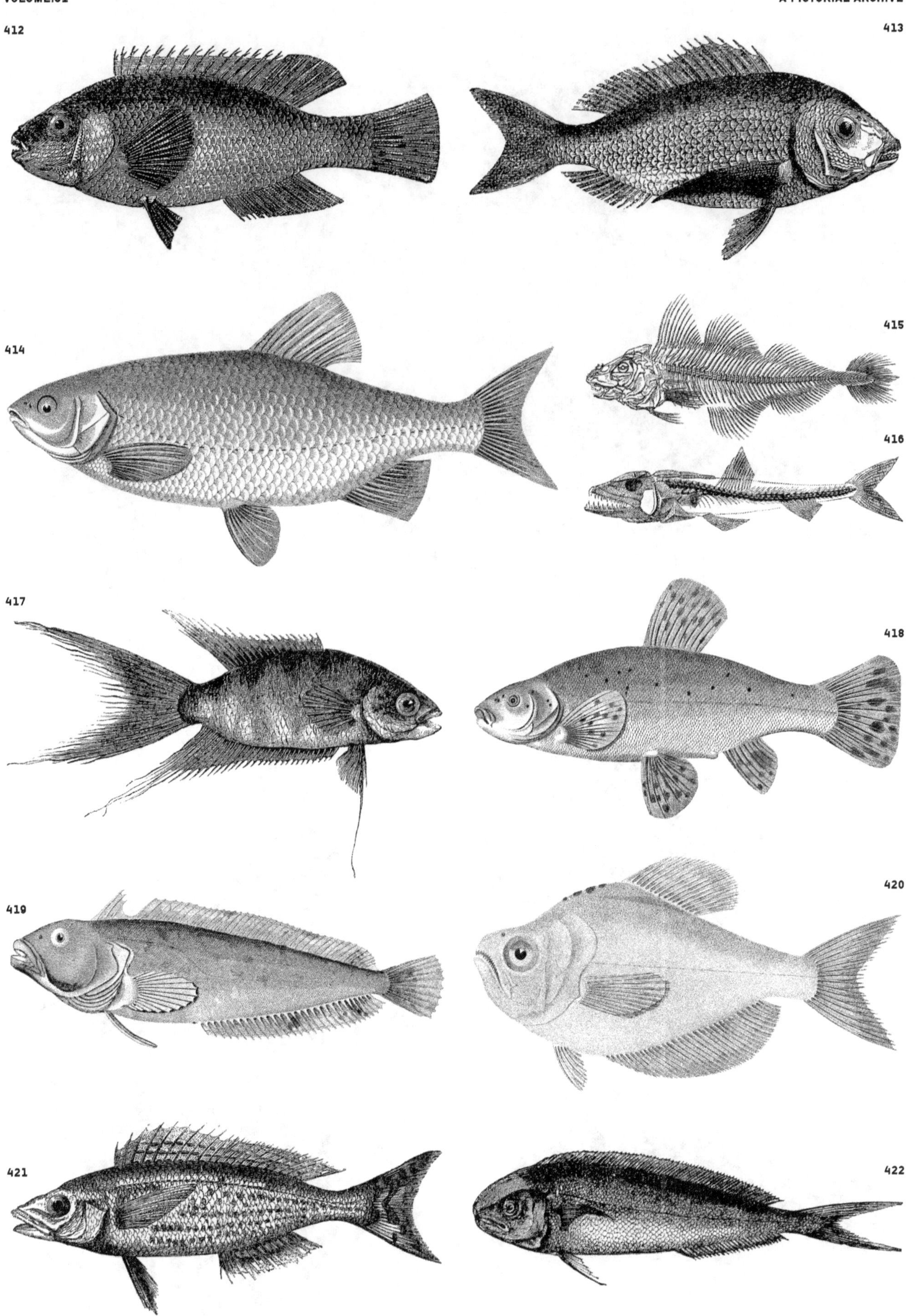

412
413
414
415
416
417
418
419
420
421
422
SEA-LIFE & MONSTERS OF THE DEEP

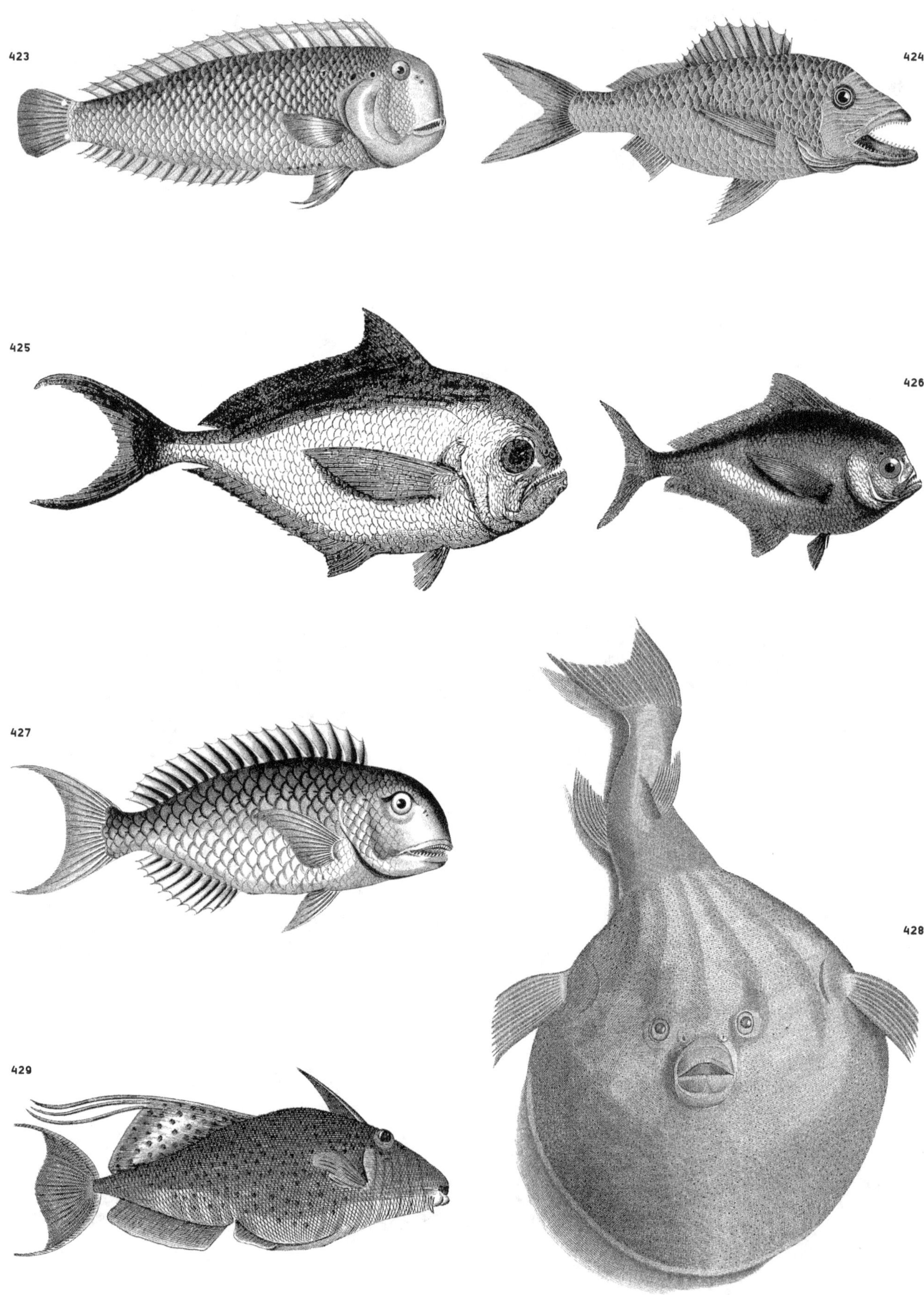

FISH

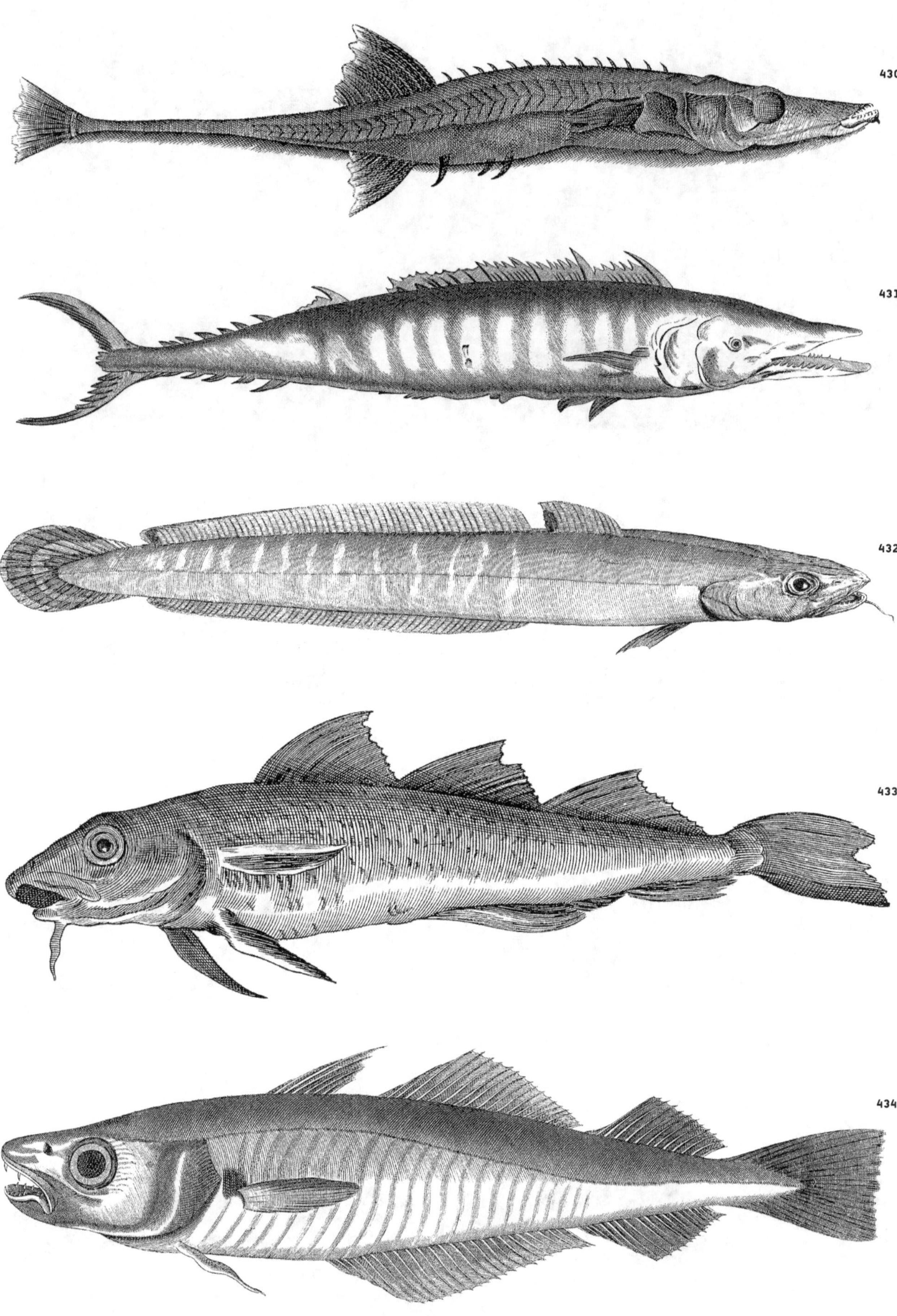

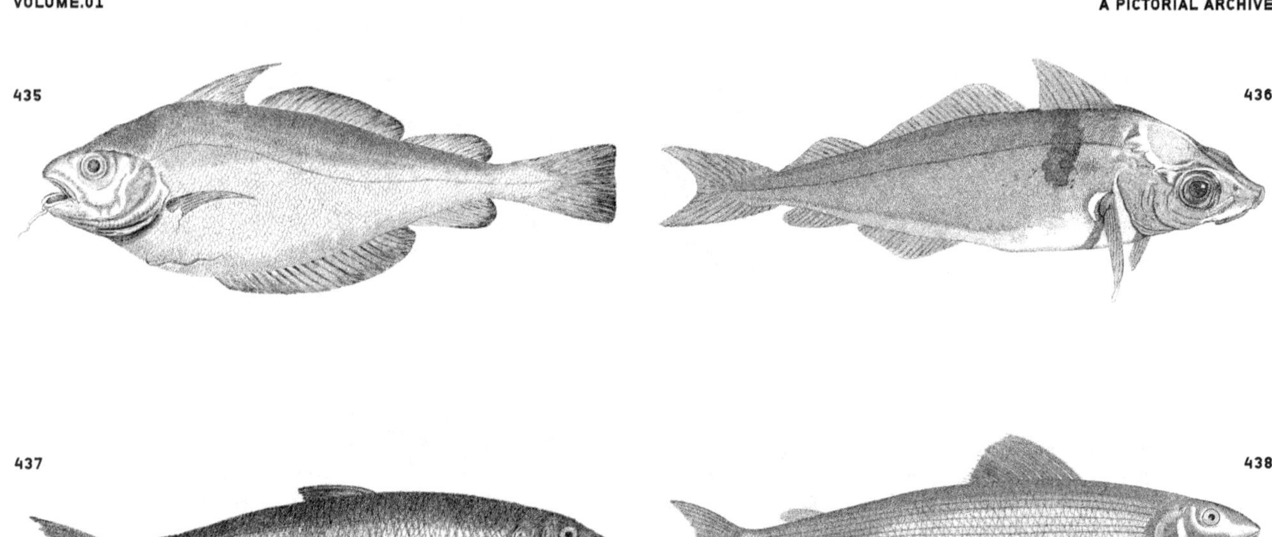

435

436

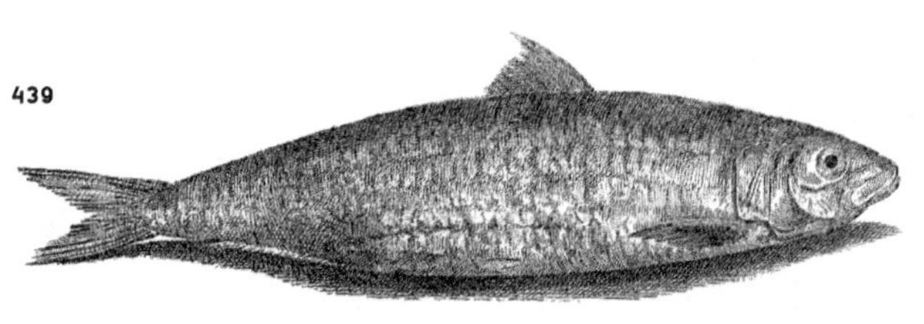

437

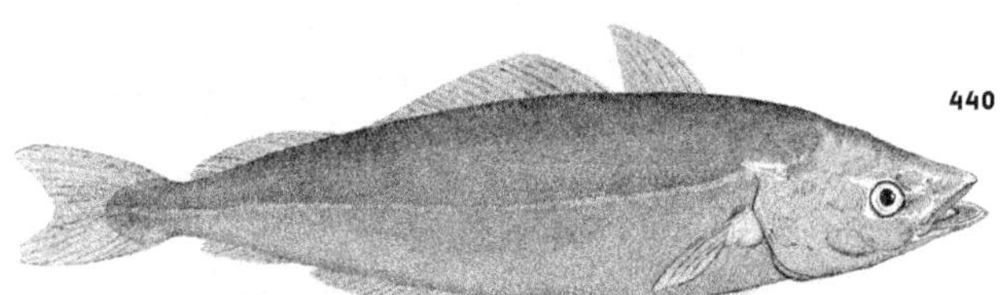

438

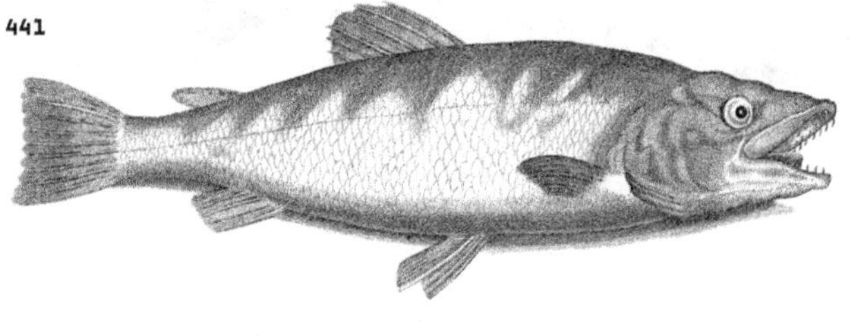

439

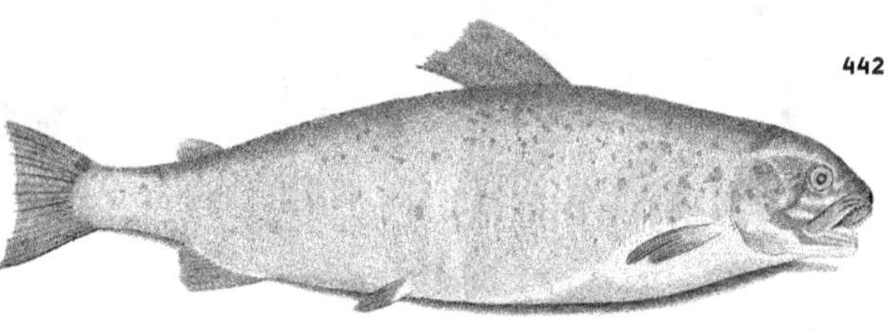

440

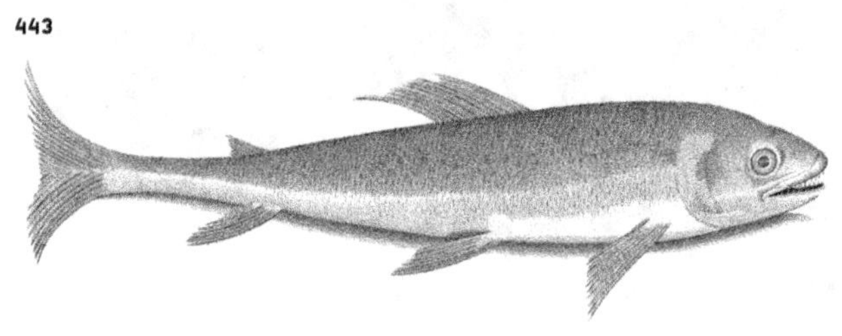

441

442

443

444

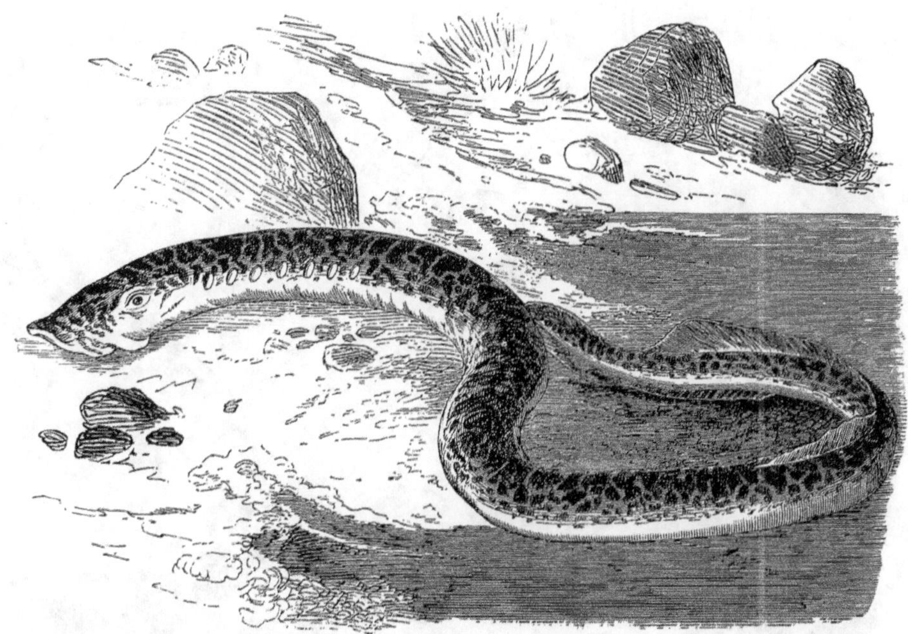

445

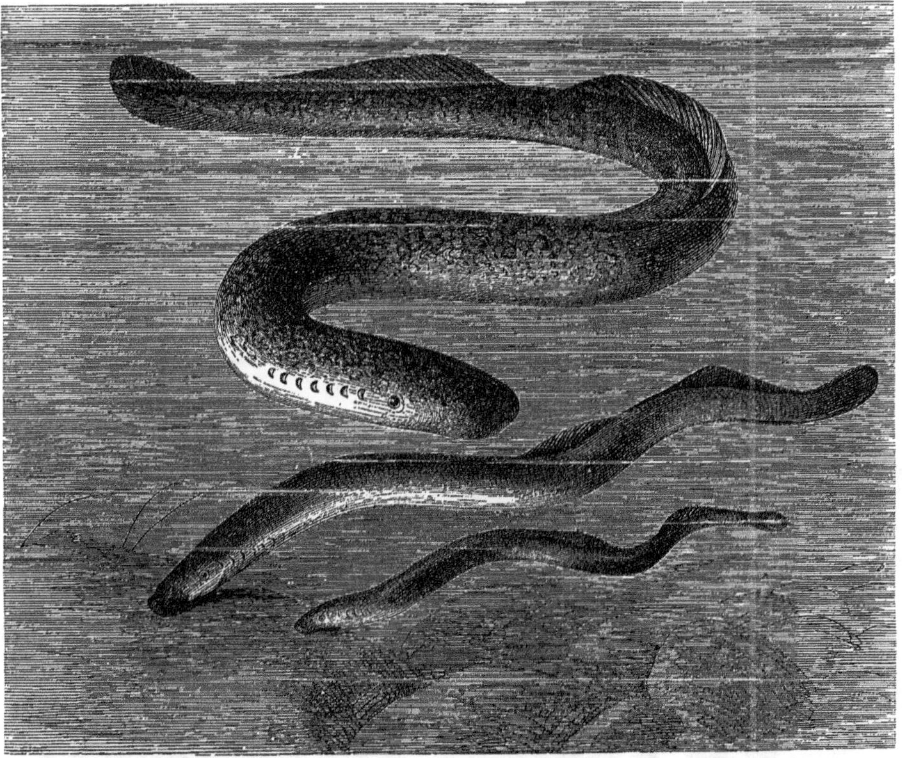

446

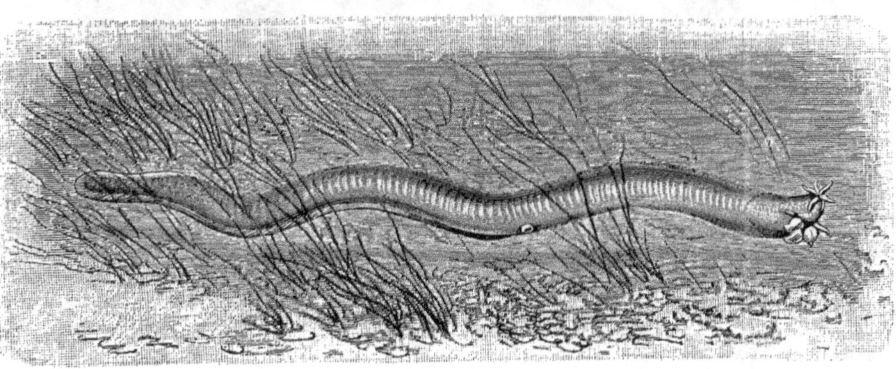

447

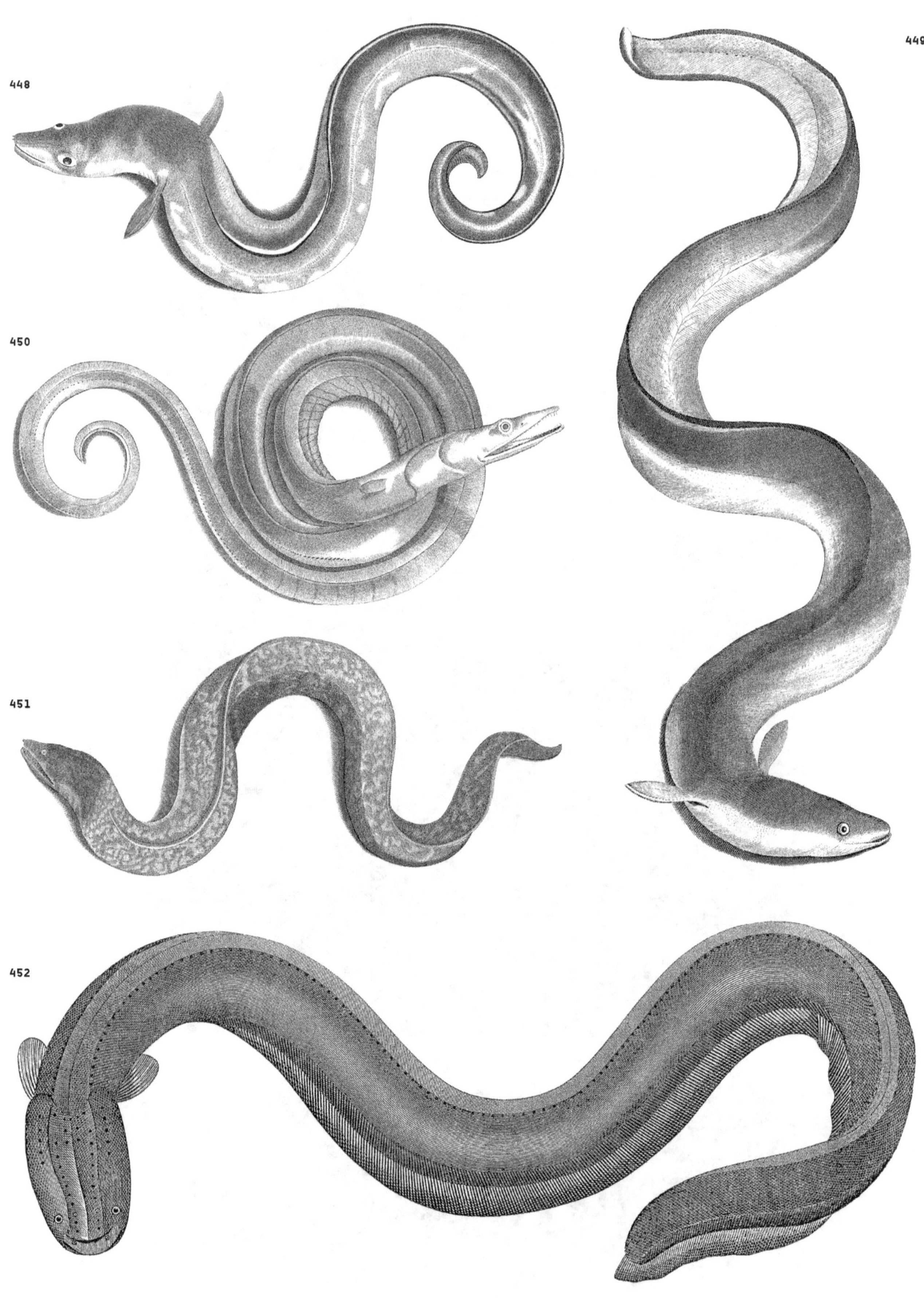

EELS

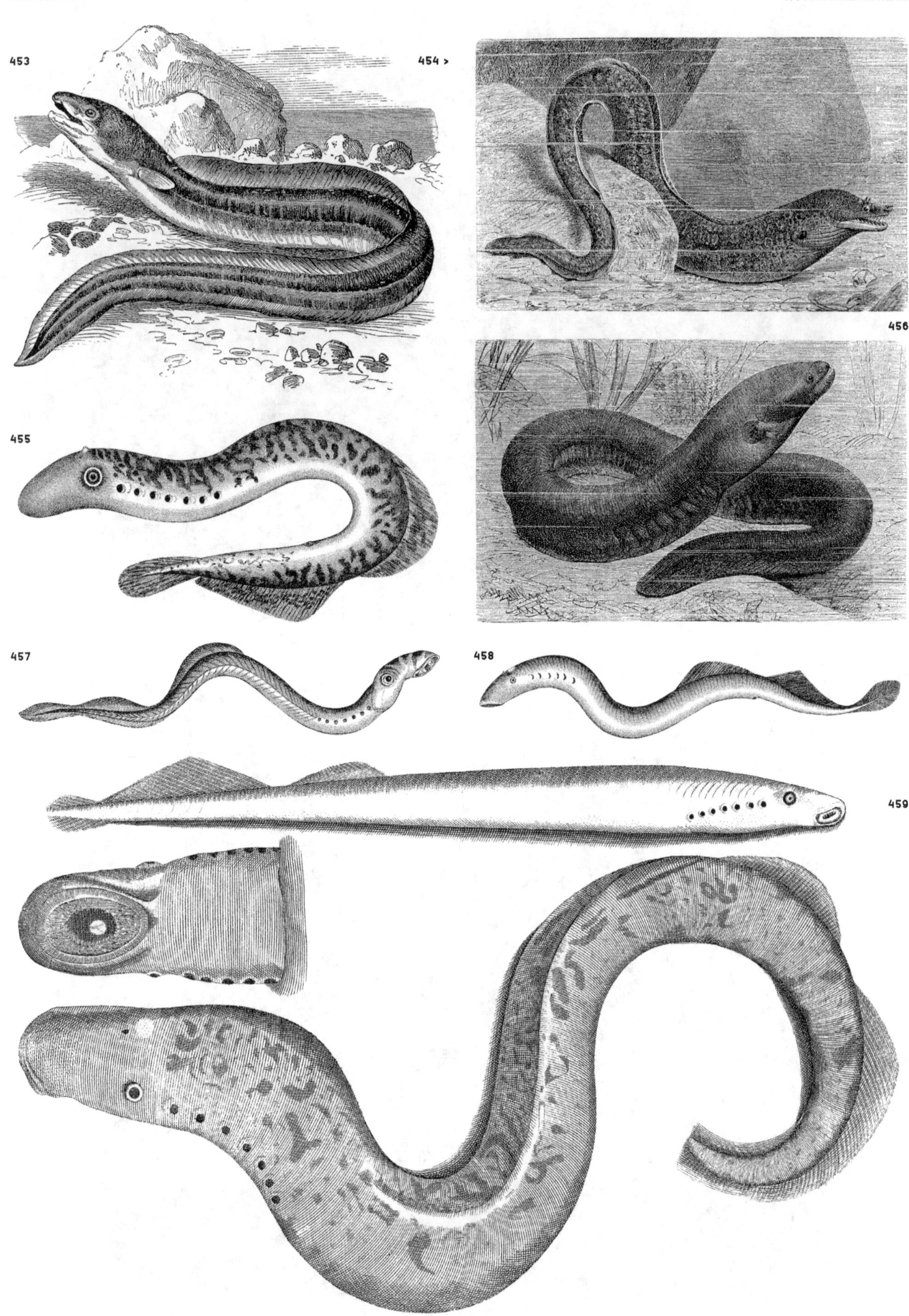

EELS

460

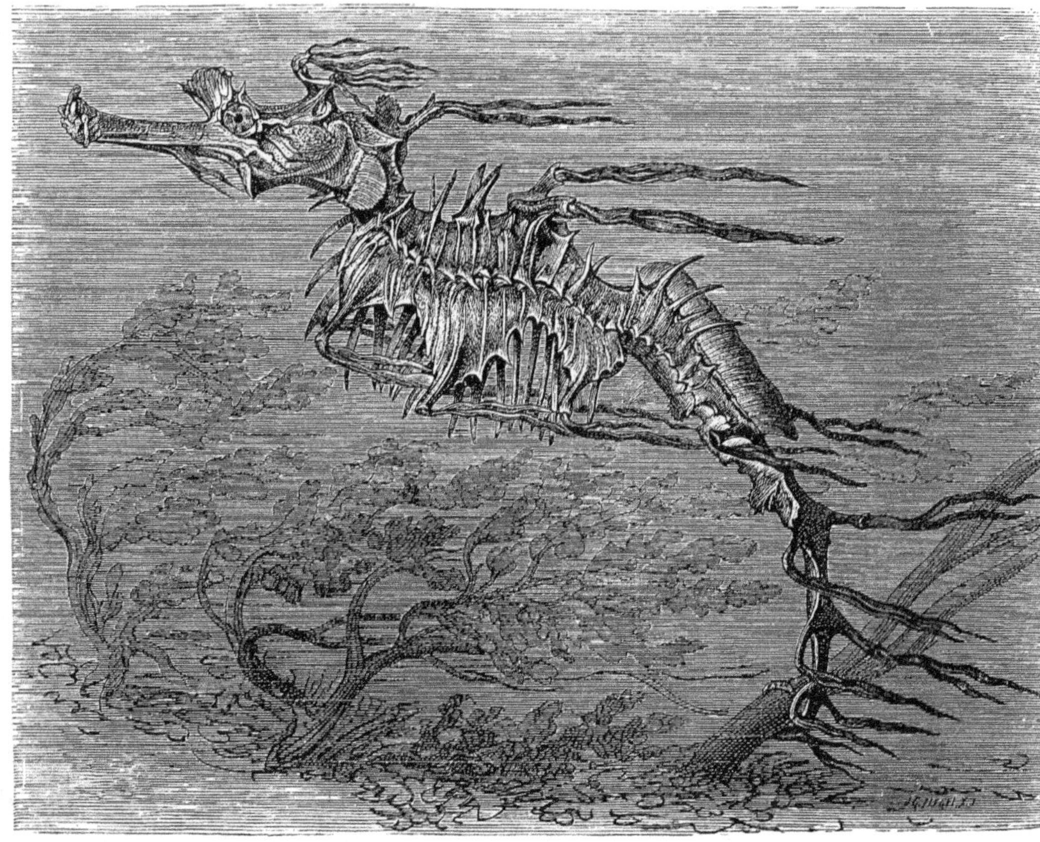

461

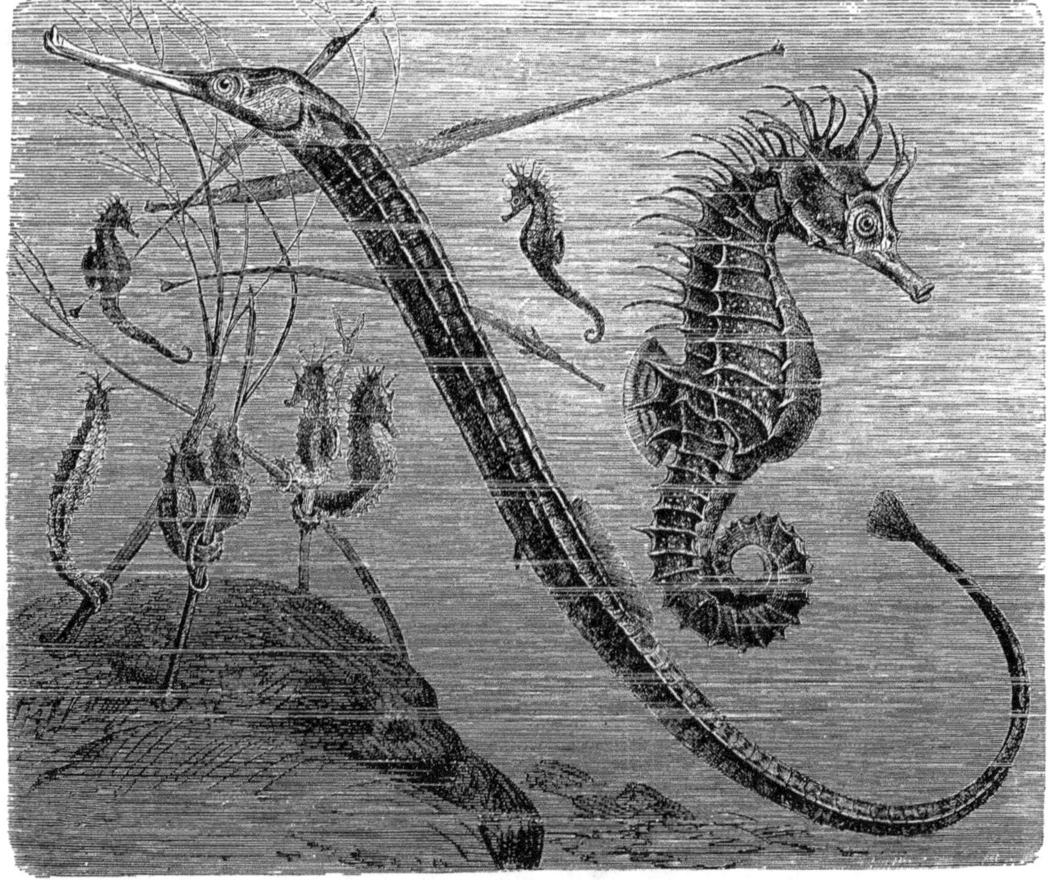

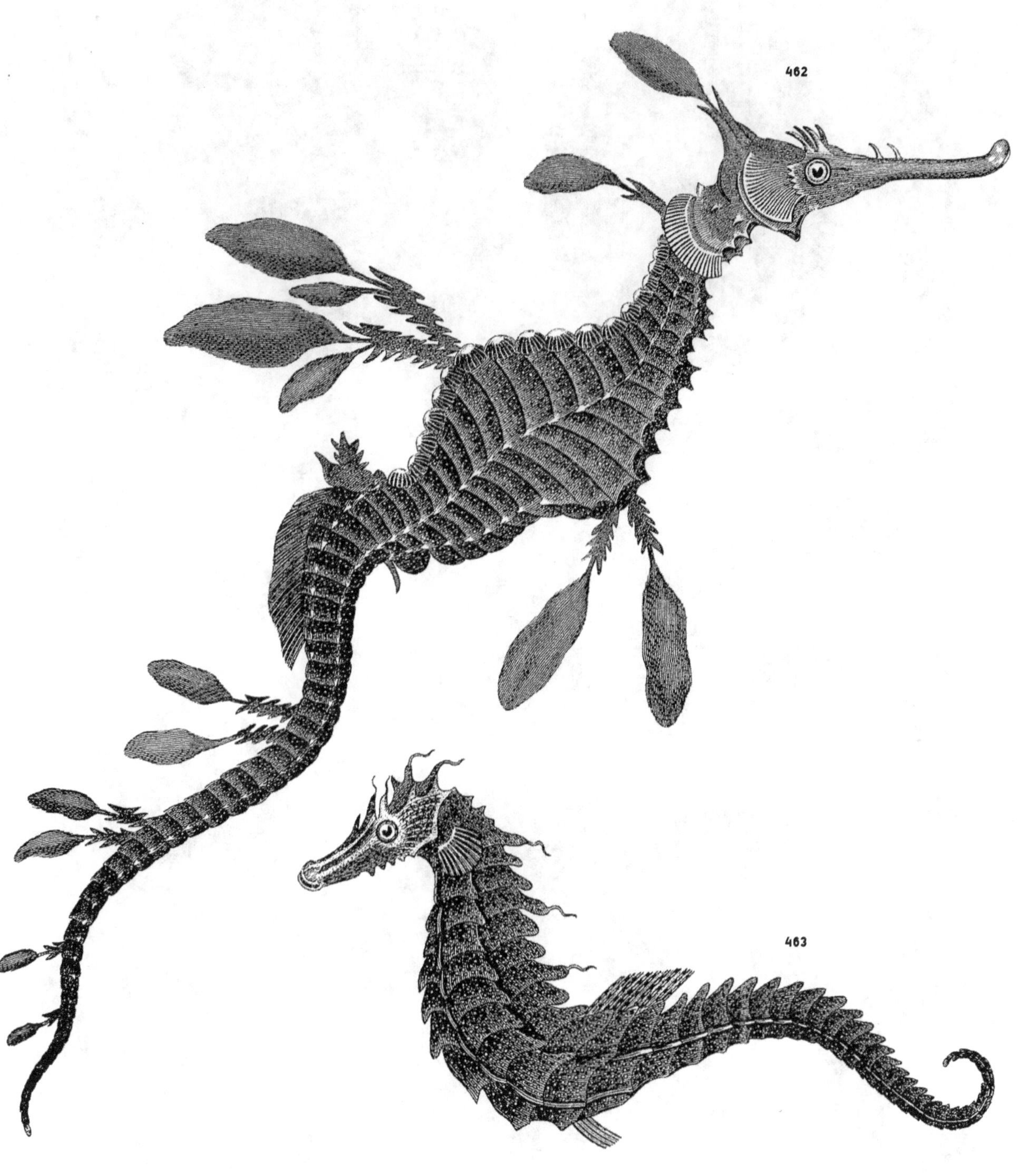

464

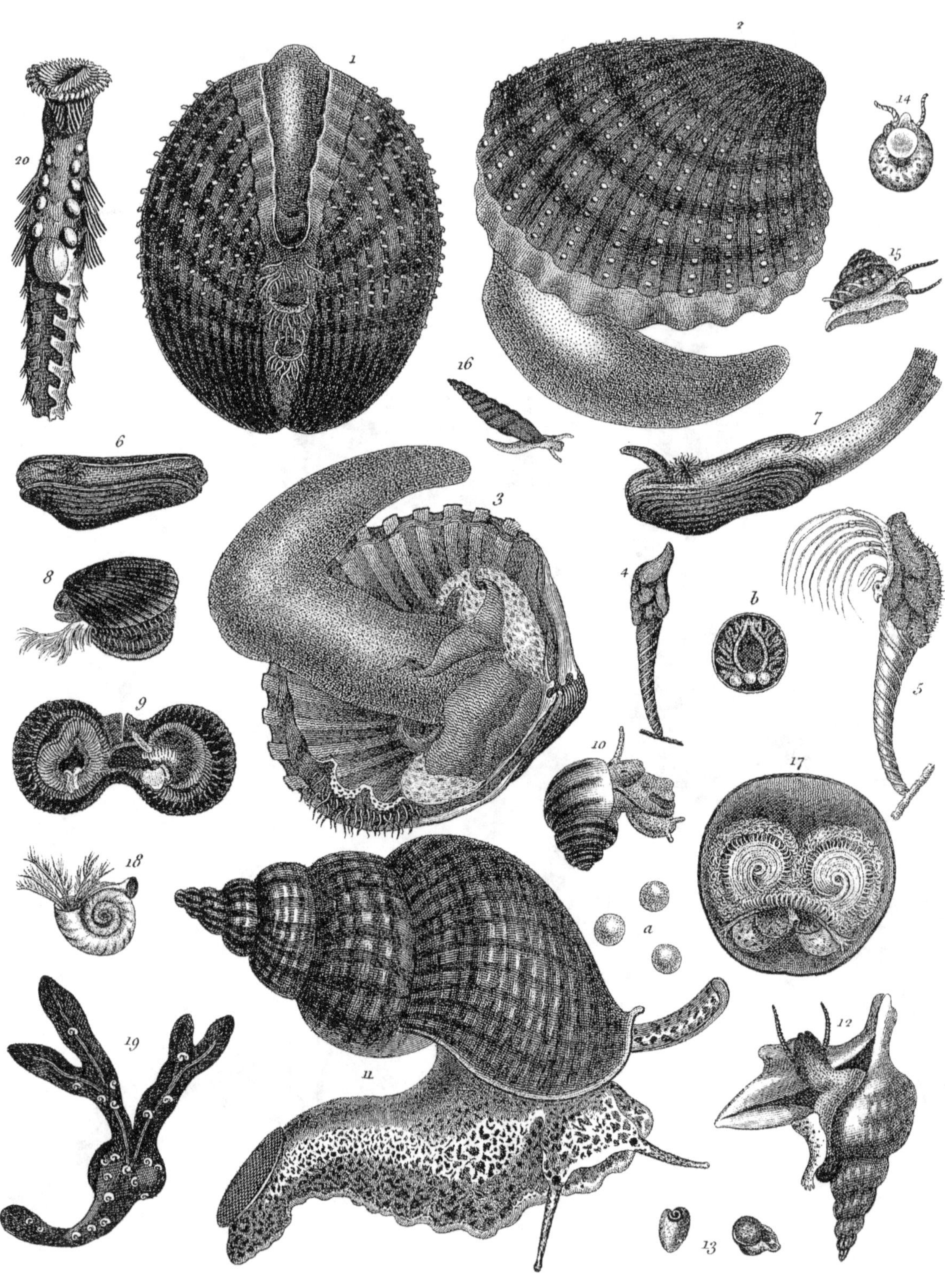

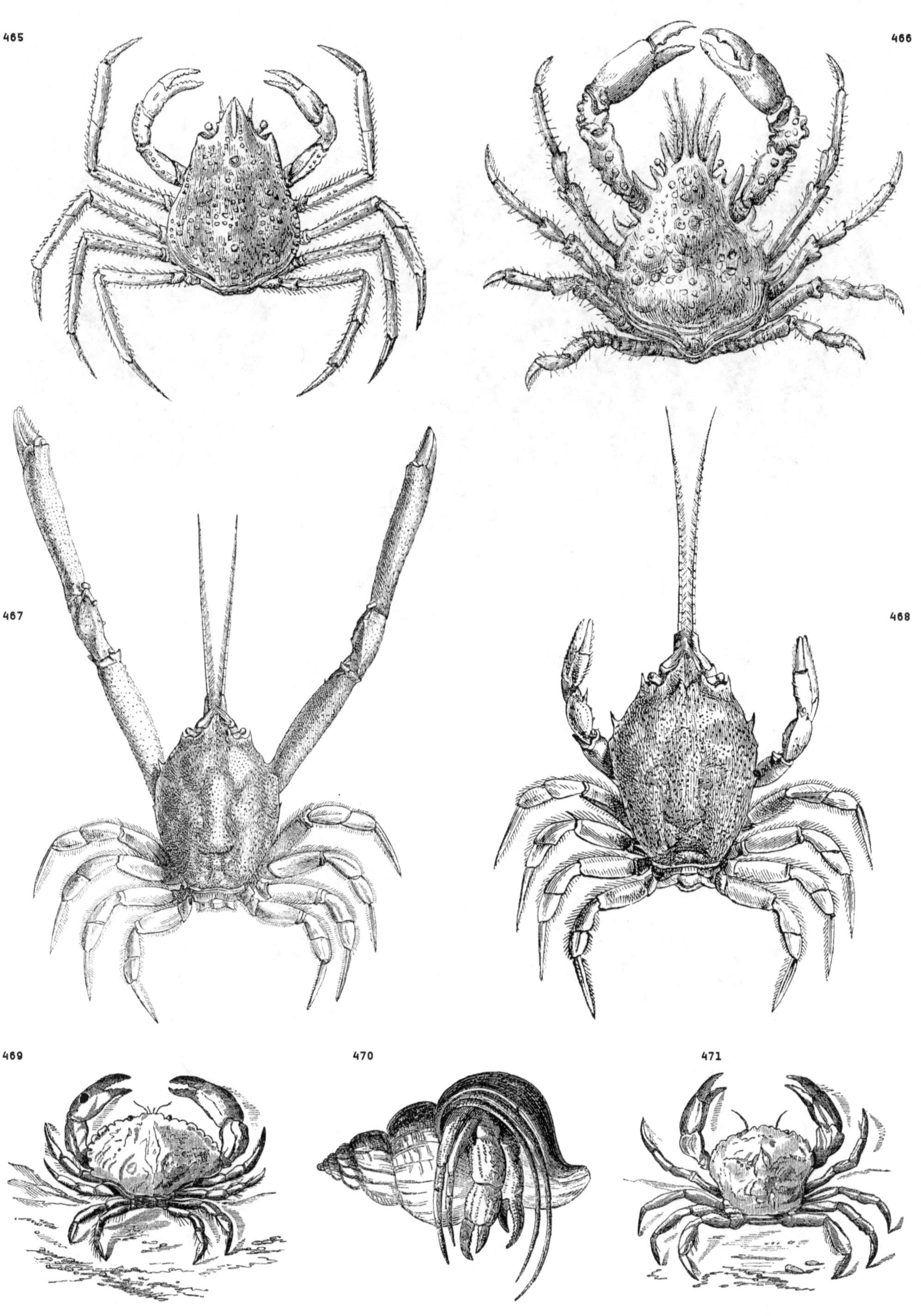

CRUSTACEANS

472

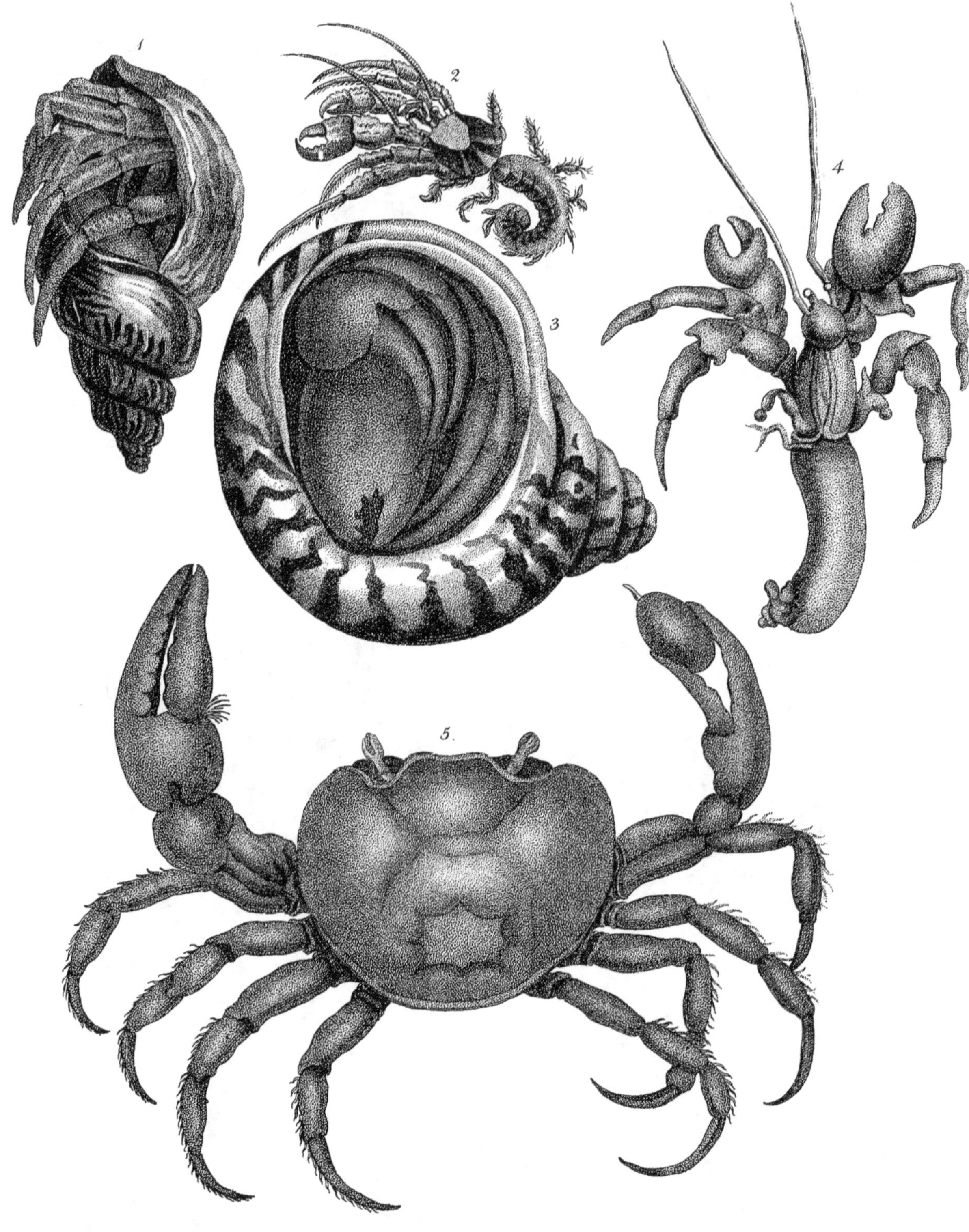

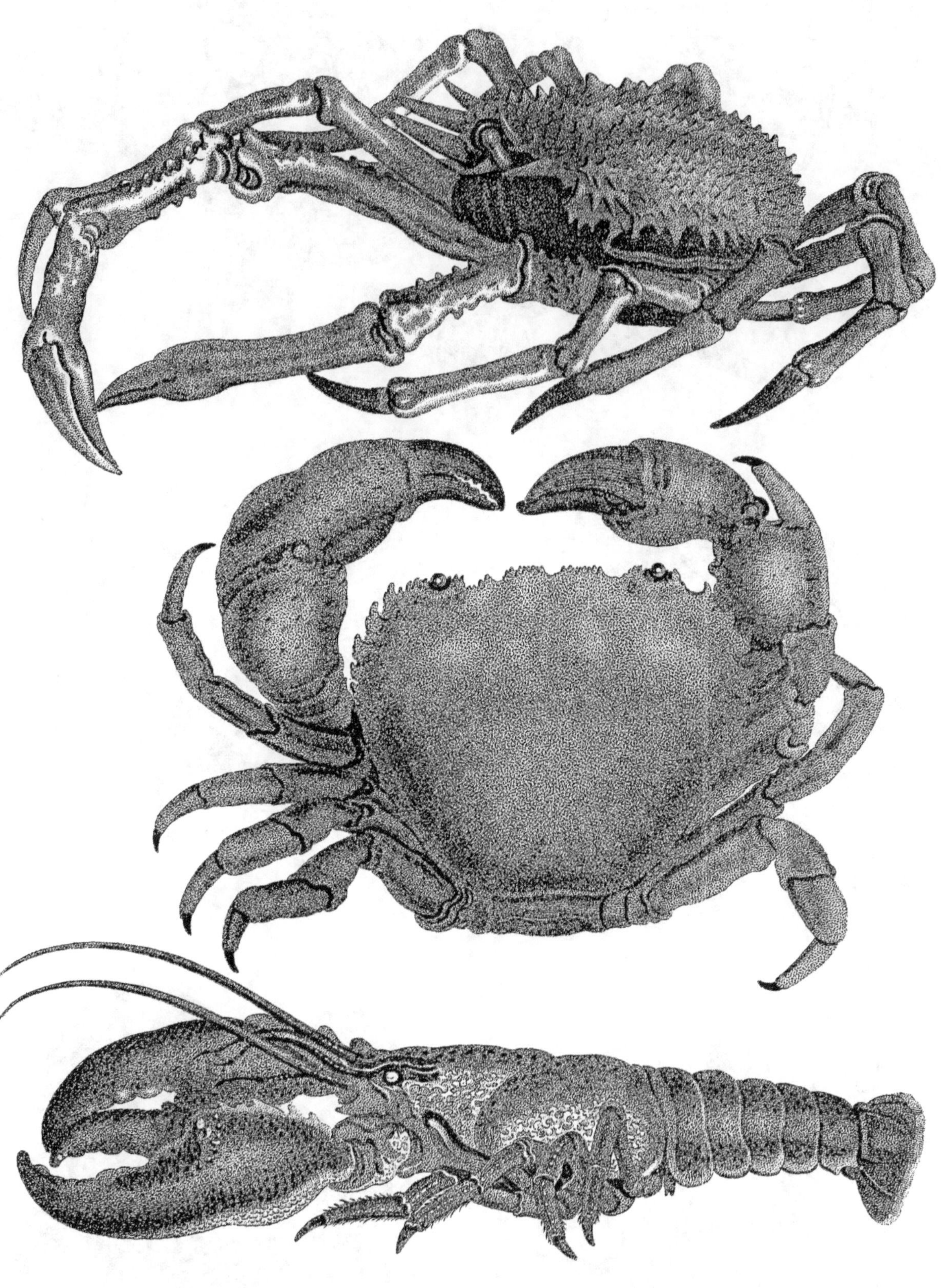

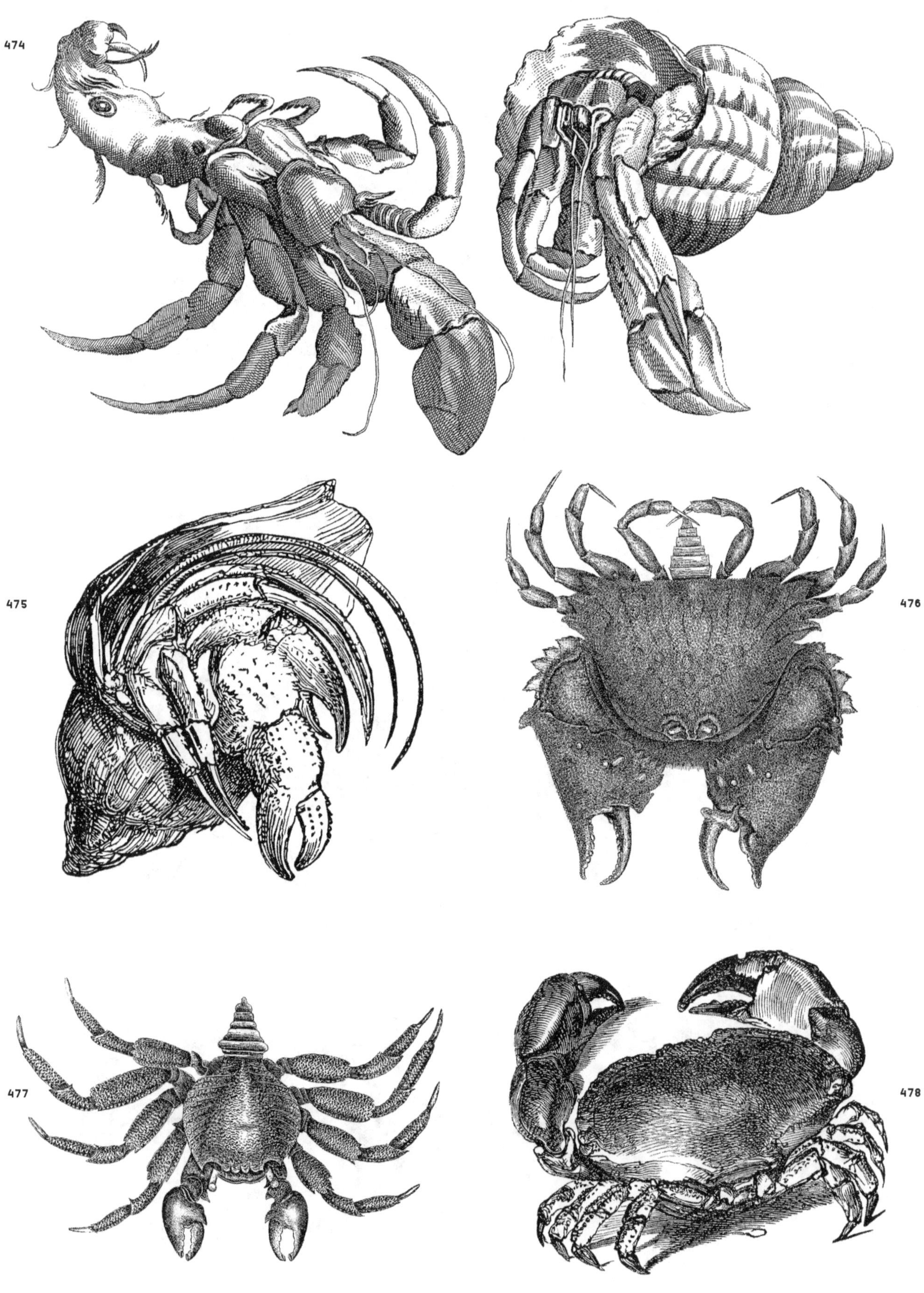

474

475

476

477

478

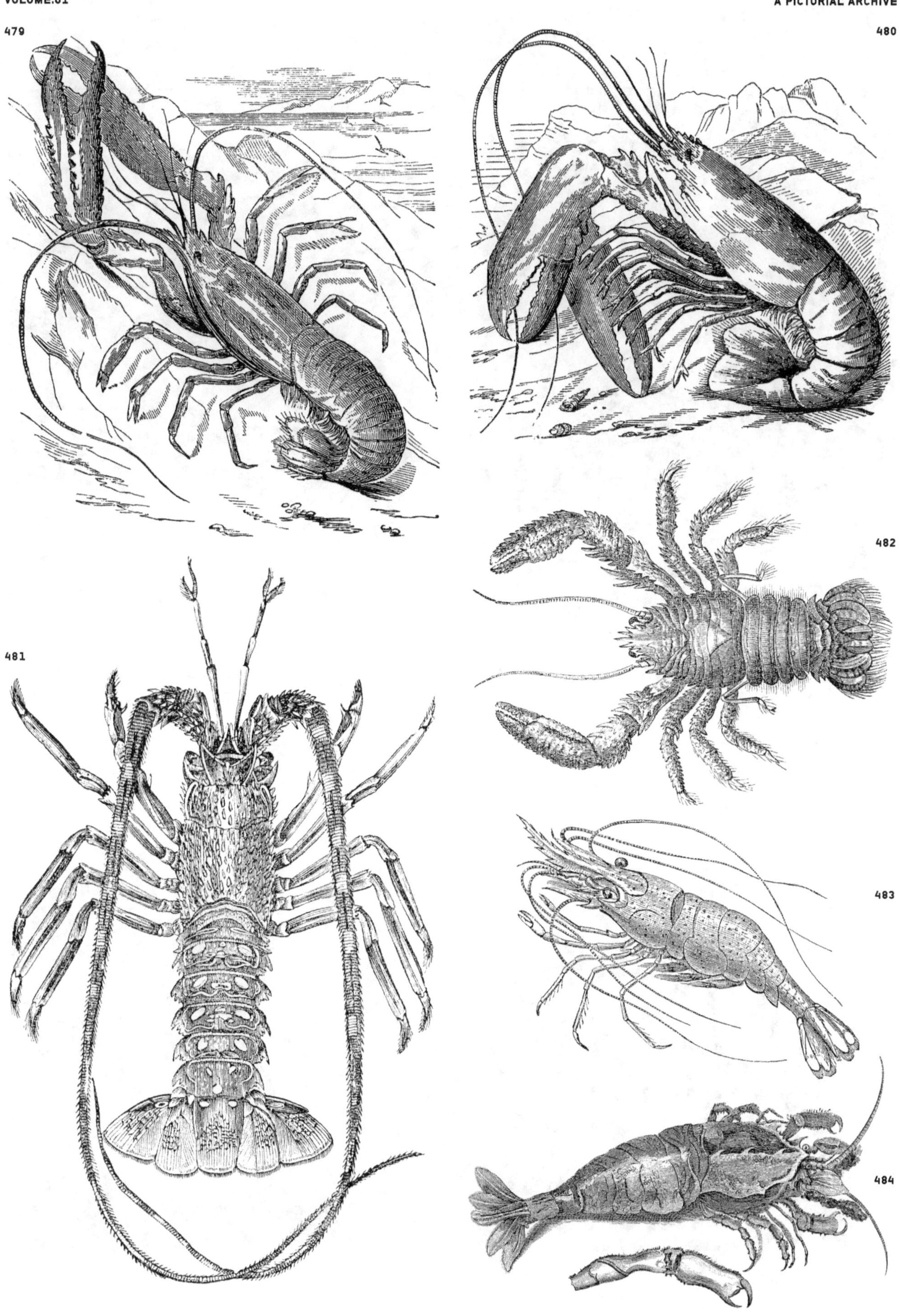

CRUSTACEANS

485

Squilla
Cancer
Cancer
Adr. Collaert
fecit et exc.
17.

486

B. Flamen fe.

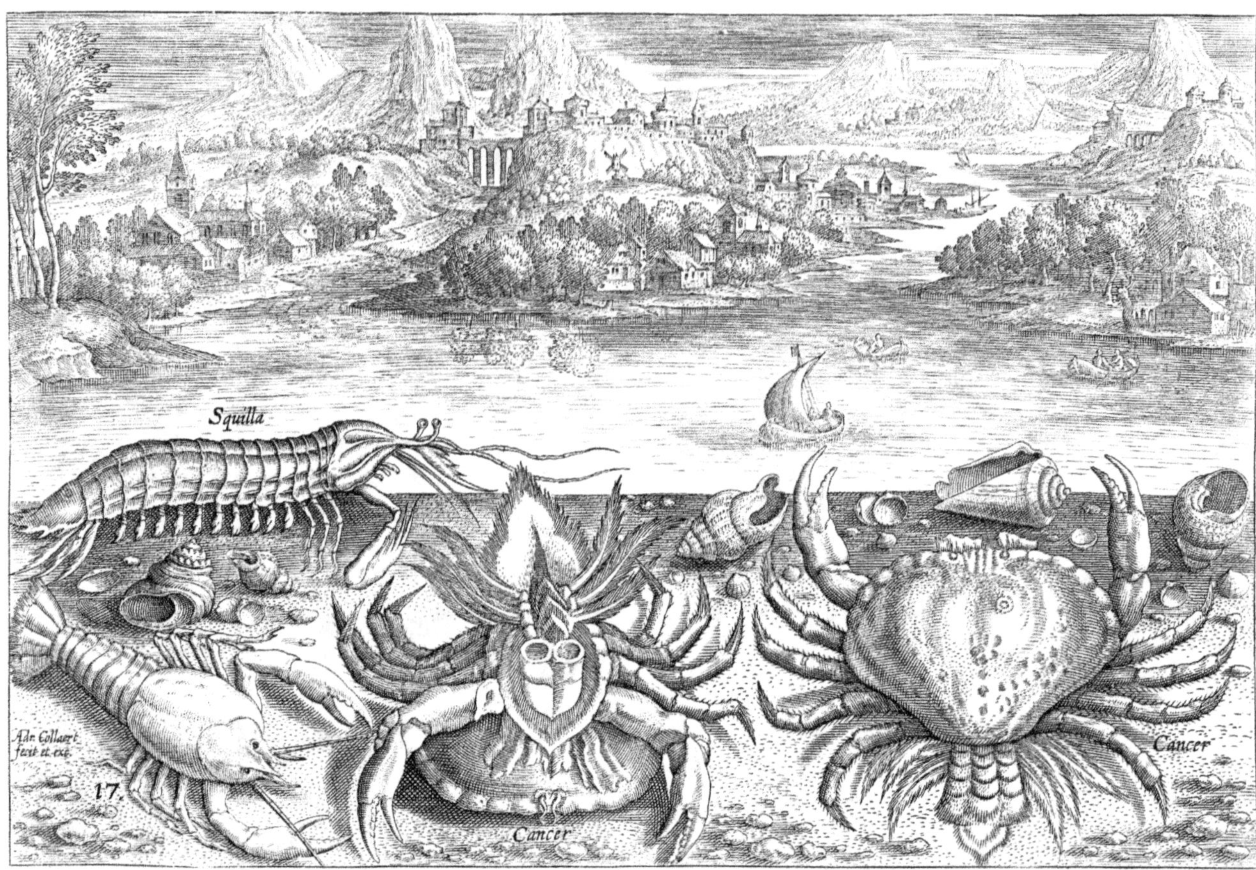

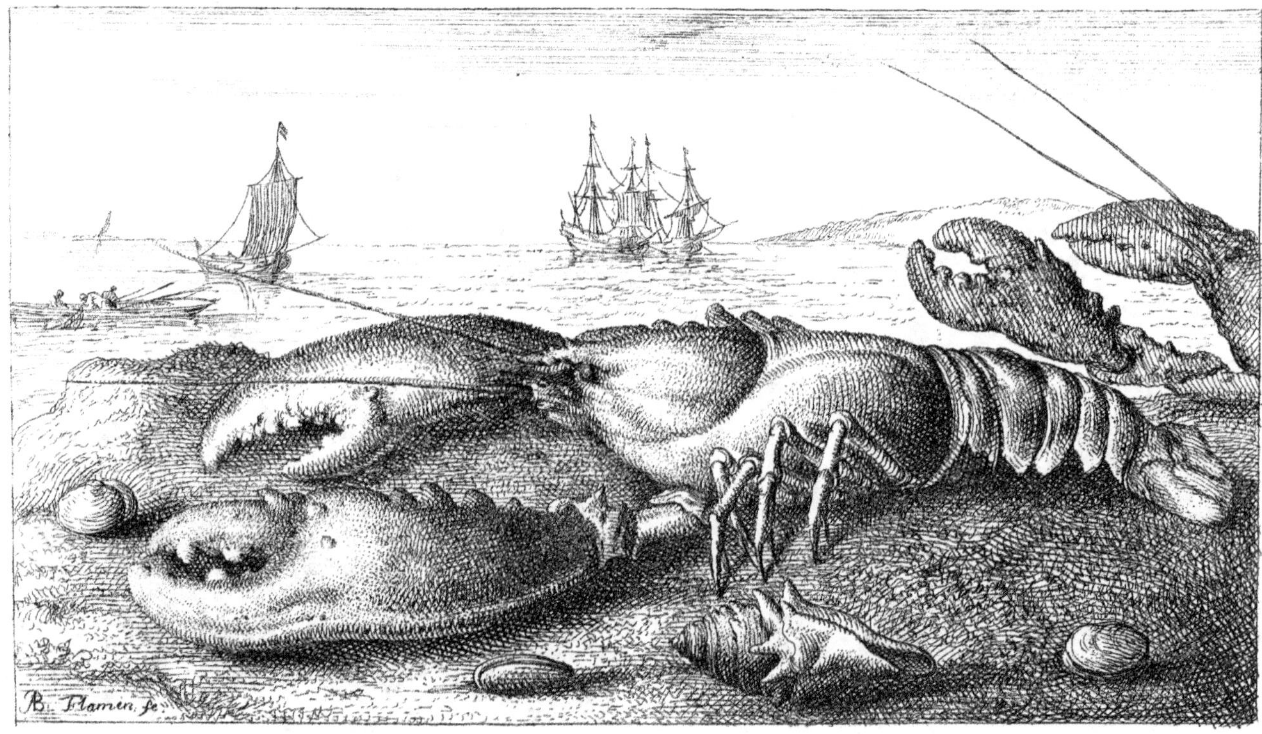

487

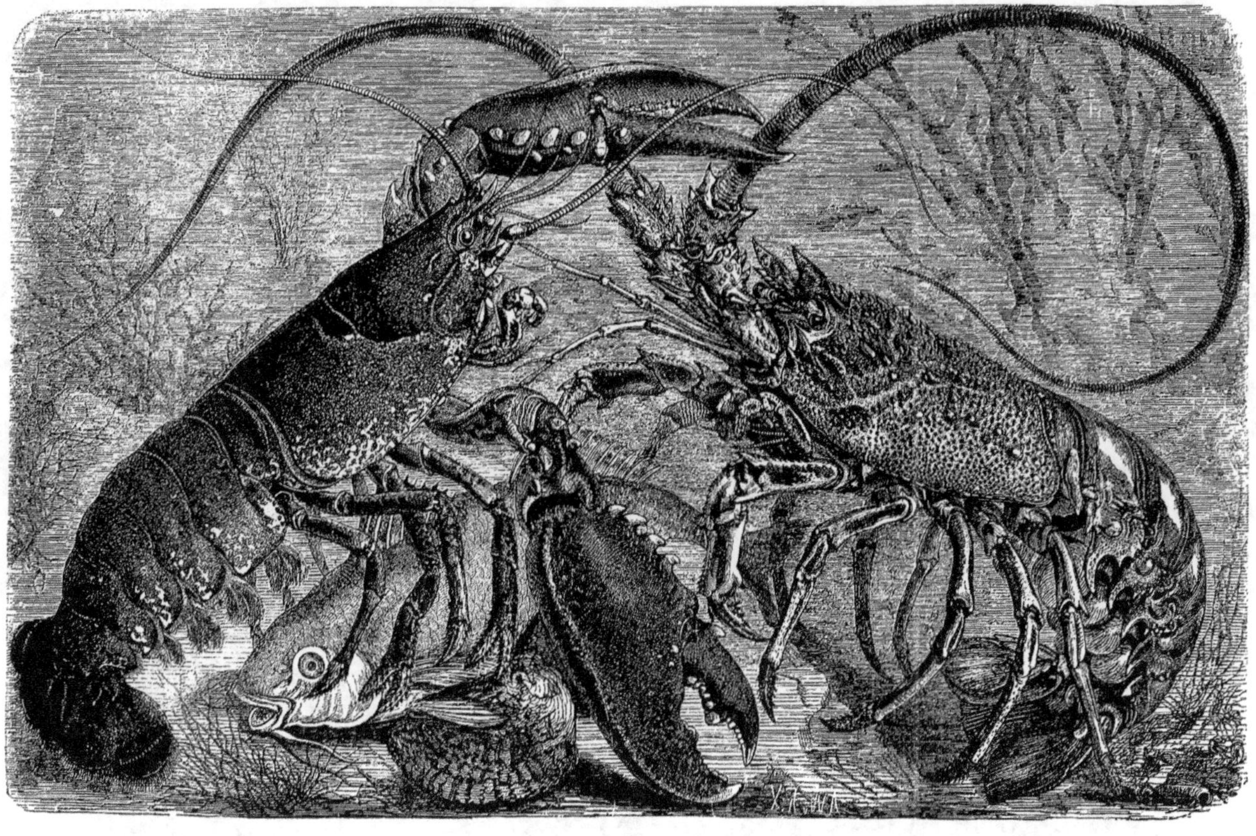

488

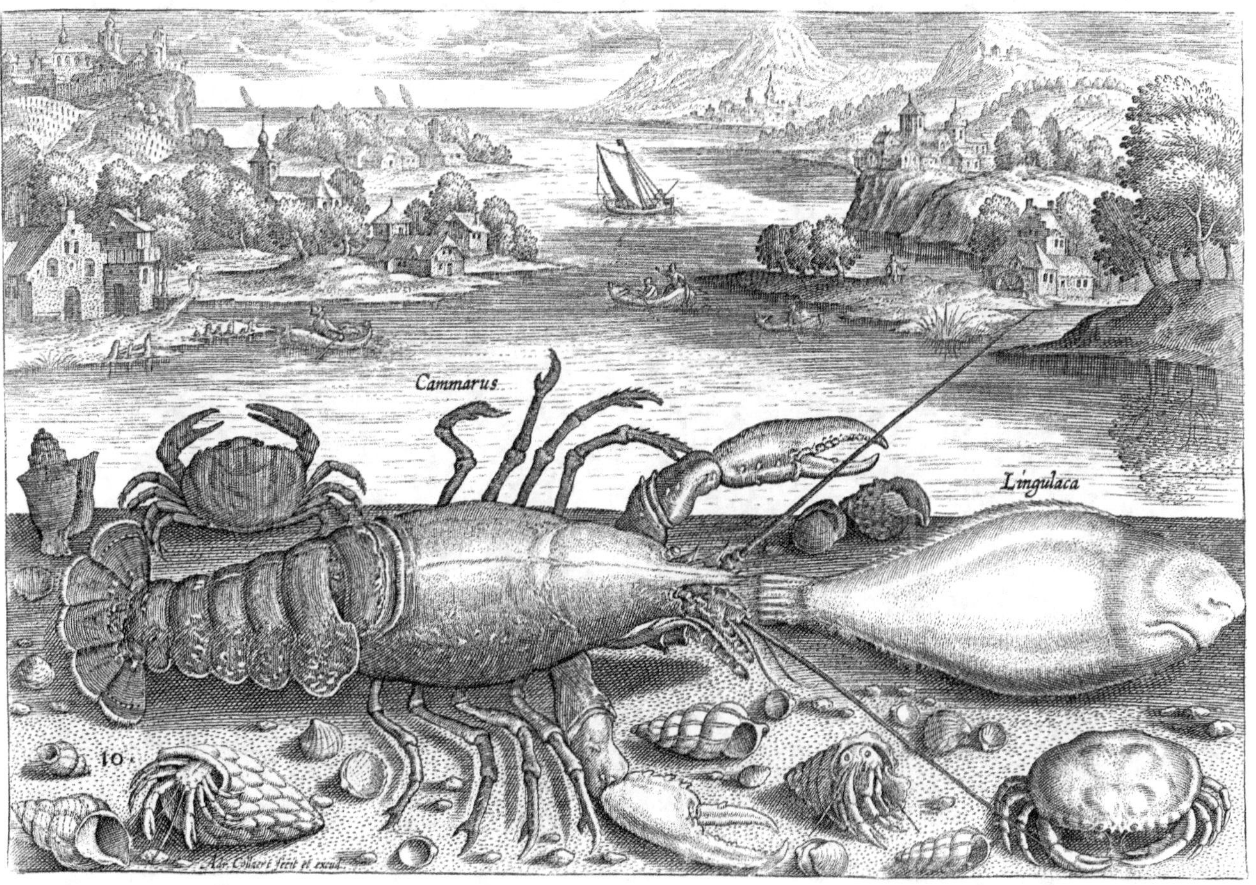

CRUSTACEANS

489

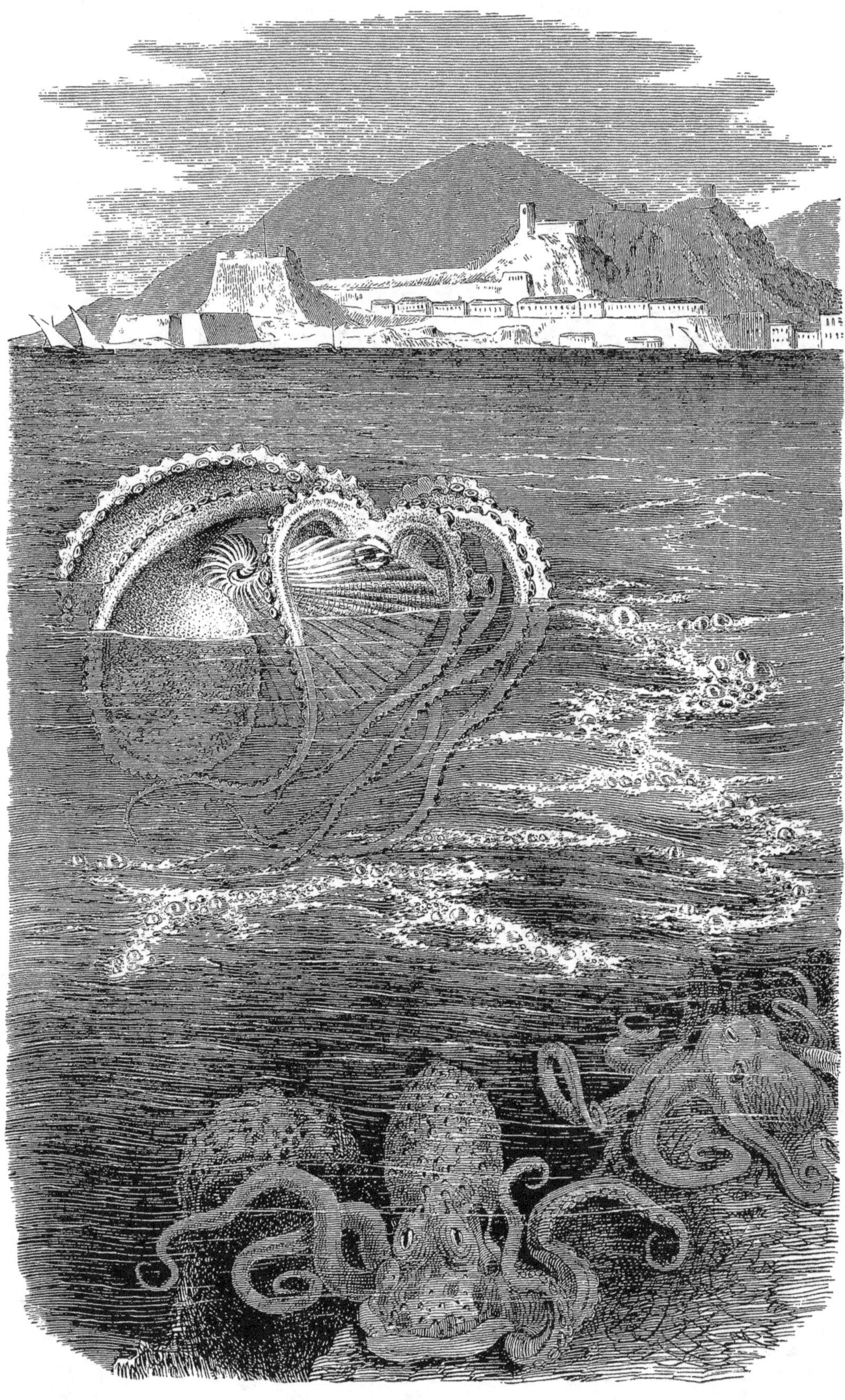

CEPHLAPODS

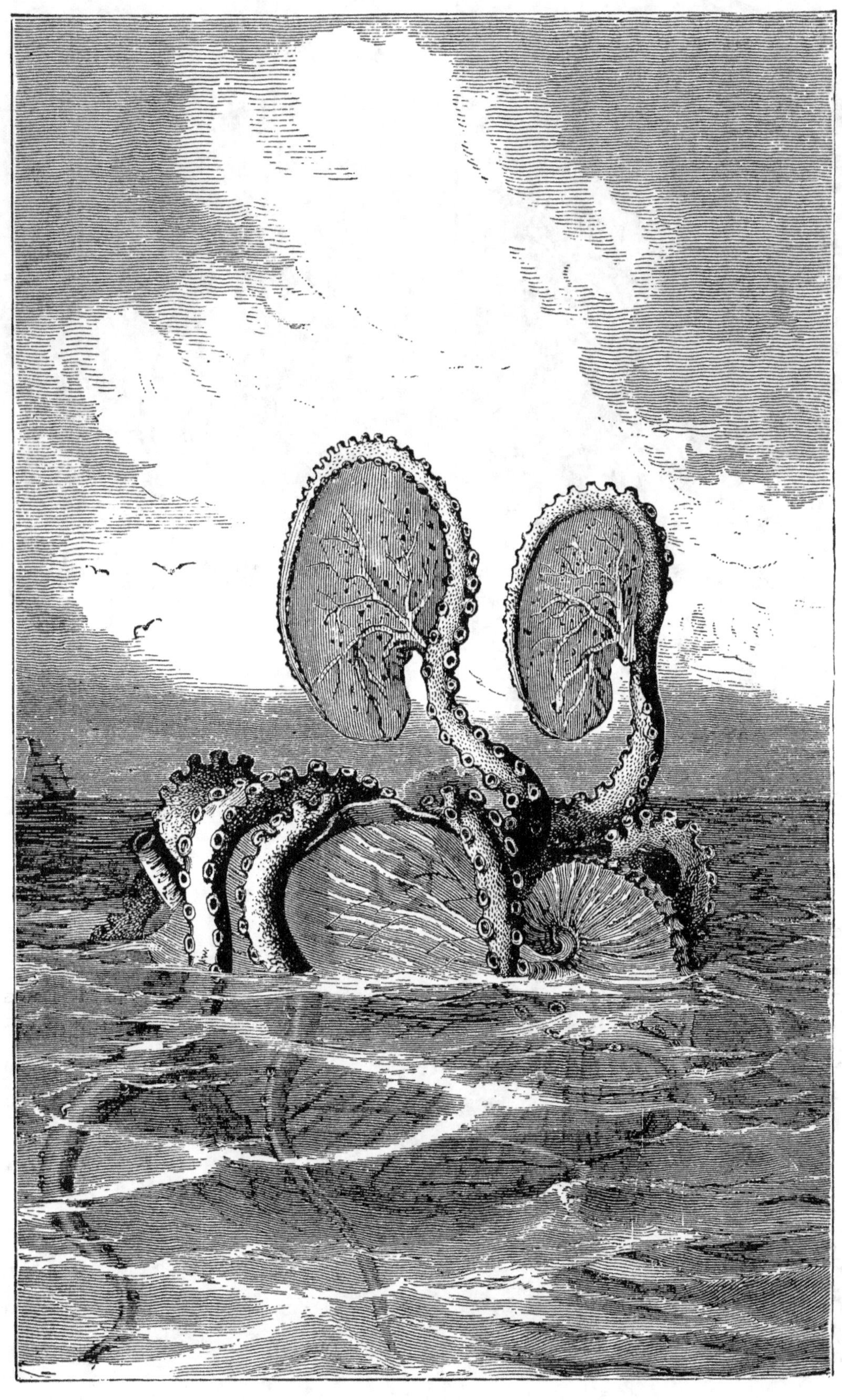

CEPHLAPODS

491

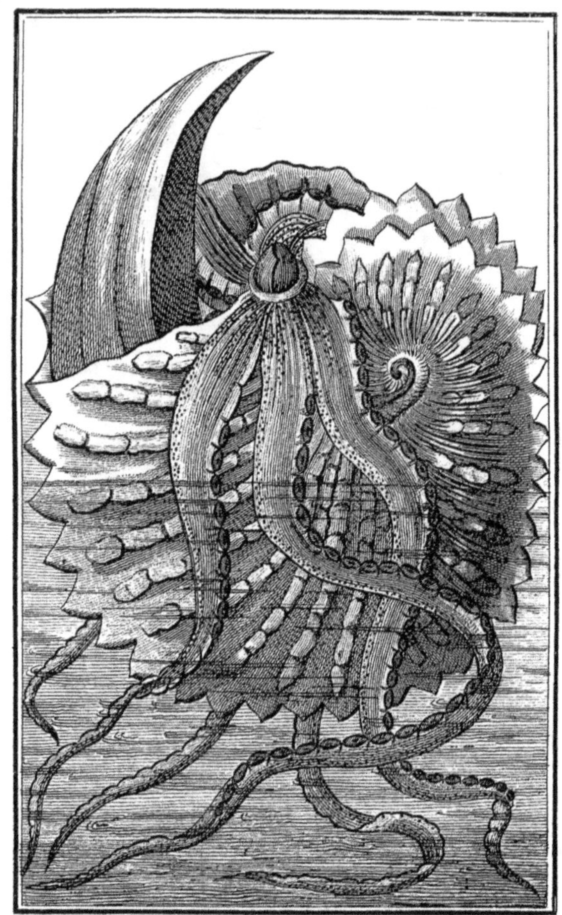

492

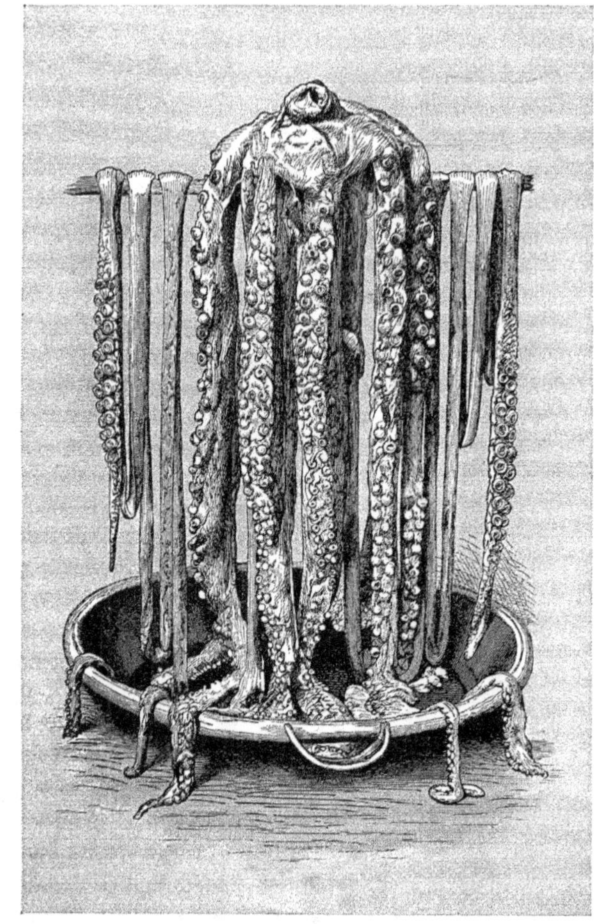

493

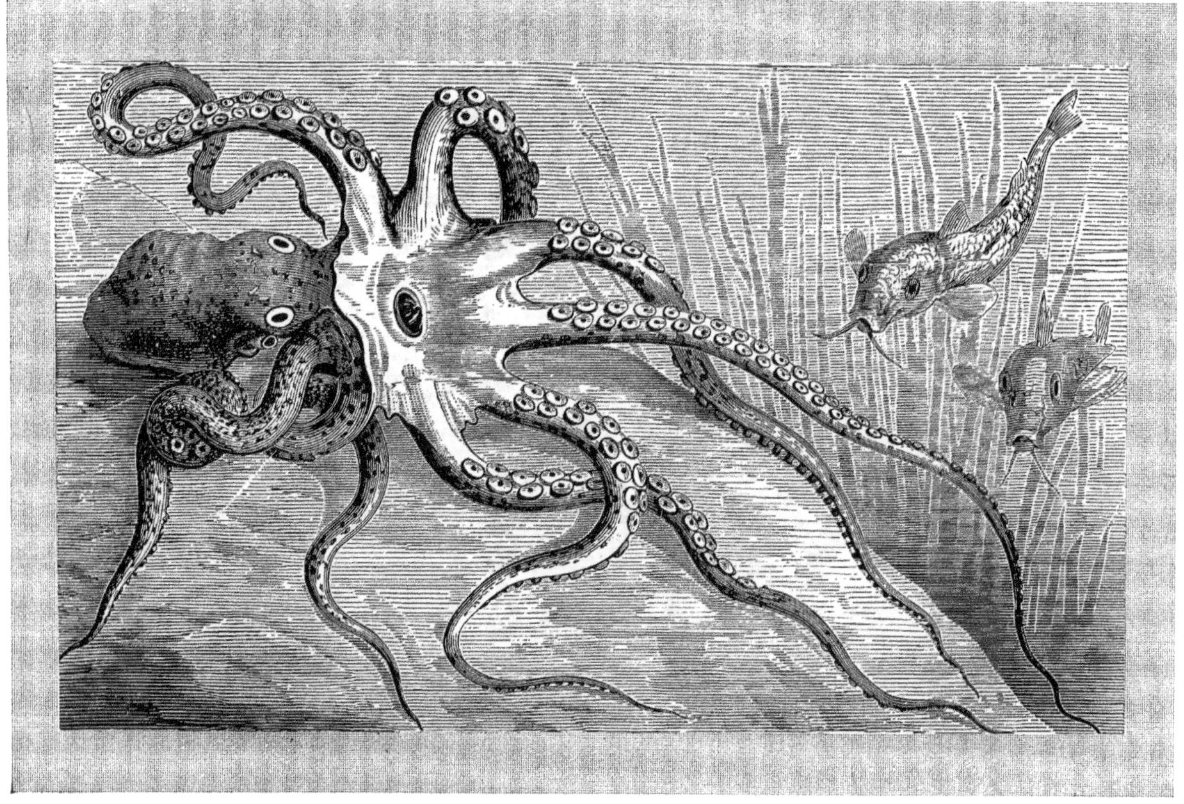

CEPHLAPODS

494

495

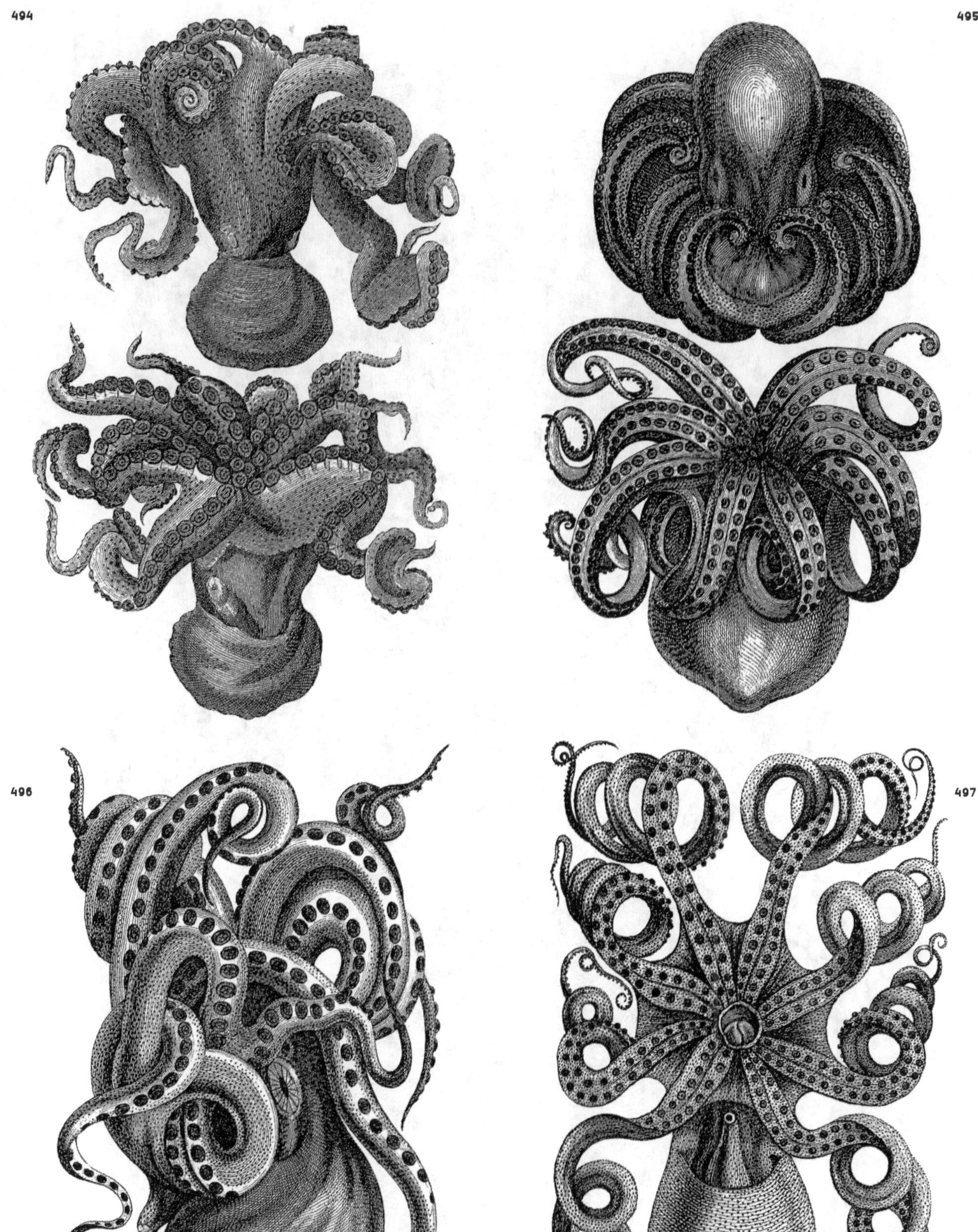

496

497

CEPHLAPODS

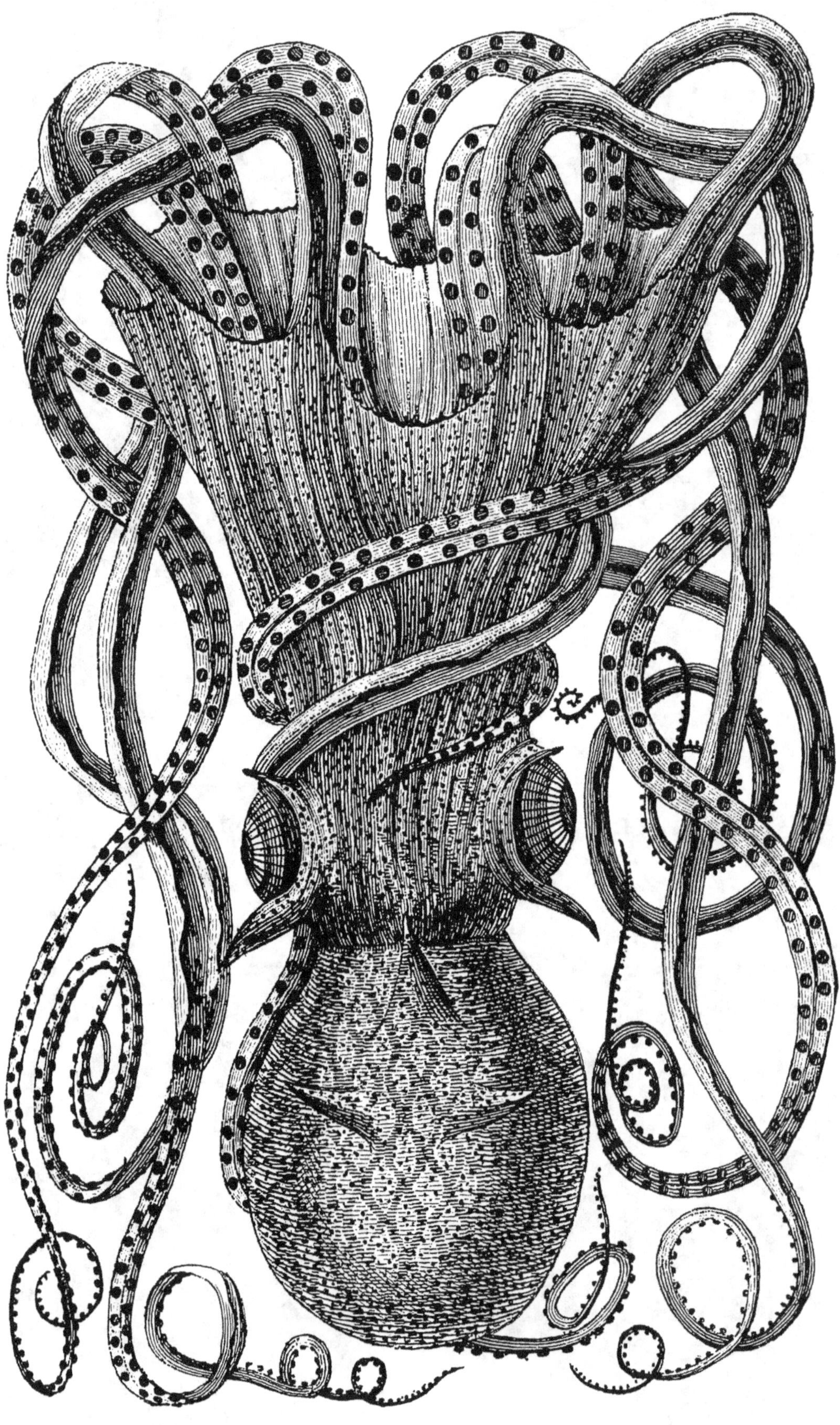

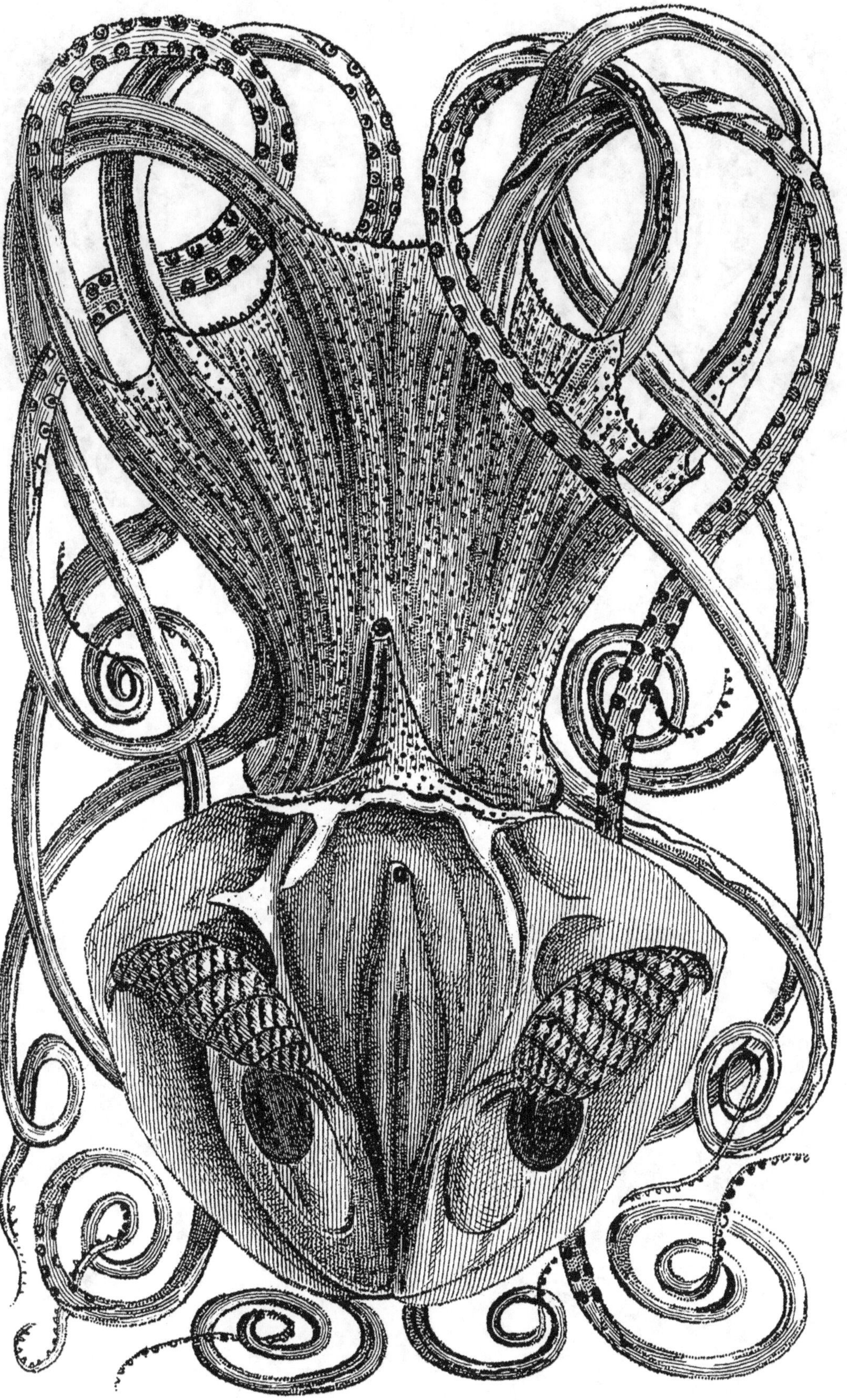

SEA-LIFE & MONSTERS OF THE DEEP

500

501

502

503

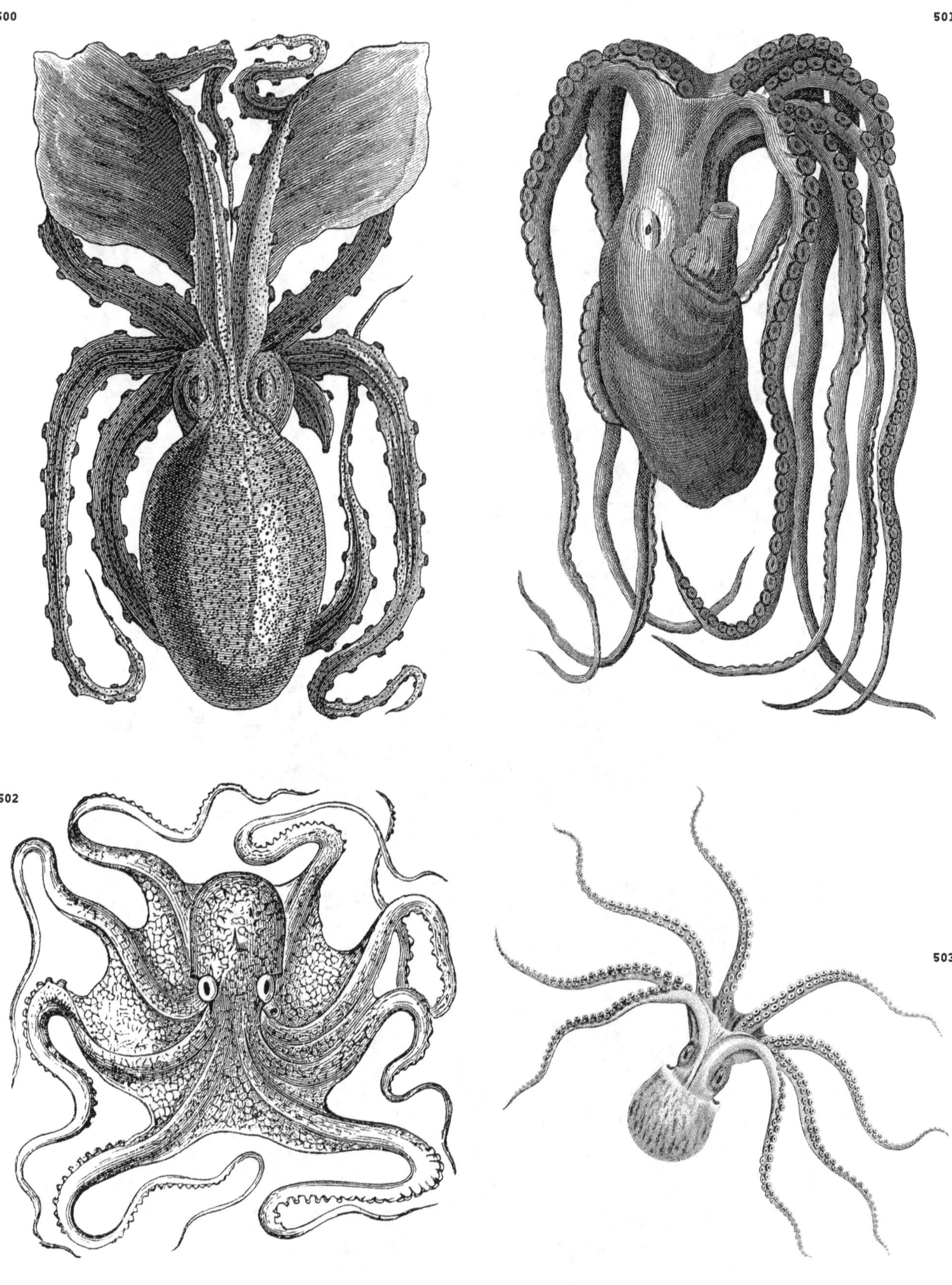

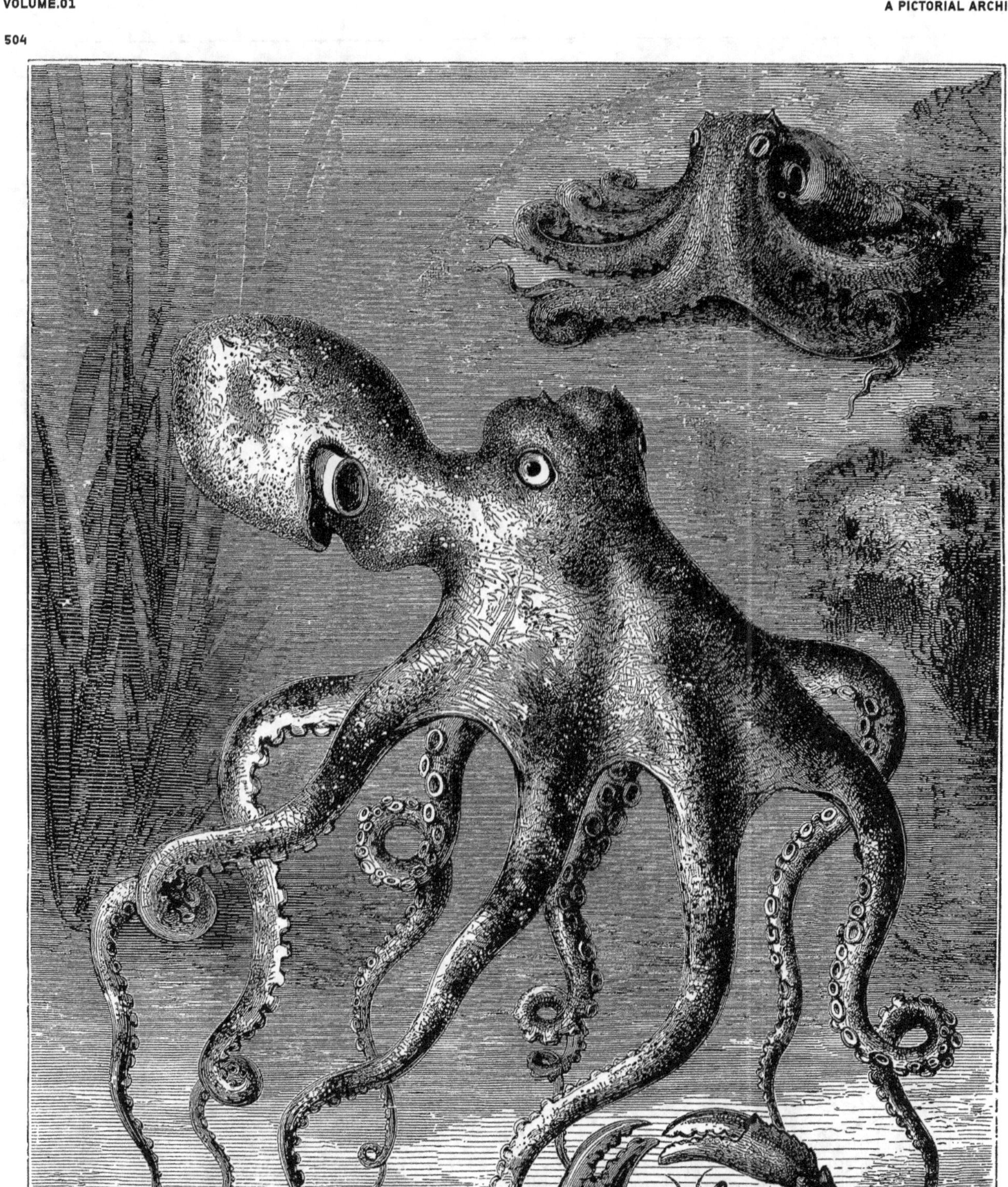

SEA-LIFE & MONSTERS OF THE DEEP

CEPHLAPODS

505

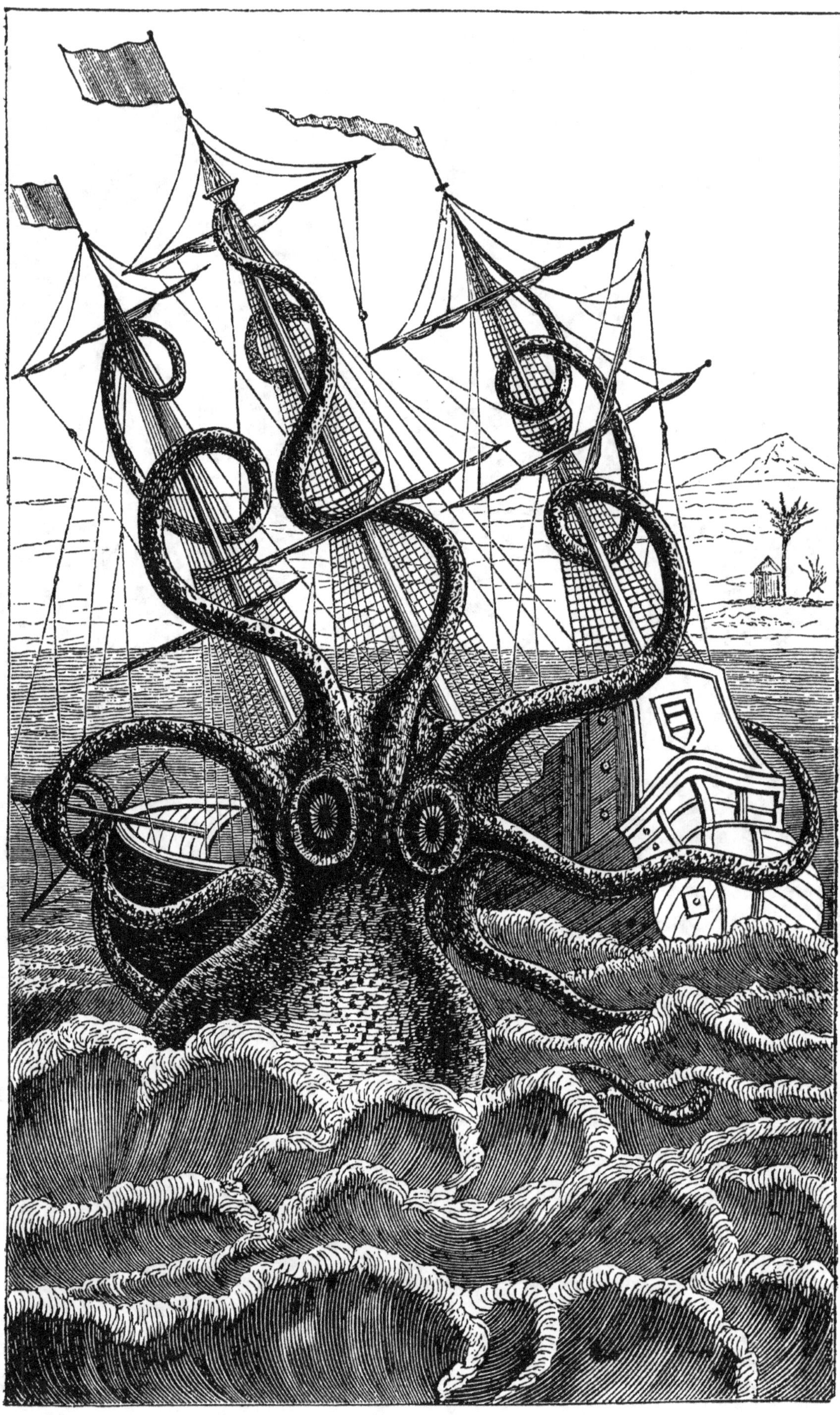

CEPHLAPODS

506

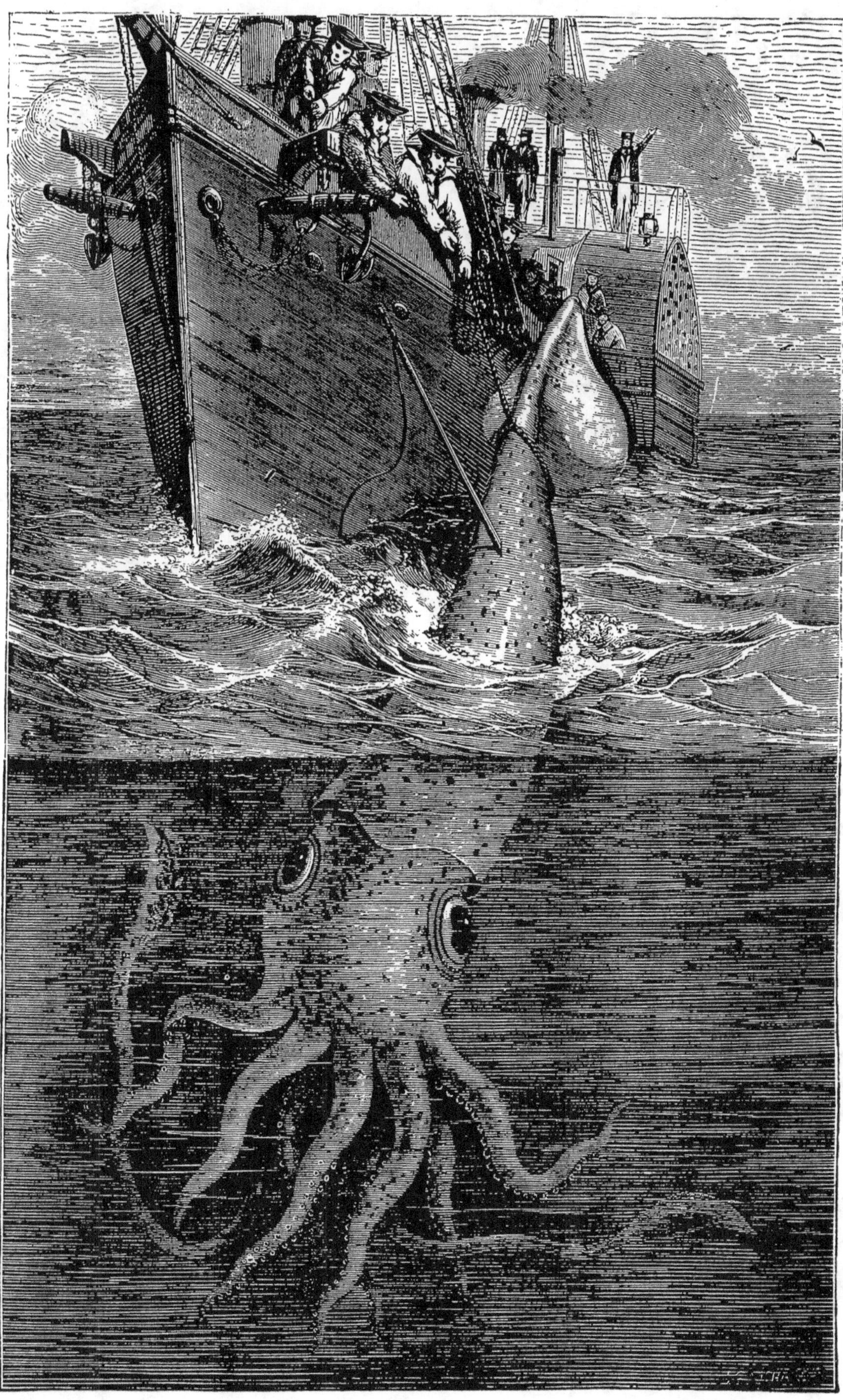

CEPHLAPODS

507

508

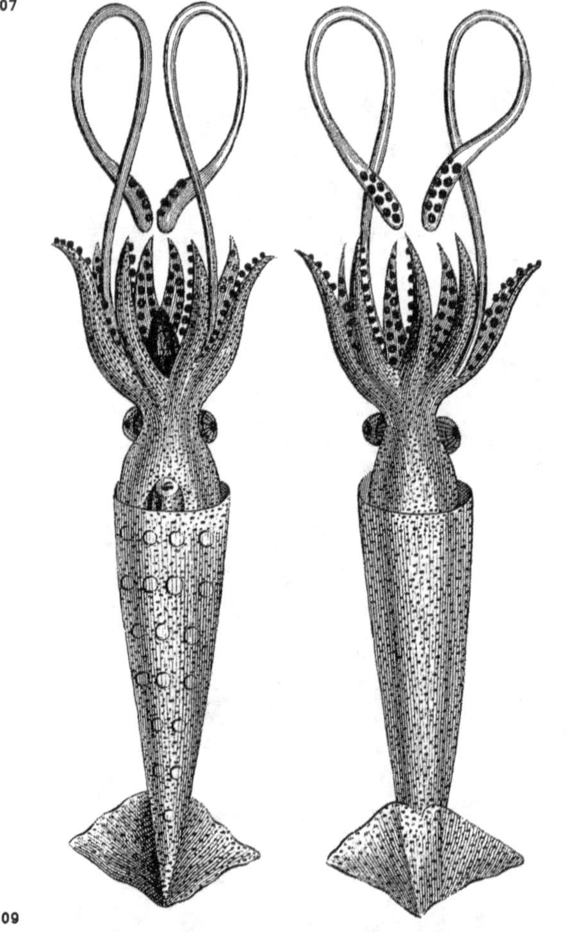

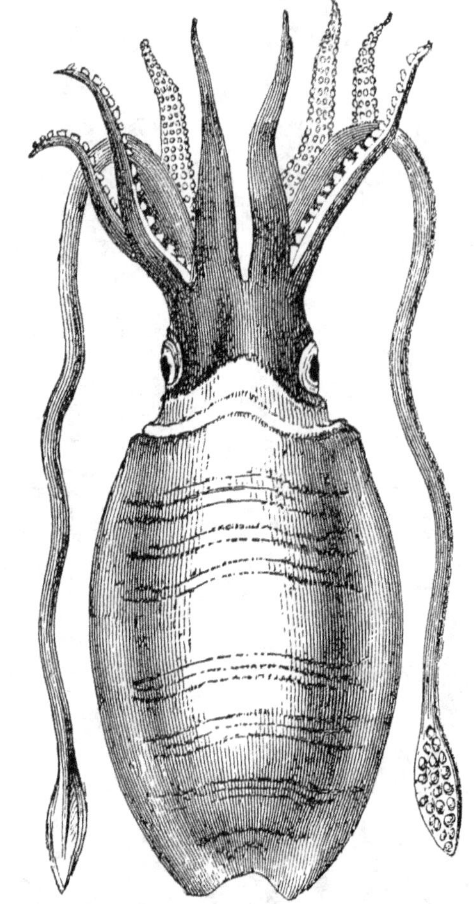

509

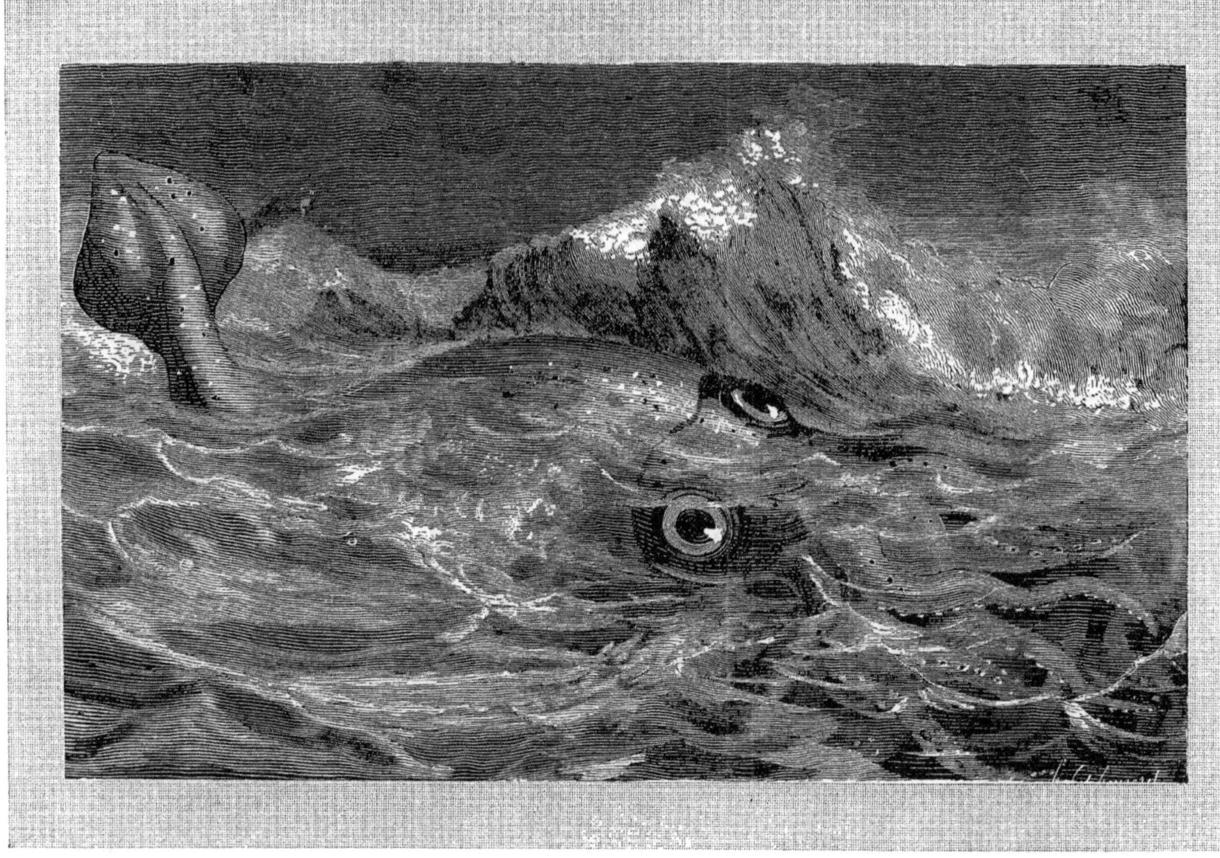

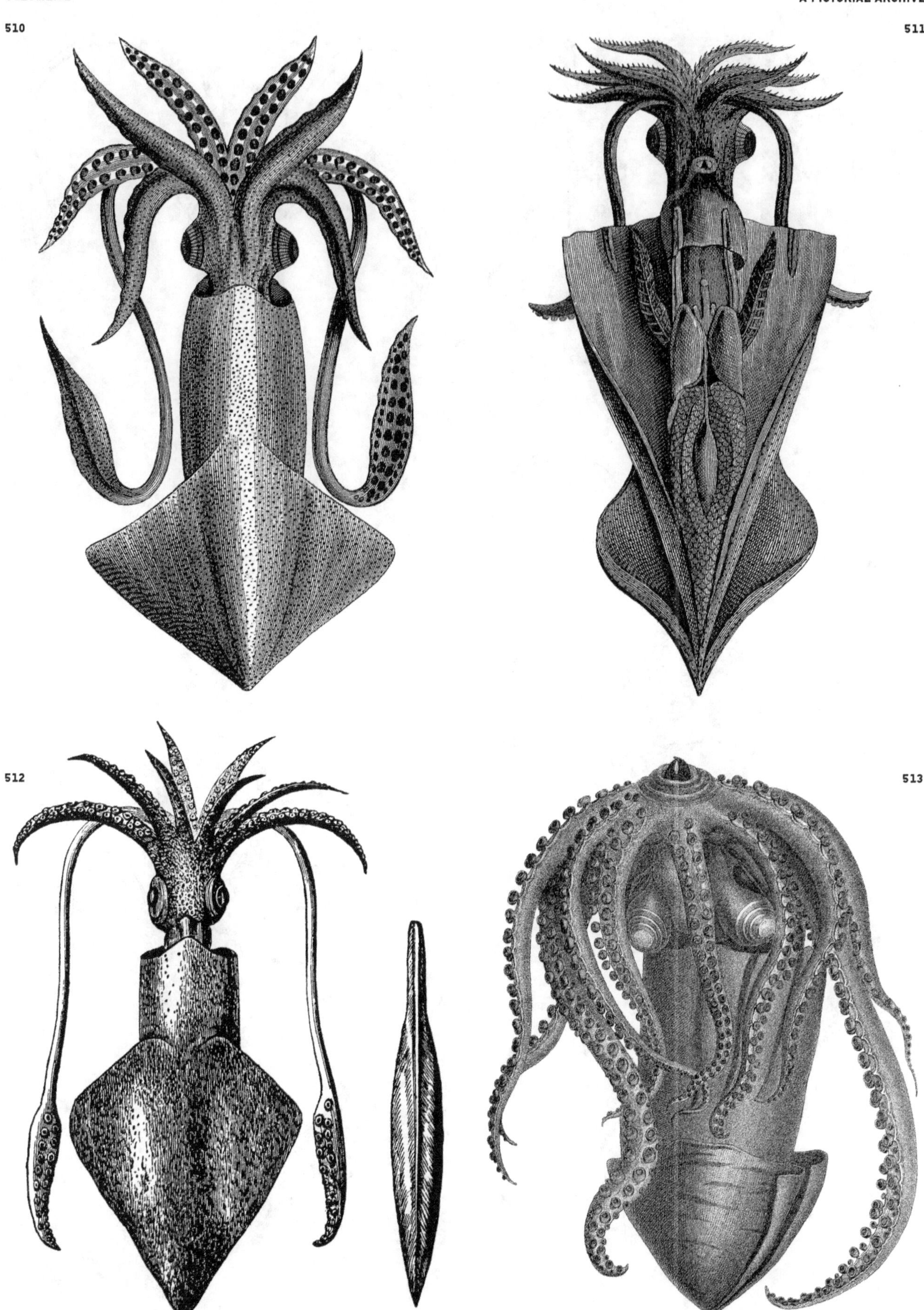

CEPHLAPODS

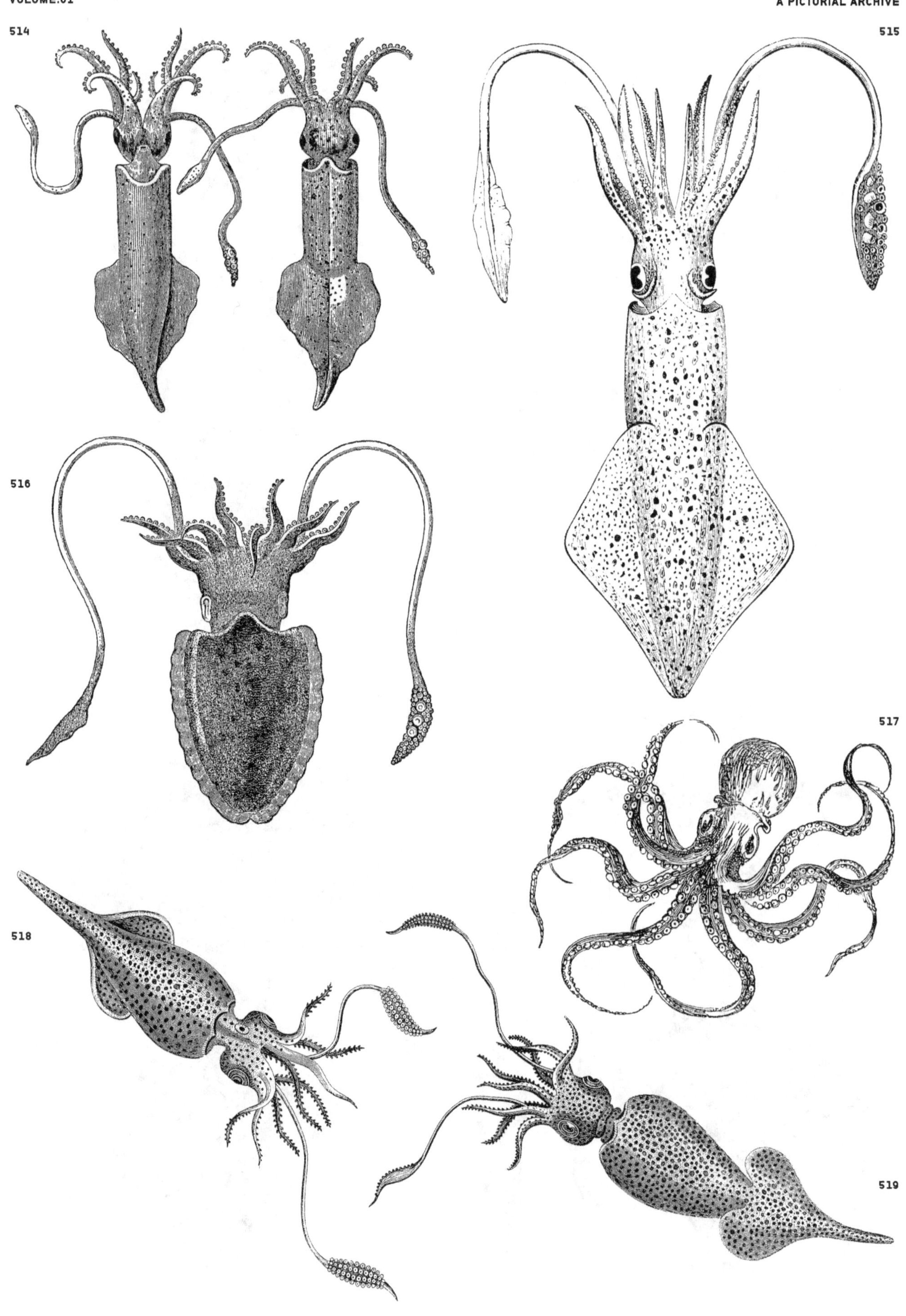

514
515
516
517
518
519

520

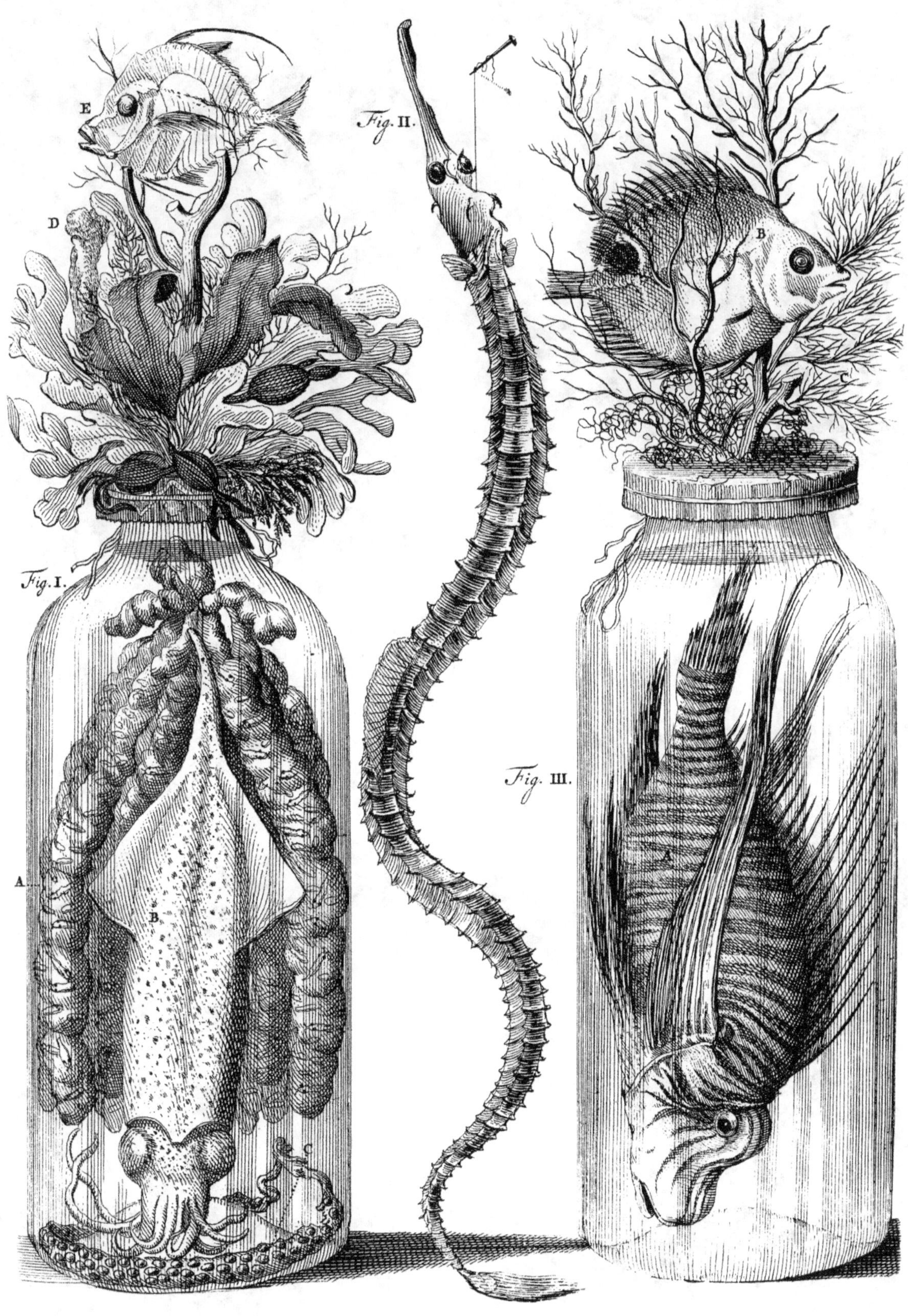

521

522

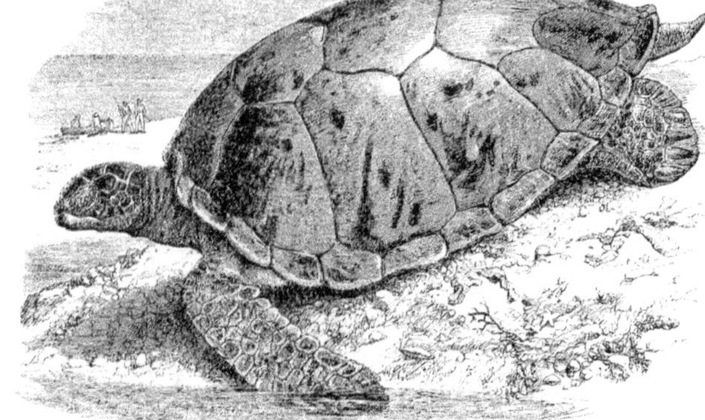

523

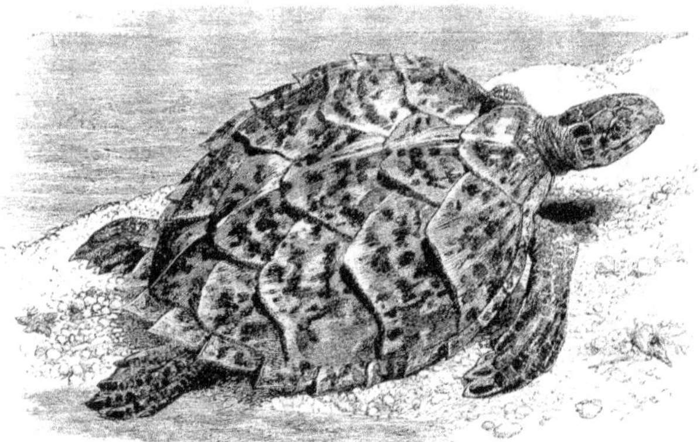

524

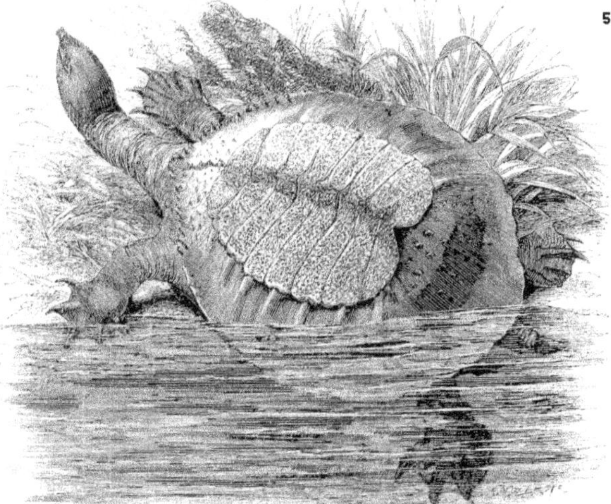

525

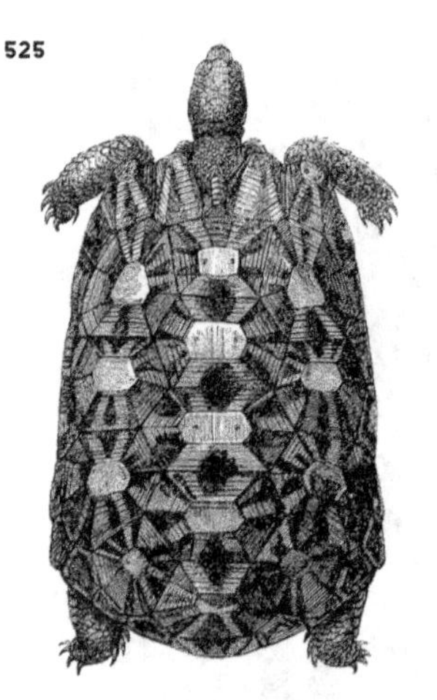

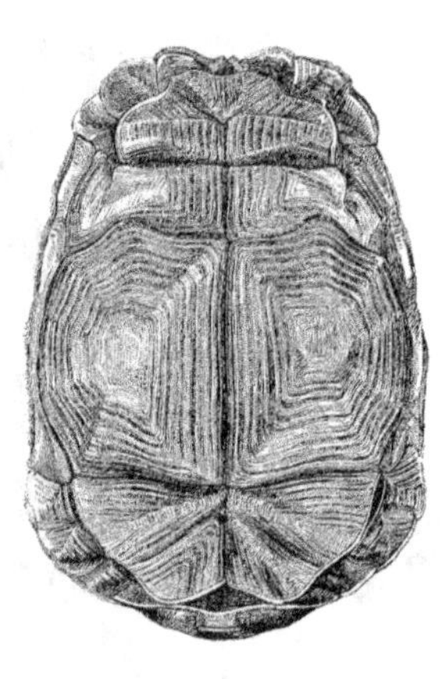

526

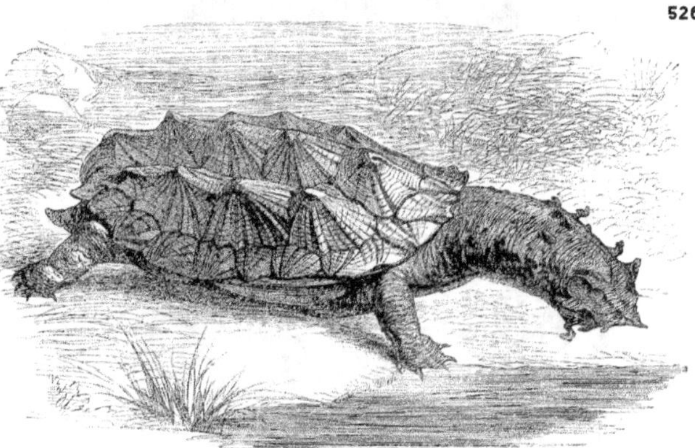

527

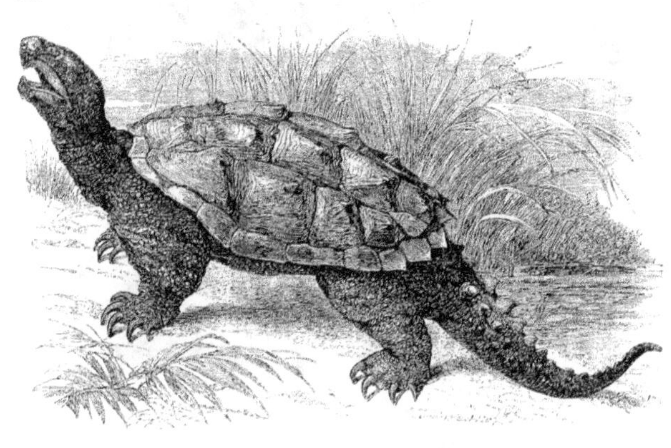

528

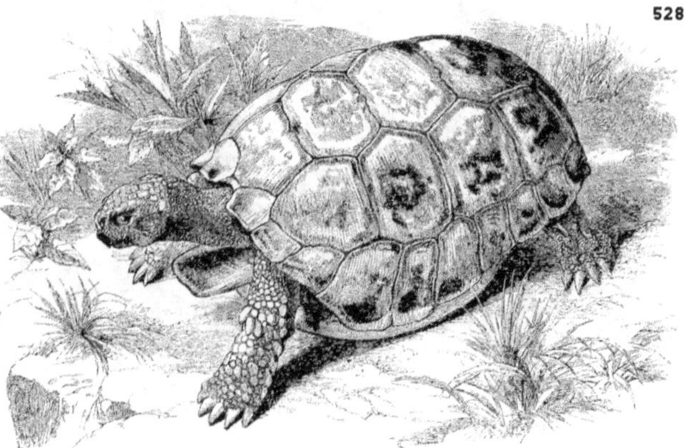

TURTLES

529

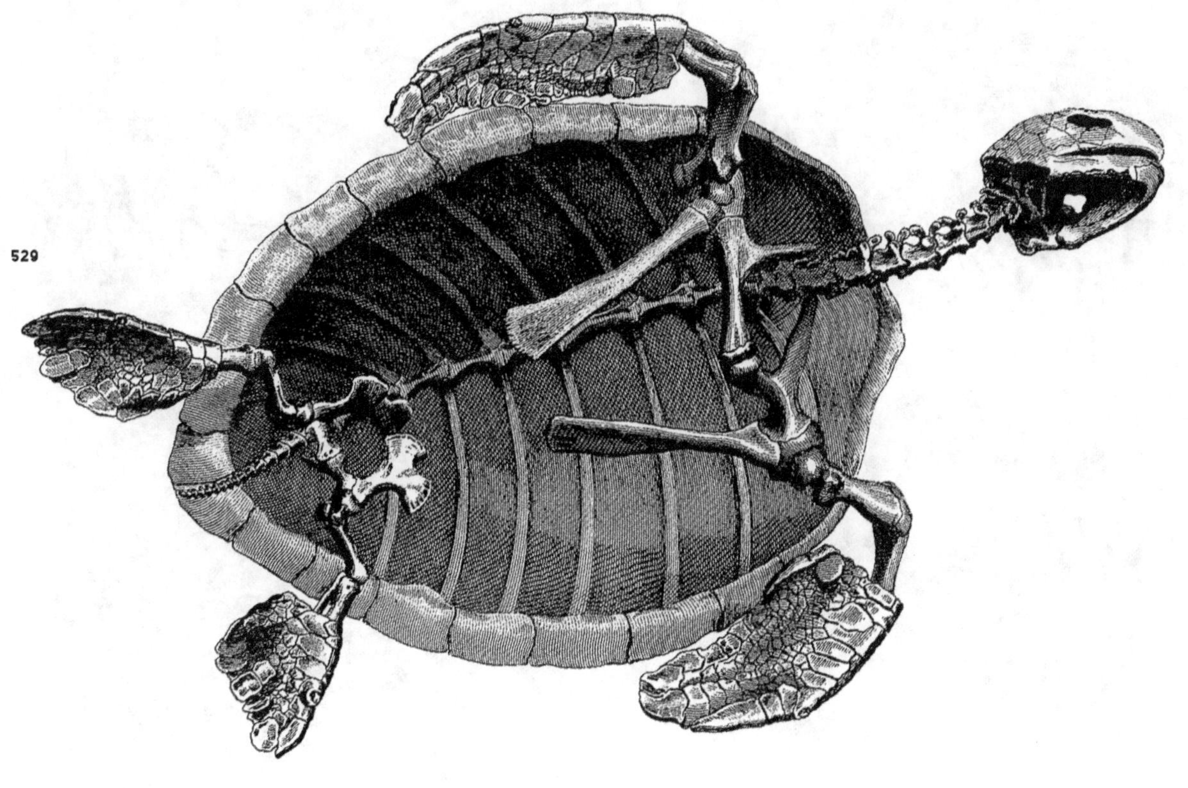

530

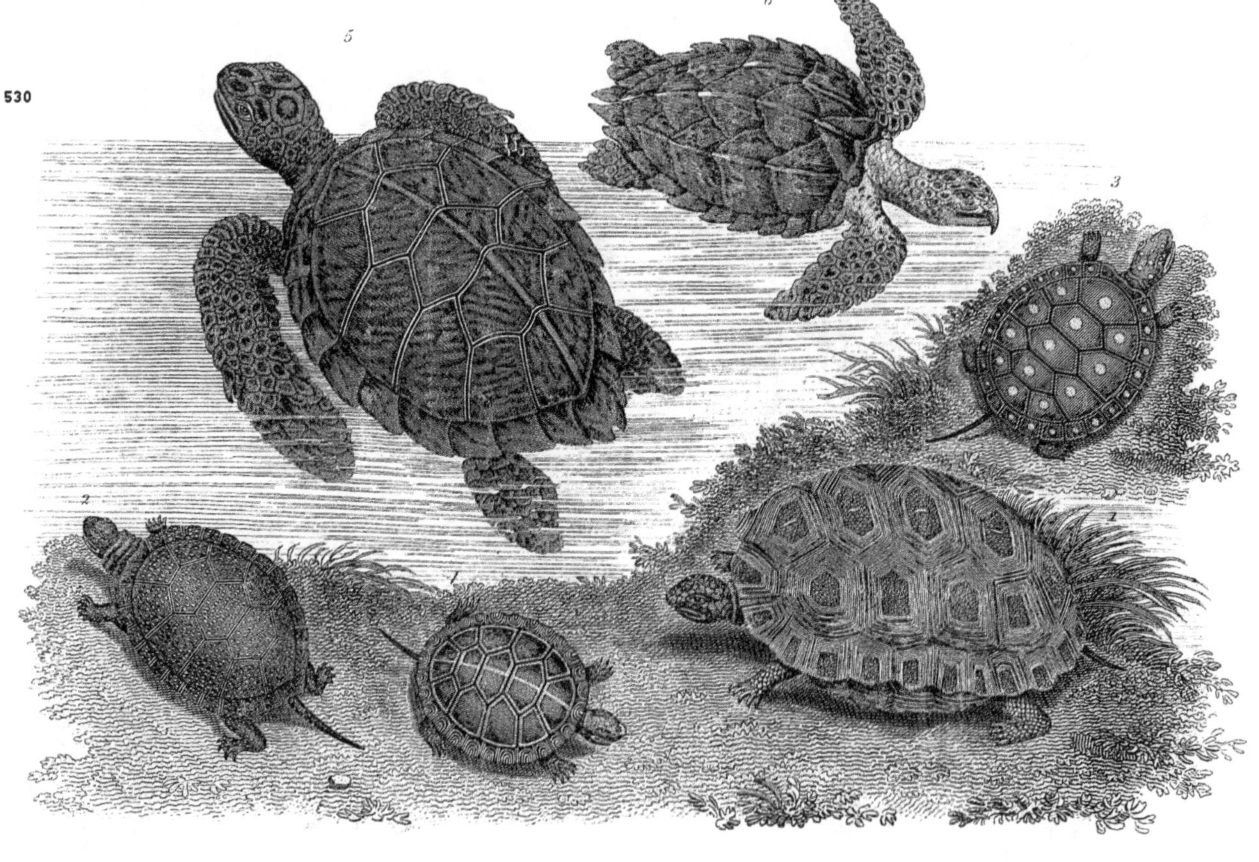

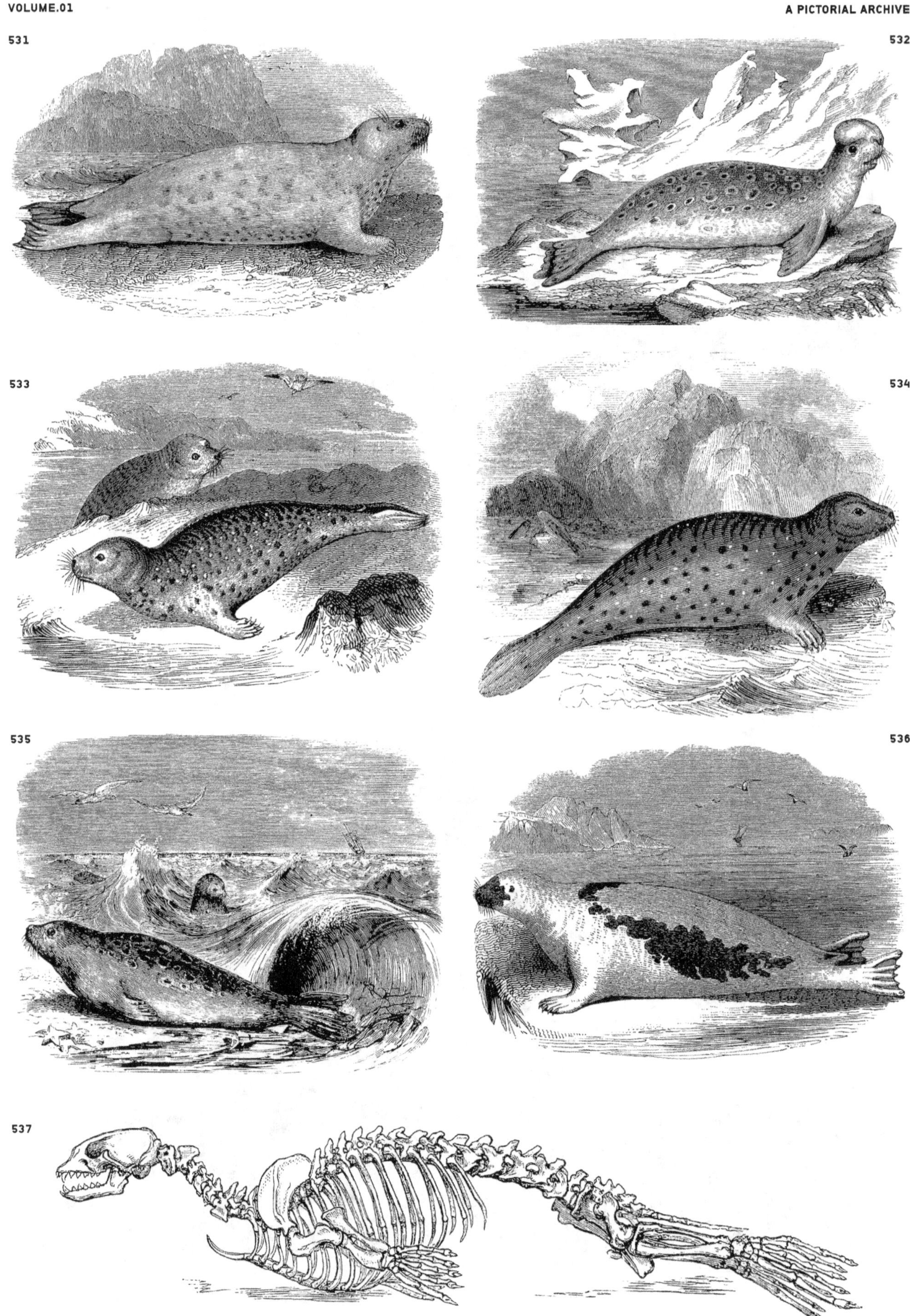

531

532

533

534

535

536

537

SEALS & WALRUSES

538

539

540

541

542

543

544

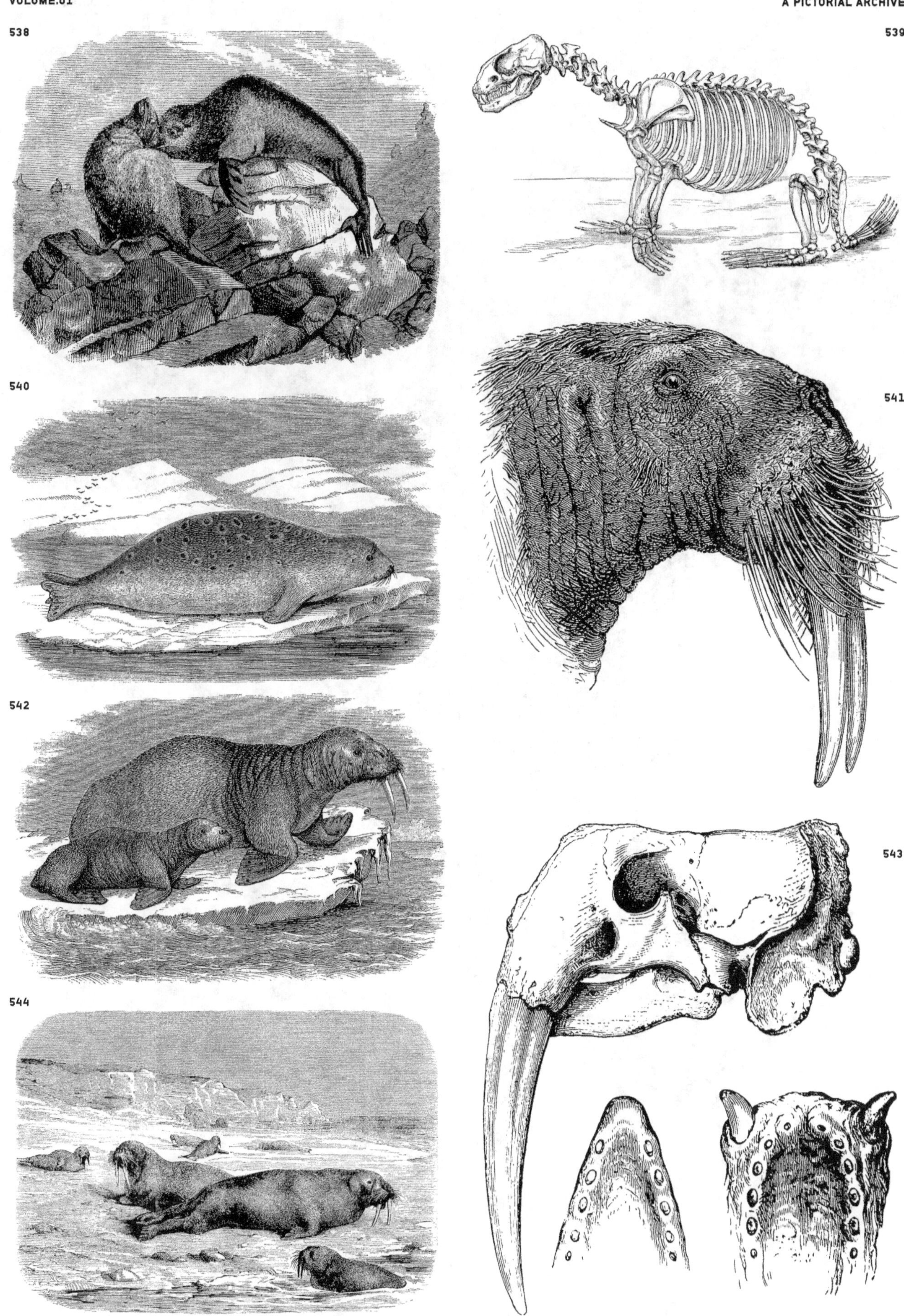

SEA-LIFE & MONSTERS OF THE DEEP

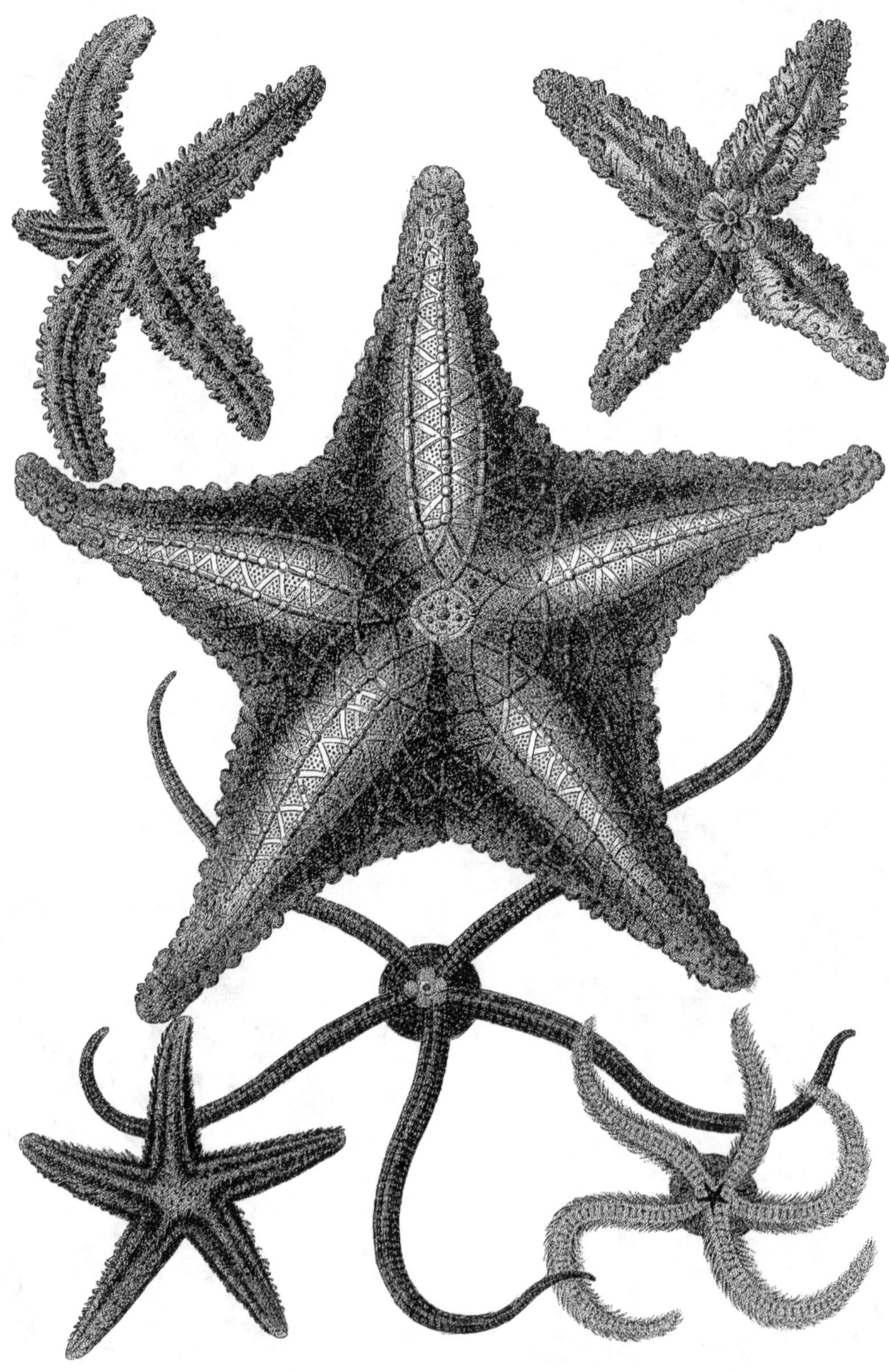

STARFISH

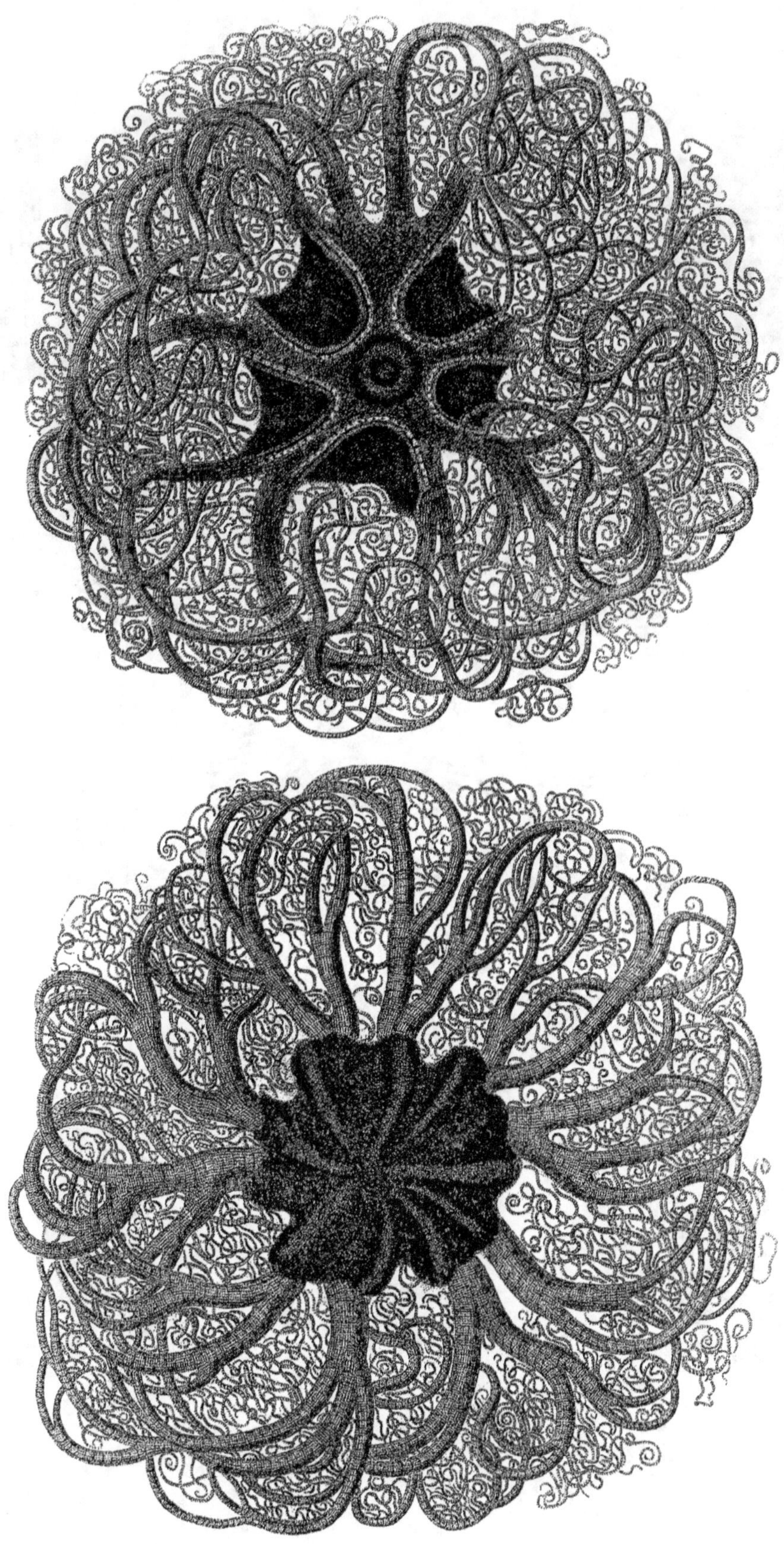

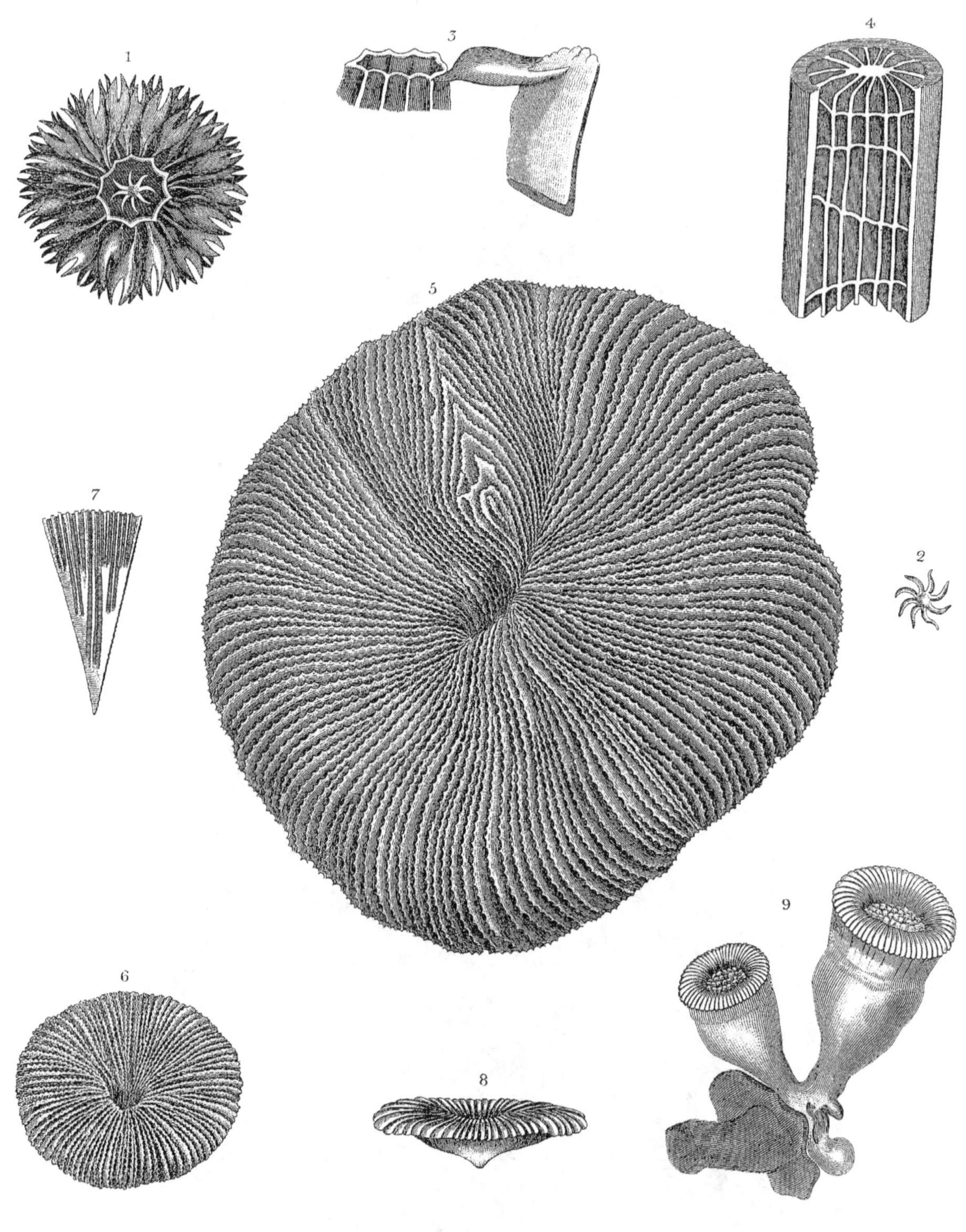

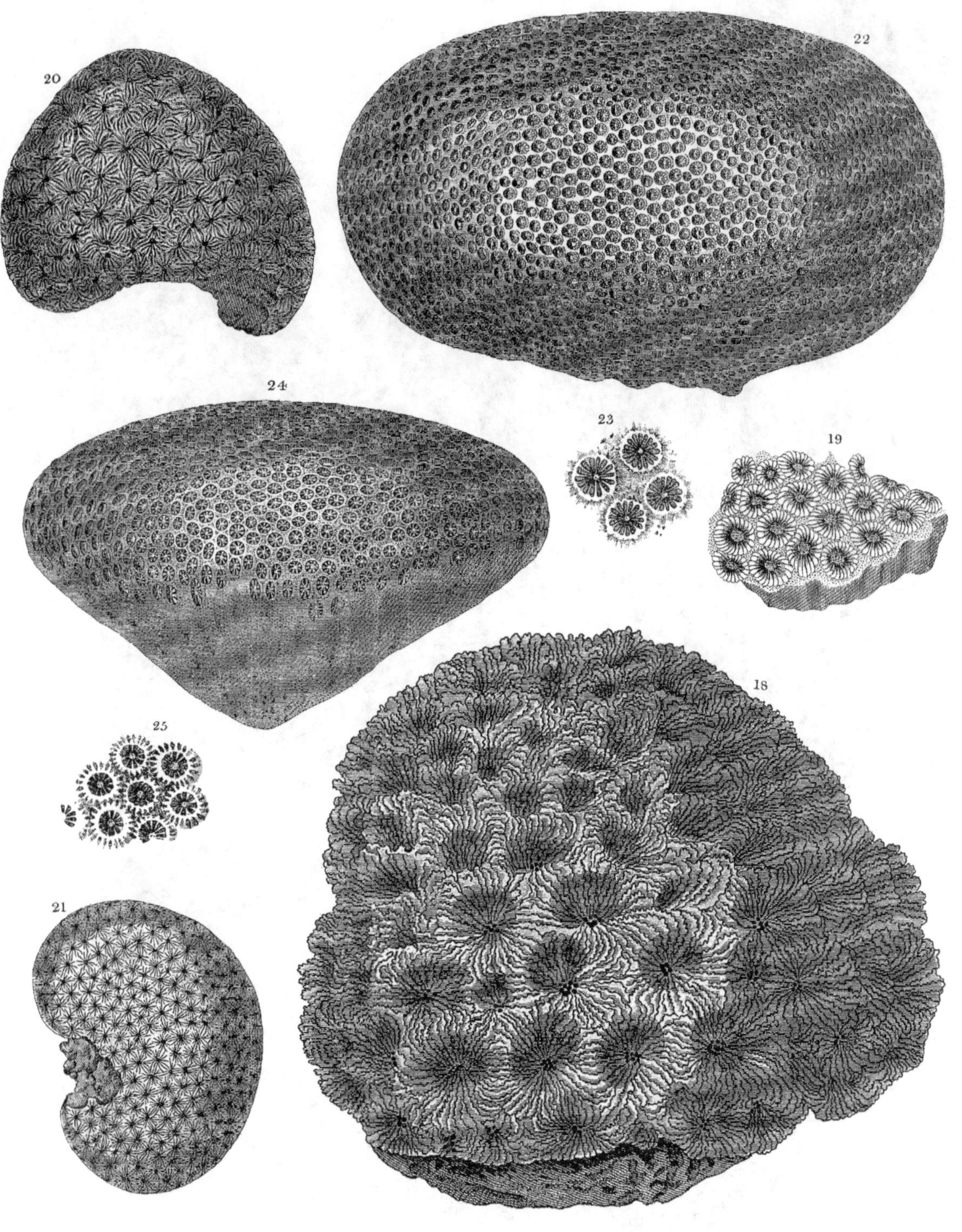

SEA-LIFE & MONSTERS OF THE DEEP

549

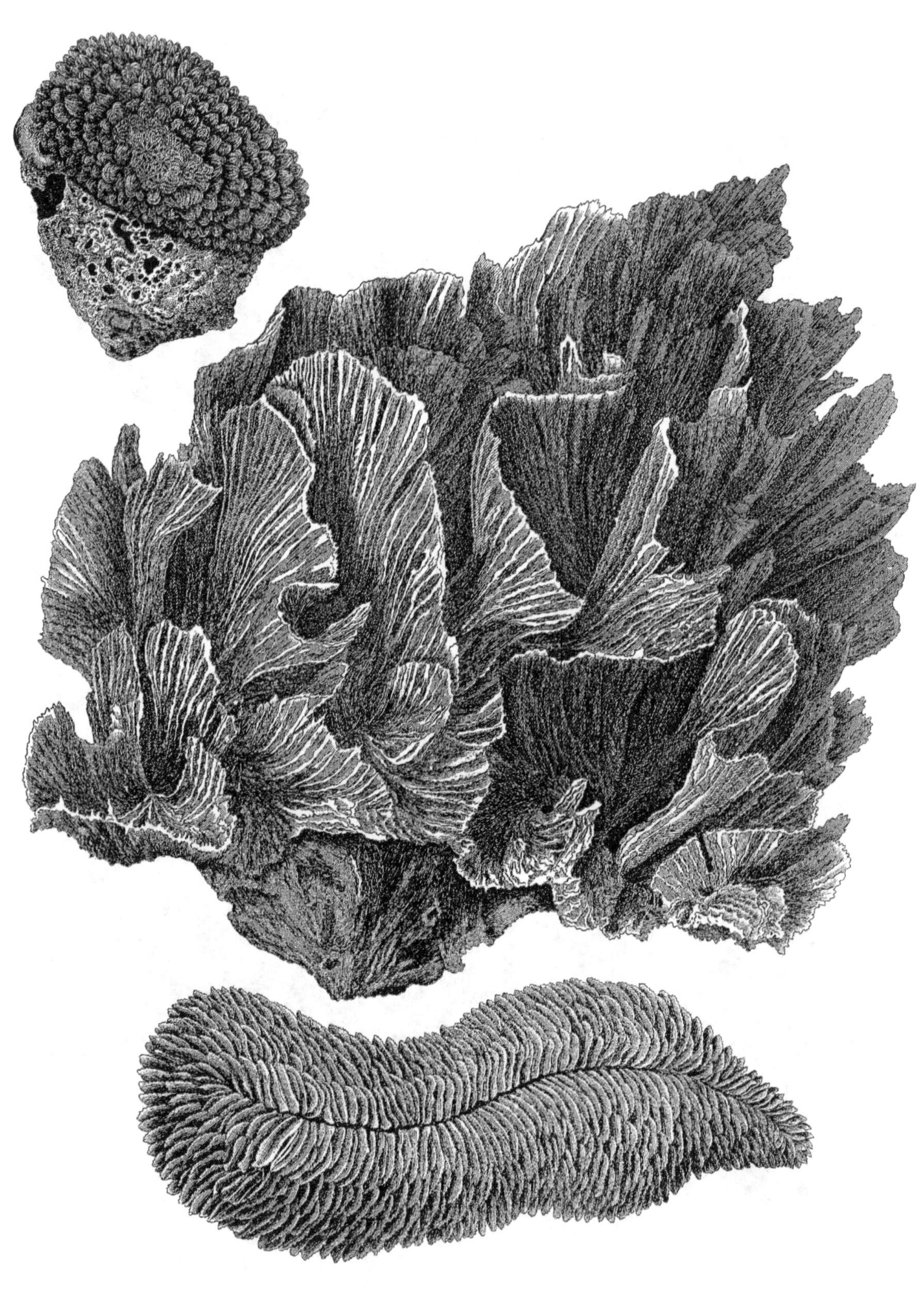

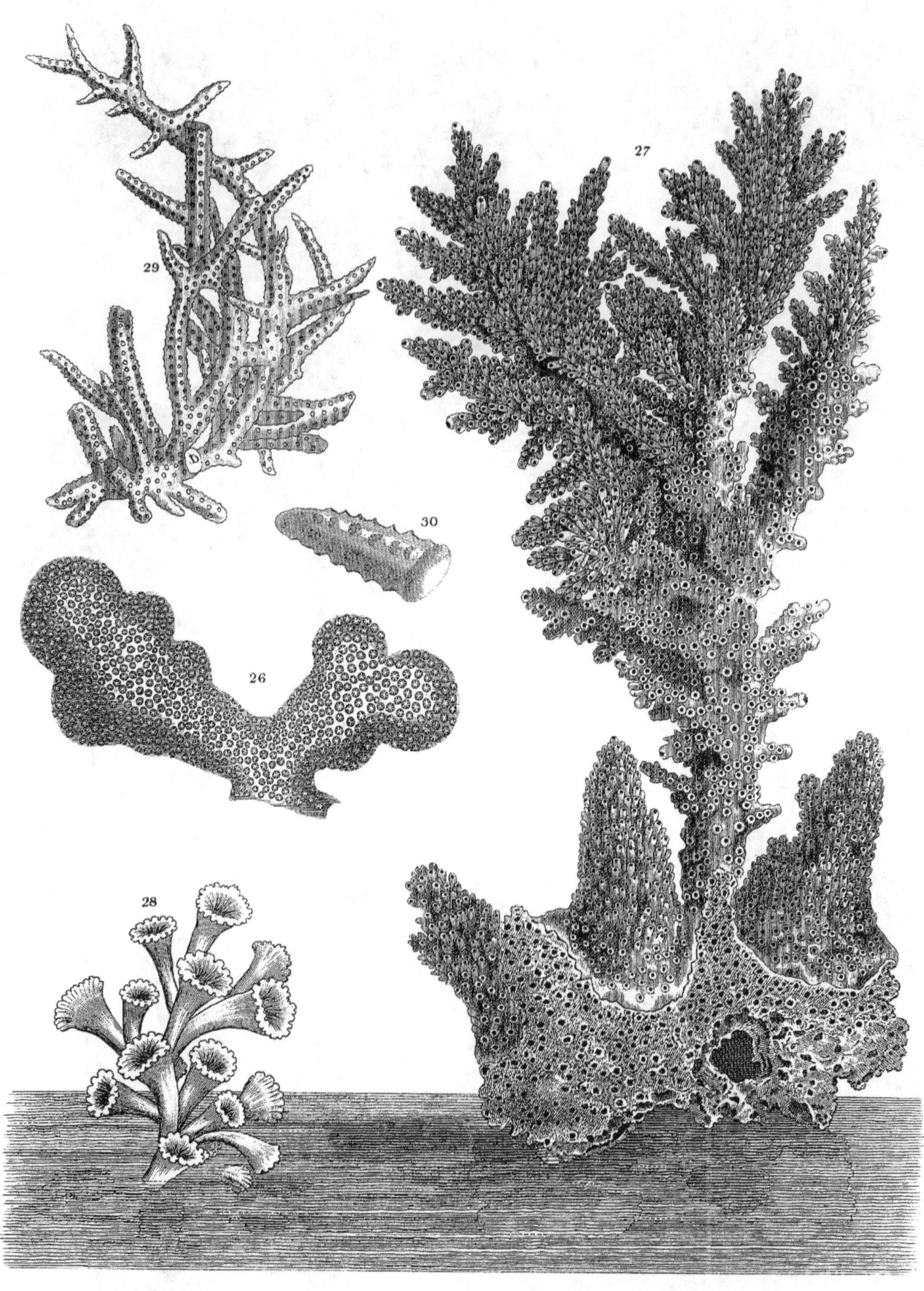
29
30
26
27
28

551

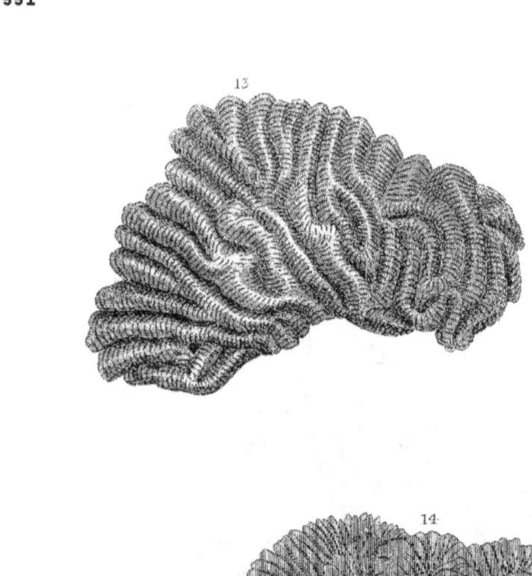

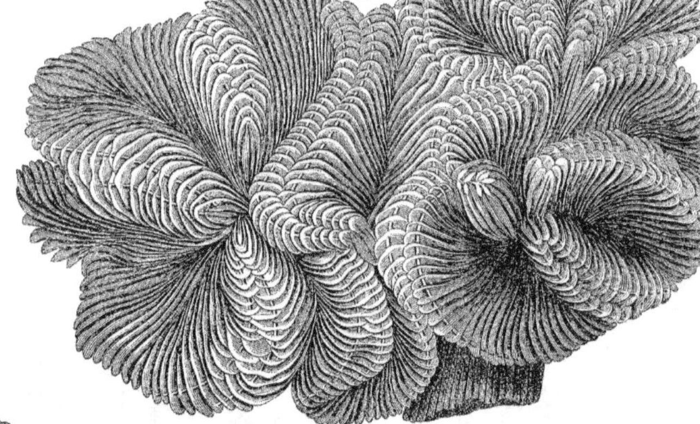

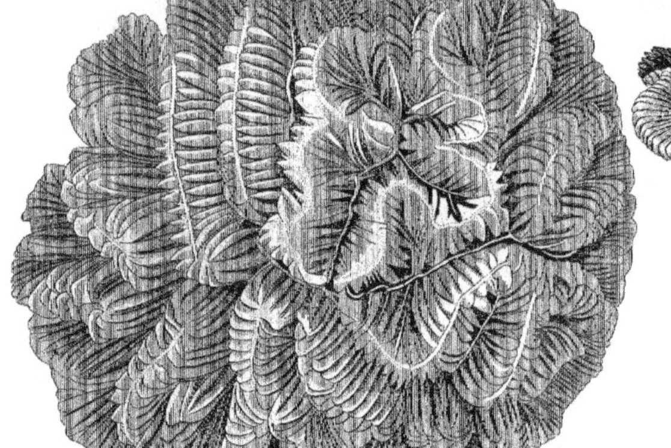

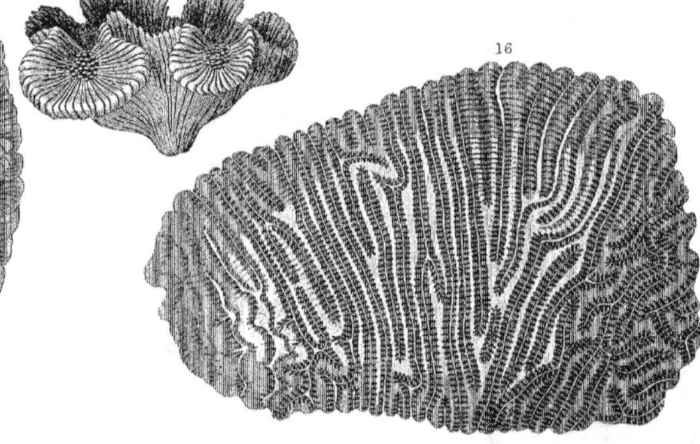

552

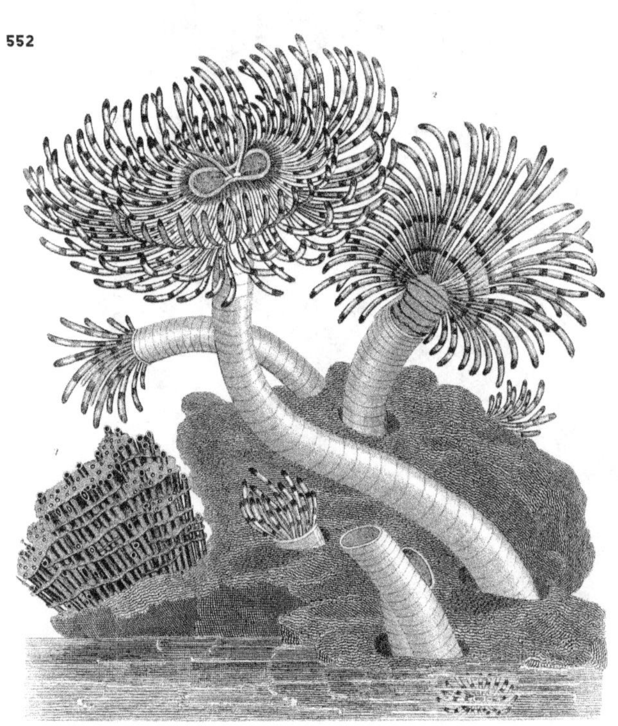

553

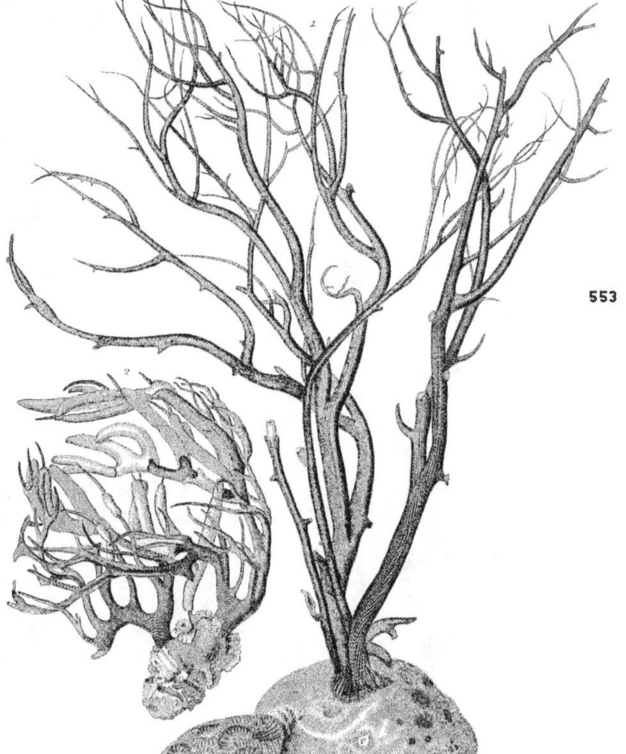

554

555

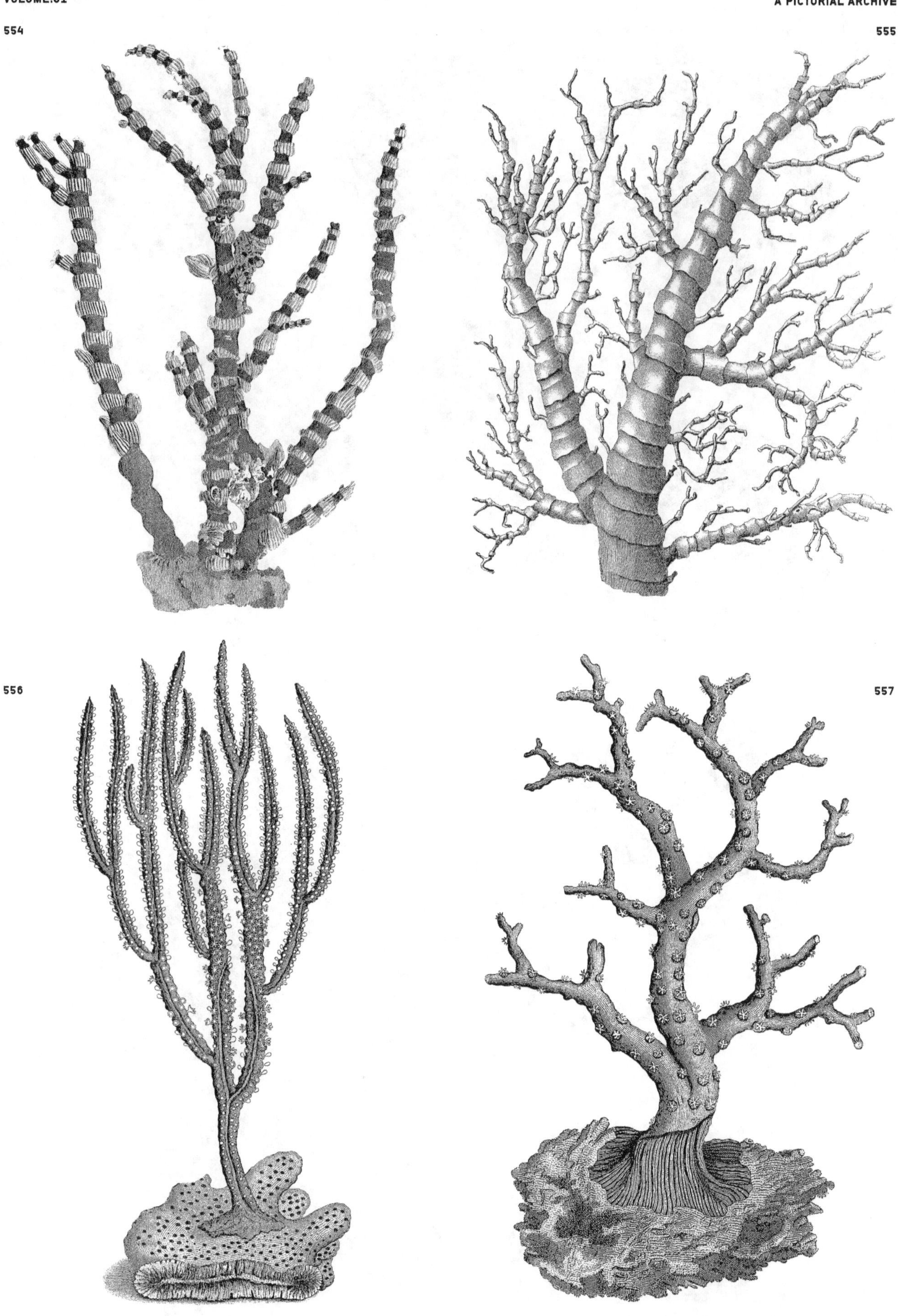

556

557

558

559

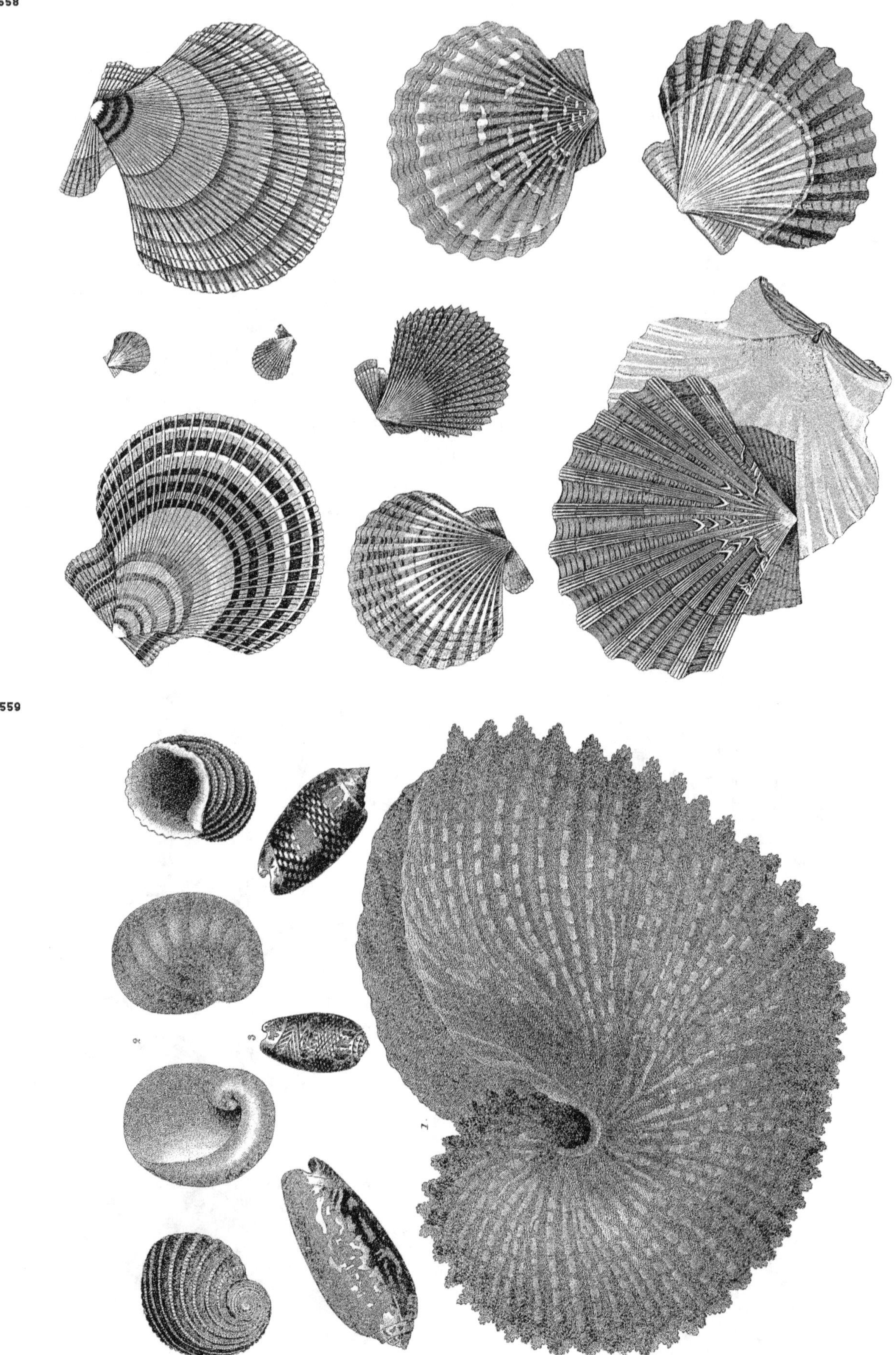

560

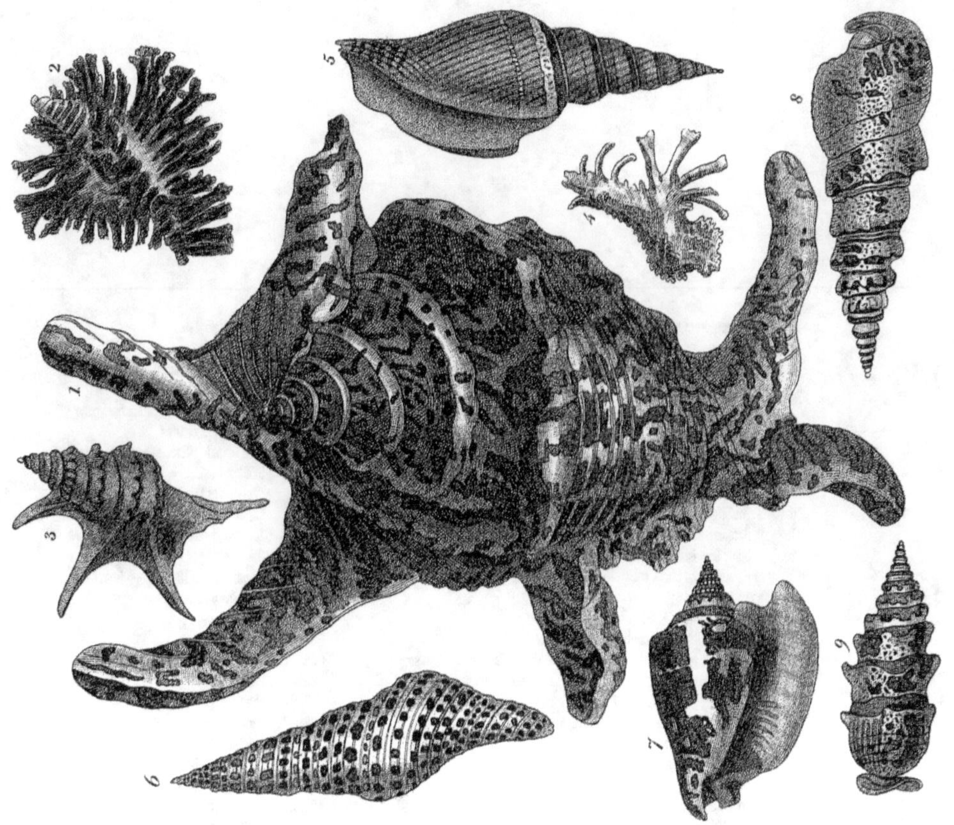

561

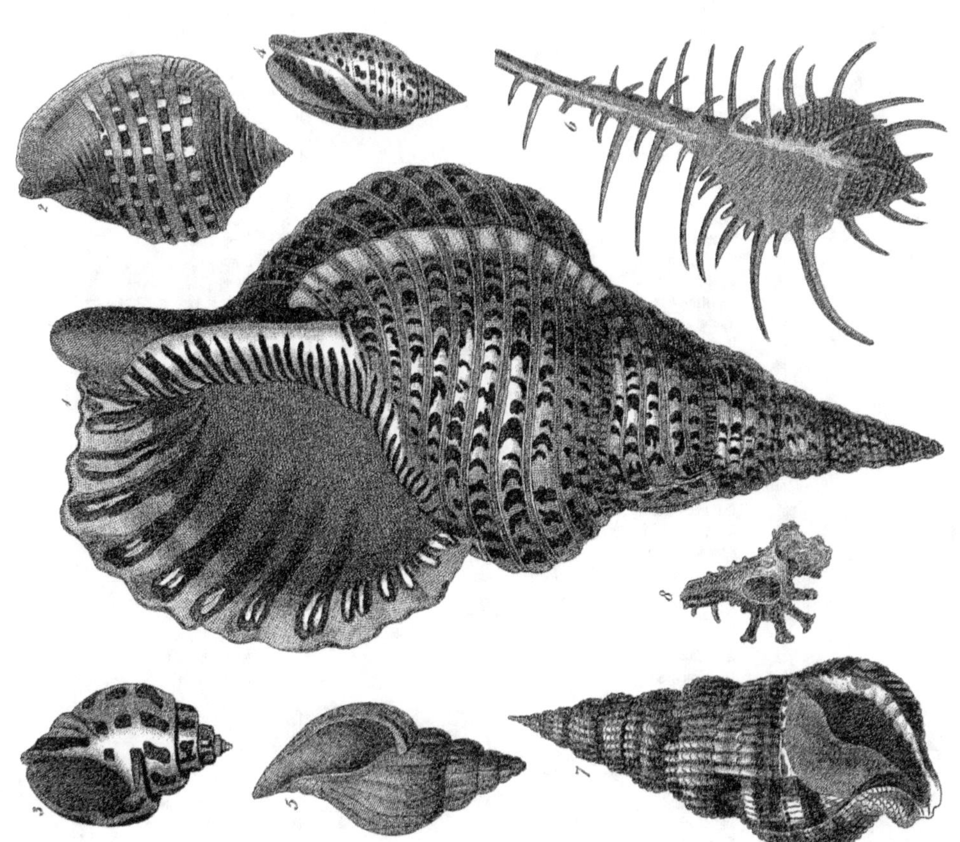

LIST OF ILLUSTRATIONS

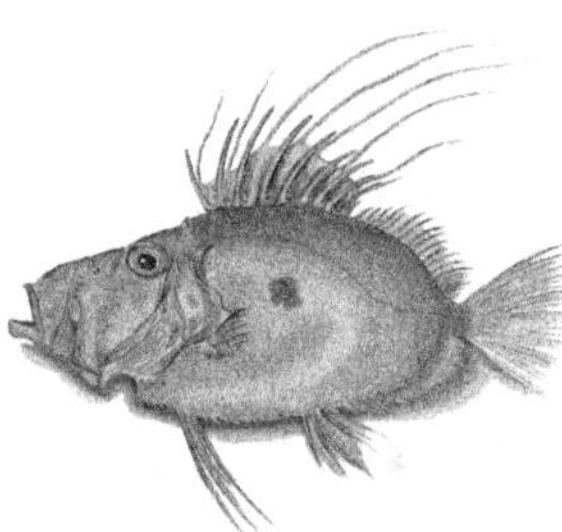
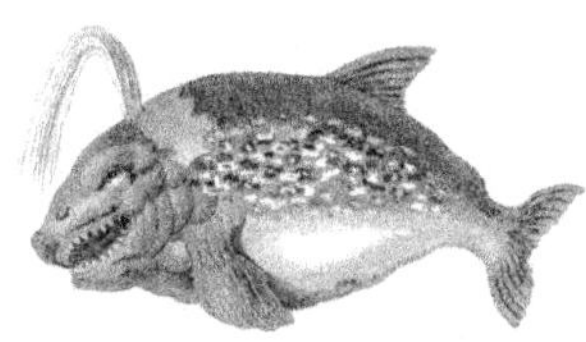
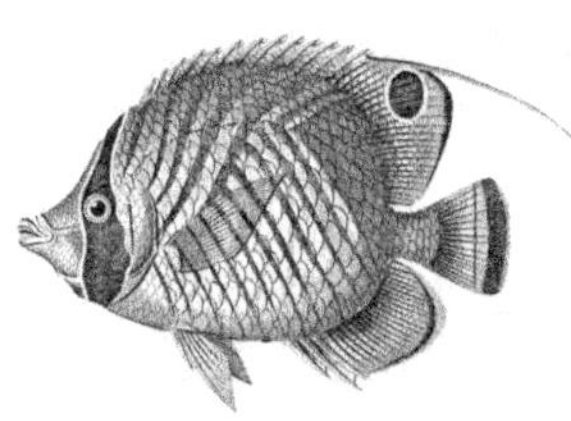
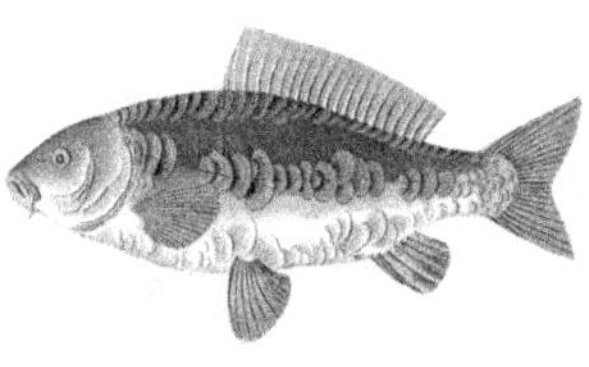
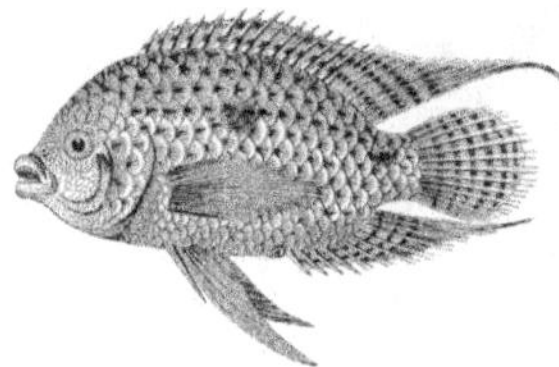

1.   Elementorum myologiae specimen, Steensen, 1669
2.   Abdominal organs, eggs of a shark
3.   The rock shark, The human shark (description from source)
4.   The Smooth Hound
5.   The Port Jackson Shark
6.   White Shark
7.   Indo-Pacific Basking-Shark
8.   The Blue Shark
9.   Lower teeth of extinct combo-toothed sharks
10.   The shark, The dotted shark, The Gaude shark (description from source)
11.   Hammer-Head Shark
12.   Spiny Dog-Fish and Smooth Hound
13.   Hammerhead Shark shown from above. Also the head of the Hammerhead Shark shown from below
14.   Centrina Supina Shark (Description from source)
15.   The Blue Shark (Description from source)
16.   1. Catalus Major Shark; 2. Catalus Minor Shark (Description from source)
17.   1. Ganis Galeus Shark; 2. Vulpecula Shark (Description from source)
18.   1. Muftelus Spinax Shark; 2. Muftelus Laevis Shark (Description from source)
19.   Lesser Spotted Dog-Fish and its eggs
20.   The Nurse Hound
21.   Common Skate and Marbled Electric Ray
22.   Dogfish Shark
23.   Thornback Skates
24.   The White Ray
25.   Halavi Ray
26.   The Thornback
27.   Skeleton of Thornback Ray
28.   Two species of fish, Skates and their eggs
29.   Thornback Ray
30.   Mirror Ray
31.   Common shovelnose ray
32.   Eagle Ray
33.   Raia Salu (Description from source)
34.   Pastinaca Salu (Description from source)
35.   Eagle Ray
36.   Torpedo Salu
37.   Squatina Salu
38.   Baleen Whales
39.   Narwhal
40.   Male Narwhal
41.   Narwhal
42.   The Sperm Whale
43.   The Sperm Whale
44.   The Blue Whale
45.   Greenland Whale
46.   Greenland Right-whale
47.   Left side of the skull of the Greenland Whale with the whalebone
48.   Skeleton of Greenland Whale
49.   Greenland Whale
50.   The Greenland or Right Whale
51.   Skeleton of Sperm-whale
52.   Hump-backed Whale
53.   The Blunt Headed Cachalot (Sperm Whale)
54.   Sperm Whale
55.   Skeleton of Sperm Whale
56.   Sperm Whale
57.   Whale Fishery
58.   The Sperm Whale
59.   Humpback Whales disporting
60.   Boat struck by a whale
61.   Lesser-Fin Whale
62.   The Common Fin-Whale
63.   Rudolph's Rorqual
64.   Lesser Rorqual
65.   Sibbald's Roqual
66.   Killer Whale
67.   Razorback Whale
68.   The Orca
69.   Pilot-Whale
70.   Sperm Whale
71.   Atlantic Right-whale
72.   Beluga Whale
73.   Hump-back whale suckling her young
74.   Killer Whale, or Orca
75.   Orca Dolphin (Description from source)
76.   Skull of the Beluga Whale
77.   Skeleton of the Greenland Right-whale
78.   Common Rorqual
79.   The Round-headed Cachalot (Sperm Whale)
80.   Dolphin
81.   Vulgar Dolphin (Description from source)
82.   Dolphins pursuing a boat
83.   Risso's Grampus
84.   Risso's Grampus
85.   Dolphin
86.   Paunchy Dolphin (Description from source)
87.   The Porpoise
88.   Skull and lower jaw of the dolphin
89.   Dolphin
90.   Two-Toothed Dolphin (Description from source)
91.   Skull and teeth of Bottle-nosed Dolphin
92.   Porpoise Dolphin
93.   Bottle-nosed Dolphin
94.   Porpoise
95.   White-beaked Dolphin
96.   White-sided Dolphin
97.   Dolphin
98.   Bodianus
99.   Bodianus Boenack
100. Angler fish
101. Angler Fish
102. Angler Fish
103. Orfus Germanorum
104. Sea Bream
105. Sea Bream
106. Group of Bream
107. Bream
108. Bream
109. A Type of Holocentrus (Squirrelfish)
110. A Type of Holocentrus (Squirrelfish)
111. Black Balistes
112. A Type of Holocentrus (Squirrelfish)
113. Remora
114. Remora
115. Remora
116. Remora
117. Remora
118. Surmullet
119. Striped Surmullet
120. Gold Spotted Surmullet
121. Three Banded Surmullet
122. Sapphirine Gurnards
123. Armed or Mailed Gurnard
124. Beaked Gurnard
125. Head of Gurnard
126. Yellow Cuirassier Fish
127. Yellow Skalpin
128. Yellow Cuirassier Fish
129. Gurnard
130. Gurnard
131. Oriental flying gurnard
132. Monkfish
133. Shortspine Thornyhead
134. Quillback Rockfish
135. Spiny Gurnard
136. Butterfly Fish
137. Butterfly Benny

138. Butterfly Blenny
139. Lumpus Anglorum (Description from source)
140. Orbis oblongus Teftudinis (Description from source)
141. Orbis Ranae Rictu Clus (Description from source)
142. Atlantic mackerel
143. Mackerel
144. Spanish Mackerel
145. Albacore
146. Red Spotted Sea Perch
147. Skeleton of a Perch
148. Japan Perch
149. Head of Perch
150. River Perch
151. Reddish Perch
152. Black Tailed Sea Perch
153. Common Bass, Sea-Perch and Stone-Bass
154. Perch
155. Climbing Perch
156. Climbing-Perch on Land
157. Pike-Perch and Common Perch
158. Larger and Smaller Danubian Perches, and Ruffe
159. Pike
160. Pike
161. Pike-Head
162. Dropped Wrasse
163. Wainscoted Wrasse
164. Punctuated Wrasse
165. Ballan Wrasse
166. Striped Wrasse
167. Rainbow Wrasse
168. Silvery Viviparous Wrasse
169. Striped Red Mullet
170. Tang Mullet
171. Notch-Lipped Mullet
172. Mullet
173. Bahama Mullet
174. Grey Mullet
175. Telescope Carp
176. Sickle Finned Carp
177. King of the Carps (description from source)
178. Group of Carp
179. Crucian Carp
180. Carp
181. Cod
182. Cod
183. Haddock, Whiting and Young Adult Cod
184. Male Salmon
185. Salmon (female)
186. Salmon
187. Salmon and Sea-Trout
188. Beaked Salmon
189. Salmon
190. Trout
191. Trout
192. May-Trout and Hucho
193. Electric Catfish
194. Wels Catfish
195. Whiptail Catfish Loricaria cataphracta
196. Sturgeon
197. Sturgeon
198. Skeleton of Sturgeon, exhibiting heteroceral tail
199. Sturgeon of Russia
200. Spoon-Beaked Sturgeon
201. Four Eyed Loach
202. Angola Loach
203. Giant and Common Sturgeon
204. Giant Loach, Common Loach and Spiny Loach
205. Head of Four-Eyed Loach
206. African Mud Fish

207. African Mud-Fish
208. Australian Lung-Fish
209. Tench
210. Brazilian Arapaima
211. Tench
212. Burbot and Wels
213. Toxotes
214. Sichel, Rapfen and Beaked Carp
215. Bichir
216. South American Mud-Fish
217. Female and Male Double-Eye
218. Tontelton Fish
219. Sea Scorpion
220. Sea Scorpion
221. Armed Bull-head
222. Sea Bull
223. River Bullhead
224. Head of Baracoota
225. Barracoota
226. Armed Bull-Head
227. Barracuda and an Angler-Fish
228. Common Bull-Heads
229. Frog-Fish
230. Pelor Filamentosum
231. Father Lasher
232. Uranoscopus Scaber
233. Pegasus
234. Bony-Pike
235. Gar-Pike
236. Common Pike
237. Garfish
238. Garfish
239. Unicorn-Fish
240. Cayman Garfish
241. Trumpet Fish or Bellows Fish
242. Cornetfish
243. Blochian
244. Viviparous Eelpout (Zoarces viviparus)
245. Band-Fish
246. Trumpet Fish
247. Viviparous Fish
248. Ribbon Fish
249. Silvery Light-Fish and Barbed Hedgehog-Mouth
250. Banks' Ribbon-Fish
251. Barbot
252. Whistle Fish
253. Ascanian Gymnetrus
254. Broad Nosed Pipe Fish
255. Cepedian Gymnetrus
256. Long Tailed Carapo
257. Striped Snakehead
258. Rufsellian Gymnetrus
259. Lancet Goby
260. Fifteen Spined Stickleback
261. Striated Serpent-Head
262. Black Smooth-Head
263. Blue-Finned Tube-Mouth
264. Indian Spiny Eel and Baikal Oil-Fish
265. Scabbard-Fish
266. Dorab
267. Hoedt's Soft-Spine
268. Risso's Thornback
269. Angel-Fish
270. Monk Fish
271. Upper Side of the Sole
272. Under Side of the Sole
273. Argus Flounder
274. Turbot
275. Malthe

276. Sea Zebra
277. English Sole
278. European Flounder
279. Flounder
280. European Plaice
281. Common Dab
282. Plaice
283. Malthe Vespertilio
284. Orbicular Porcupine Fish
285. Pennant's Globe-Fish
286. Puffer Fish
287. Oblong Porcupine Fish
288. Tetrodon Fahaka-Floating Belly Upward
289. T.Lagocephalus
290. Porcupinefish
291. Porcupinefish
292. Porcupinefish
293. Porcupinefish
294. Porcupinefish
295. Smooth Toadfish
296. Porcupinefish
297. Scorpionfish
298. Boxfish
299. Boxfish
300. Boxfish
301. Boxfish
302. Boxfish
303. Boxfish
304. Ostracion Quadricornis
305. Prickly Balistes
306. Parrot Fish
307. Smooth Trunk Fish
308. Tile-Fish
309. Three Coloured Chetoton
310. Sea Camel
311. File-Fish
312. Beaked Trunk Fish
313. Wrasse
314. Triggerfish
315. Triggerfish
316. Triggerfish
317. Triggerfish
318. Triggerfish
319. Triggerfish
320. Sea Swallow
321. Mesogaster
322. Flying-Fish
323. Flying Fish
324. Flying Fish
325. Under Swordfish
326. Swordfish
327. Spotted Indian Sword-Fish
328. A fisherman attacked by a swordfish
329. Japanese Saw-Fish
330. Sword Fish
331. Picked Dog Fish
332. Skeleton of extinct fringe-finned shark, showing diphycercal tail
333. Bornean Feather-Back
334. Lump-Sucker and Viviparous Blenny
335. Lump Sucker
336. Lump Fish
337. Star-Gazer and Weaver
338. Cataphracted Cuirassier
339. Cataphracted Cuirassier
340. Sun Fish
341. Mola Mola
342. Herring
343. Haddock

SEA-LIFE & MONSTERS OF THE DEEP

LIST OF ILLUSTRATIONS

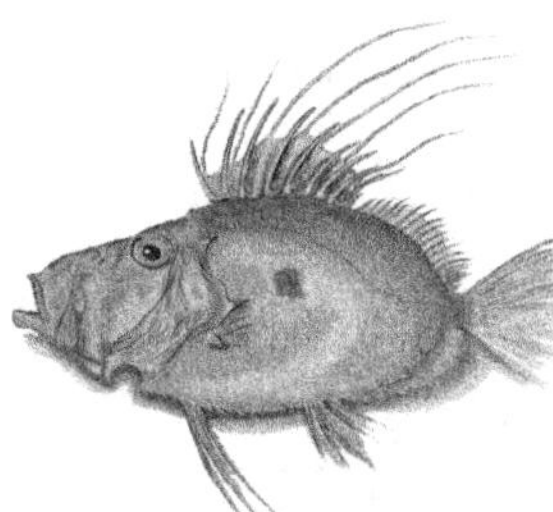

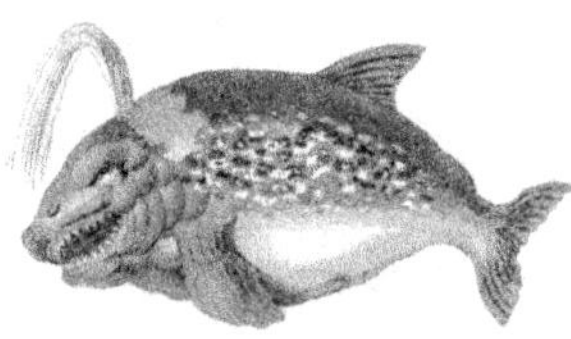

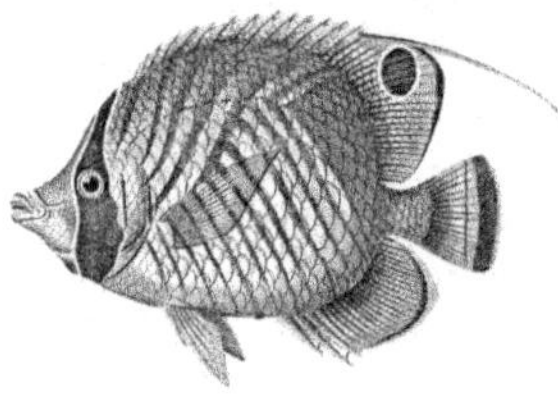

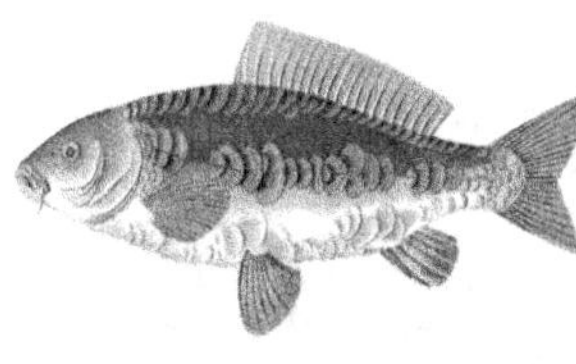

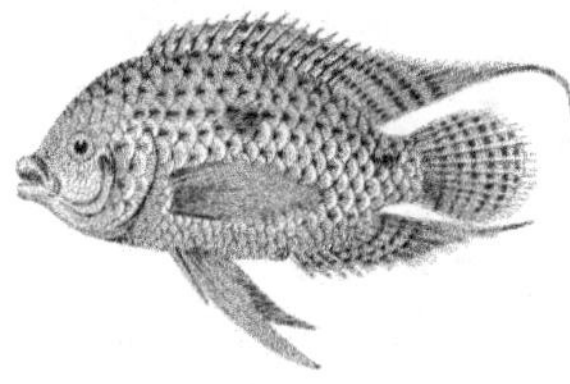

344. Pteraclis
345. John Dory
346. John Dory
347. John Dory
348. Bristled Chetodon
349. Sickle Banded Chetodon
350. Platax
351. Angelfish
352. Band Fish of Surat
353. Z.Gallus
354. Vespertilio Chetodons
355. A Group of Scaly Finned Fishes
356. Mahi Mahi
357. Angelfish
358. Dorada
359. Doctor-Fish
360. Opah
361. Snipe-Fish
362. African Herring
363. Gurami
364. Sea Pike
365. Ten Spined Sticklebacks
366. Malabar Pike
367. Pollack
368. Pike
369. Scabrous Bullhead
370. New Zealand Gastrochisma
371. Skipjack
372. New Zealand Trachichthys
373. Silver Striped Herring
374. New Zealand Thorny-Nose
375. Mastacembelus ophidium
376. Mastacembelus ophidium
377. Common Mackerel and Horse-Mackerel
378. Plumiers Goby
379. Mackerel
380. Group of White-Fish
381. Maigre
382. Pilot-Fish
383. Group of Spine-Finned Fish
384. Grayling and Charr
385. Kentucky Blind-Fish
386. Bow-Fin
387. Sand-Smelt and Cuvier's Square-Tail
388. Peter's Beaked Fish and Slender Pikelet
389. Common Smelt
390. Australian Knife-Jawed Fish
391. Australian Long-Fin
392. Sargo and Gilt-Head
393. Chisel-Jaw and Moon-Eye
394. Antarctic Chimaera
395. Arctic Chimaera
396. Tristram's Chromid
397. Spotted Firm-Fin
398. Piraya
399. Roach
400. Phosphorescent Sardine
401. Japanese Chirus
402. Oblique-Spined Blenny
403. Three Finned Amia
404. Bass
405. Sprat
406. Common Meagre
407. Epibulus Insidiator
408. Bleeker's Plesiops
409. Grayling
410. Rhodeus Amarus
411. Maigre
412. Gilthead

413. Braize
414. Cyprinus
415. Skeleton of the Haddock
416. Skeleton of a Saurodont Fish
417. Elegant Long-Fin
418. Golden Tench
419. Blennius
420. Kurtus indicus - Indian humphead
421. Kingfisher Smaris
422. Coryphaena
423. Five Finger Marked Coryphena
424. Ruffe
425. Ray's Sea-Bream
426. Ray's Bream
427. Blue Coryphena
428. A species of boxfish
429. Triggerfish
430. Aculeatus marinus major schonfeldy (Description from source)
431. Wahoo
432. Ling
433. Asellus varius Schonfeldij (Description from source)
434. Whiting
435. Whiting (Description from source)
436. Haddock
437. Herring
438. Grayling
439. Pilchard
440. Cole Fish
441. Salmon
442. Salmon
443. Salmarinus Salu (Description from source)
444. Arctic char
445. The Sea Lamprey
446. Sea-Lamprey, River-Lamprey and Small-Lamprey
447. Hag-Fish
448. Conger Eel
449. European eel
450. Serpens Marinus Salviani (Description from source)
451. Muraena Salviam
452. Electrical Eel
453. Conger Eel
454. Mediterranean Muraena
455. The Sea Lamprey copy
456. Electric Eel
457. The Silver Lamprey
458. The River Lamprey
459. Lamprey
460. Fucus-Like Sea-Horse
461. Great Pipe-Fish and Short-Snouted Sea-Horse
462. Weedy Sea Dragon
463. Seahorse
464. Testaceous, or Shell Worms
465. The Spider Crab
466. Four Horned Spider Crab (male)
467. The Masked Crab (male)
468. The Masked Crab (female)
469. European green crab
470. Hermit Crab
471. A Crab
472. 1. Soldier Crab; 2. Soldier Crab out of the Shell; 3. Hermit Crab; 4. Hermit Crab out of the Shell; 5. The Land Crab
473. The Cristatus Crab, the Pagurus Crab & the Common Lobster
474. Hermit crab with and without shell
475. Hermit Crab
476. Rough Shelled Crab
477. Red Mottled Crab
478. Common Crab
479. Norwegian Lobster
480. The Common English Lobster

481.   Spiny Lobster
482.   The Squat Lobster
483.   Prawn
484.   A large crustacean (crab) next to an enlarged detail of its leg. Etching.
485.   Some crustaceans on the beach, Adriaen Collaert, after 1598 - 1618
486.   Lobster on the Beach, Albert Flamen, 1664
487.   Lobster and Spring Lobster
488.   A fish and some crustaceans on the beach, Adriaen Collaert, after 1595 - 1618
489.   The Paper Nautilus and The Octopus
490.   The Nautilus
491.   The Nautilus
492.   Head and Tentacles of a giant calamary
493.   Octopus and its prey
494.   Cirrhous Octopus
495.   American Octopus
496.   Common Octopus
497.   Common Octopus
498.   Fraizé Octopus
499.   Fraizé Octopus
500.   L'argonaute (Description from source)
501.   Musk Octopus
502.   The Octopus Vulgaris
503.   Common Octopus
504.   Common Octopus
505.   "Le Poulpe Colossal" The Giant Kracken by de Montfort
506.   Gigantic Cuttle Fish Hooked by a French Steamer Ship off the Coast of Tenerife
507.   The Pelagonian squid (Description from source)
508.   Common Sepia
509.   Giant calamary afloat
510.   The Common Calamari
511.   Dissected Calamari Squid
512.   The Common Squid and its internal horny shell or pen
513.   Helminth
514.   Calamary (Squid)
515.   European Squid
516.   Common Cuttlefish
517.   Cuttle
518.   Front of Cuttlefish
519.   Back of Cuttlefish
520.   Jars containing fish, squid
521.   Hawks-Bill Turtle
522.   Green Turtle
523.   Hawksbill Sea Turtle
524.   Snapping Turtle
525.   Above and below views of the Pyxis
526.   The Matamata
527.   Alligator Terrapin
528.   Gopher Tortoise
529.   Skeleton of water tortoise (description from source)
530.   Six species of turtle and tortoise
531.   Grey Seal
532.   Hooded Seal
533.   The Common Seal
534.   The Seal
535.   The Ringed Seal
536.   Greenland or Harp Seal
537.   Skeleton of Seal
538.   A seal fight
539.   Skeleton of Otaria, or Eared Seal
540.   Ringed or Marbled Seal
541.   Head of Walrus
542.   Walrus
543.   Skull and Dentition of Walrus
544.   Walruses on the ice
545.   Starfish
546.   Magellanic Starfish
547.   1-4 Formation of the Madrepora Animal; 5-9 Madrepora of the First Division
548.   Madrepora of the Fourth Division
549.   Madrepora of the second Division

550.   Madrepora of the Fith Division
551.   Madrepora of the Third Division
552.   1. Tubi Musica; 2. Tubu Magnifica (Description from source)
553.   1. Gorgonia Antipathes; 2. Gorgonia Muricata
554.   Isis Hippuris, the Black Coral of India
555.   Isis Ochracea, the East-Indian Coral
556.   Gorgonia Ceratophyta
557.   Gorgonia nobilis
558.   Various species of Scallop
559.   1. Paper Nautilus; 2. Venus's Ear and other sea ears; 3. Cylindri or Olives
560.   1. A Rock Shell; 2-4. A Porrhais; a Devil, a Pelican's Foot & a Spider; 5.
Rhombus; 6. a Ditto, the Lover of Babel; 7. Alatoe, orwinged shell; 8-9. Erucas
561.   1. The Triton or Trumpet of Mar; 2. The Wry-Mouthed; 3. Umbilicated; 4.
Plicated; 5. Guttered Whelks; 6. The Longistora; 7. A Strombus; 8. Purpura (Description
from source)

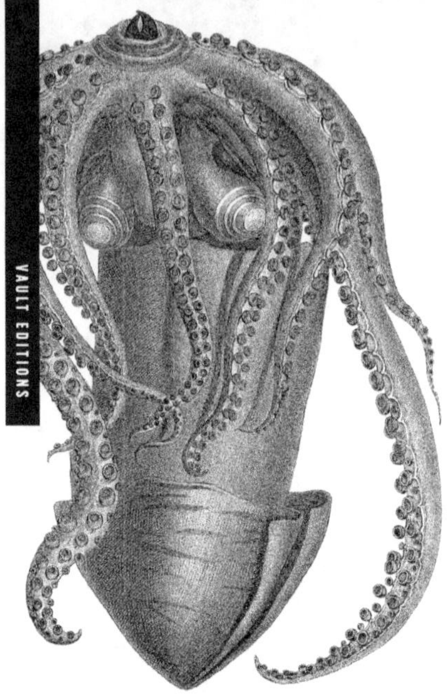

LEARN MORE

At Vault Editions, our mission is to create the world's most diverse and comprehensive collection of image archives available for artists, designers and curious minds. If you have enjoyed this book, you can find more of our titles available at vaulteditions.com.

REVIEW THIS BOOK

As a small, family-owned independent publisher, reviews help spread the word about our work. We would be incredibly grateful if you could leave an honest review of this title wherever you purchased this book.

JOIN OUR COMMUNITY

Are you a creative and curious individual? If so, you will love our community on Instagram. Every day we share bizarre and beautiful artwork ranging from 17th and 18th-century natural history and scientific illustration, to mythical beasts, ornamental designs, anatomical illustration and more. Join our community of 100K+ people today— search @vault_editions on Instagram.

DOWNLOAD YOUR FILES

STEP ONE

Enter the following web address in your web browser on a desktop computer.

www.vaulteditions.com/pages/sea

STEP TWO

Enter the following unique password to access the download page.

sear4857372sxda

STEP THREE

Follow the prompts to access your high-resolution files.

TECHNICAL ASSISTANCE

For all technical assistance, please email: info@vaulteditions.com

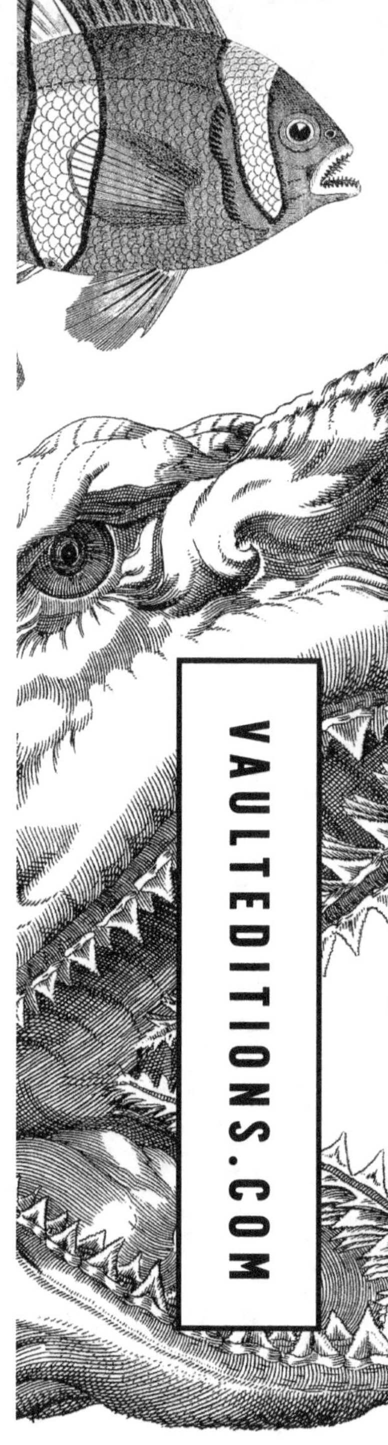

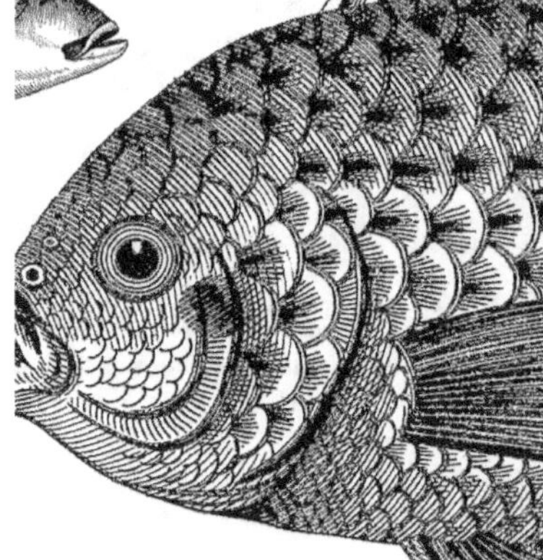

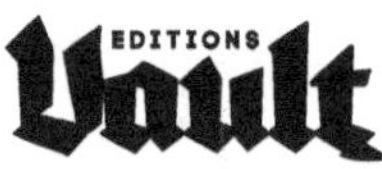